Democracy and Rights in Canada

Don Carmichael
Tom Pocklington
Greg Pyrcz

Harcourt Brace Jovanovich, Canada
Toronto Orlando San Diego London Sydney

Canadian Cataloguing in Publication Data

Carmichael, D.J.C.
    Democracy and rights in Canada

Includes bibliographical references.
ISBN 0-7747-3124-9

1. Civil rights – Canada.   2. Canada – Politics
and government.   I. Pocklington, T.C. (Thomas C.).
II. Pyrcz, Gregory E.   III. Title.

JC599.C3C37 1991   323'.0971   C90-095224-5

Acquisitions Editor: *Sheila Malloch*
Developmental Editor: *Anne Venables Eigner*
Editorial Co-ordinator: *Marcel Chiera*
Editorial Assistant: *Kerry Gibson*
Copy Editor: *John Eerkes*
Cover and Interior Design: *Daniel Kewley*
Typesetting and Assembly: *Q Composition Inc.*
Printing and Binding: *Webcom Limited*

∞   This book was printed in Canada on acid-free paper.

2 3 4 5   95 94 93 92

PREFACE

Students coming to the academic study of politics for the first time usually bring with them knowledge gained from prior social studies and some political practice. They know something of the causal contexts of political action and of their histories, and they have almost all experienced some forms of political conflict. The conflict may have involved the authority others exercise over their lives, the rights of men and women in society, the nature of just treatment, or issues such as censorship or the right to life. Most students know something of the Canadian Charter of Rights and Freedoms and of the basic idea of democratic politics, and most have enjoyed some experience in stating what they think about the public decisions made in their society.

This book was motivated by the belief that Canadians' understanding of the link between democratic principles and individual or societal rights needs to be developed and enriched. The goal of developing this understanding has often been ignored or overlooked by those who seek to develop the citizen's interest in public affairs in an attempt to elicit emotional responses. Although having students state their opinions is important psychologically, these exercises leave students ill-prepared to develop cogent and compelling arguments.

The following chapters provide exercises in the "language of democracy and rights" by discussing a number of issues that are persistently interesting to Canadians. The debates revolve around the deep protection of individual rights, the pursuit of a citizenry's general welfare, and the possibility of a more demanding form of democracy. Each chapter, except Chapter 1, contains an essay on a topic and a shorter critique that further demonstrates the complexity of the topic. The critiques do not consider all the criticisms that might be aimed at the essays but provide students with departure points for further discussion.

It is hoped that this book will enhance the ability of students to see how their understandings of issues are affected by commitments to often-competing principles and modes of reasoning, and especially, in Canada, by underlying conceptions of democracy and rights.

Acknowledgements

We wish to express our gratitude to colleagues who critically assessed this book and to those who patiently suffered through its completion. As well, we wish to acknowledge the interest and confidence that the people at HBJ–Holt showed in developing this work for the undergraduate community. Most of all, we wish to acknowledge the significant contribution that our students made in motivating, by their interest, the writing of such a book, and in their comments upon its contents in earlier drafts. Greg Pyrcz's collaboration in this project was made possible by a number of summer research grants offered through the auspices of Acadia University.

Don Carmichael
Tom Pocklington
Greg Pyrcz

Publisher's Note to Instructors and Students

This textbook is a key component of your course. If you are the instructor of this course, you undoubtedly considered a number of texts carefully before choosing this as the one that will work best for your students and you. The authors and publishers of this book spent considerable time and money to ensure its high quality, and we appreciate your recognition of this effort and accomplishment.

If you are a student, we are confident that this text will help you to meet the objectives of your course. You will also find it helpful after the course is finished, as a valuable addition to your personal library. So hold on to it.

As well, please don't forget that photocopying copyright work means the authors lose royalties that are rightfully theirs. This loss will discourage them from writing another edition of this text or other books, because doing so will simply not be worth their time and effort. If this happens, we all lose—students, instructors, authors, and publishers.

And since we want to hear what you think about this book, please be sure to send us the stamped reply card at the end of the text. This will help us to continue publishing high-quality books for your courses.

CONTENTS

.

CHAPTER 1

Thinking About Democracy and Rights

In 1976, in a free vote in the House of Commons—a vote in which the members were not required to vote along party lines—capital punishment was abolished in Canada. It was a narrow victory, 130 to 124, and soon thereafter, with increasing intensity, public opinion called for a reversal of the decision. By the middle of the 1980s, public opinion polls were consistently showing that a majority of the Canadian electorate favoured the restoration of capital punishment. In 1984, the Progressive Conservative Party, most of whose members expressed support for the reinstatement of capital punishment, won a landslide victory in a federal election. Nevertheless, in June 1987, when the issue was again put to a free vote in the House of Commons, the opponents of capital punishment were again victorious, in a vote of 148 to 127.

The issue of capital punishment raises basic questions about rights and democracy. Concerning rights: Is capital punishment a violation of a person's basic right to life? Is there any such thing as a right to life? Could it be that people do have a right to life, but that they forfeit it when they commit particularly heinous crimes? Is it really possible for people to forfeit basic rights? Do fallible human beings have the right to decide that a person should be put to death, or is capital punishment just an evasive and dishonest way to describe murder by the state? Concerning democracy: Should the majority rule in all cases? Are representatives bound to express the will of their constituents, or should they sometimes (or always) act on the basis of their conscience or informed judgment? In matters of intense concern, such as capital punishment, should the issue be decided by a direct vote by the electorate?

The prominence of issues relating to democracy and rights is the rule rather than the exception in Canadian political life. In the past decade, Canadians have been presented with a battery of such issues in the realm of biomedical ethics. The most prominent of them is abortion. "Pro-lifers," convinced that fetuses have a right to life from the moment of conception onward, are set against "pro-choicers," who emphasize the right of women to control their own bodies. Do fetuses have a right to life? Do women have an unqualified right to control their own bodies?

The abortion issue has also raised fundamental questions about the principles of democracy. In January 1988, the Supreme Court of Canada declared unconstitutional the "moderate" abortion law that had been in effect since June 1969. This raised the question whether it is consistent with democratic principles that a court should play such a pivotal role in deciding an important and controversial issue of public policy. Both pro-lifers and pro-choicers have engaged in illegal activity in support of their convictions. Most notably, Dr. Henry Morgentaler has performed abortions in open defiance of laws that he regarded as iniquitous. His actions raise the question when, if ever, it is permissible for citizens of democracies to act illegally for political purposes.

Abortion is not the only biomedical issue that raises questions of rights and democracy. Advances in medical technology now permit human life to be prolonged well past the point at which, not long ago, a person would have been considered dead. Other advances now make possible the shaping of human life in marvellous ways. These developments raise profound questions about the grounds and limits of anyone's rights to produce and terminate life and also about the proper role of democratic processes in answering such questions.

No book about Canadian political life in the 1990s would be complete without a brief mention of constitutional issues. In 1982, Canadians acquired a Charter of Rights and Freedoms. Endless disputes revolve around the question whether the rights specified in the Charter are sufficient. Of particular concern is the section 33.1 of the Charter, which allows the federal Parliament and provincial legislatures to override significant parts of the Charter. Doubts have been expressed that the Charter sufficiently respects the rights of women, Native people, and homosexuals, who are not even mentioned in the sections of the Charter that deal with equality rights.

There are grounds for concern, too, about the democratic credentials of the Constitution Act, of which the Charter is a part. First, the Constitution Act, 1982, was formulated and presented to the Canadian public as a *fait accompli* by a group of first ministers without significant public involvement. Second, the Meech Lake Accord continued the practice of private constitution-making by heads of governments. Third, the provisions for amending the Act threaten to formalize the process of constitutional amendment as a matter of bargaining among first ministers without substantial popular consultation.

The primary purpose of this book is to encourage and assist readers to think seriously and critically about the nature of their citizenship, and especially about the posture they should adopt toward the institutions, processes, practices, and policies of Canadian governments. Its intent is to draw attention to basic principles. Although a focus on rights and democracy is not the only way in which basic principles can be explored, it provides an apt point of entry for considering many of the central issues of Canadian political life.

In each chapter, the authors assess and make recommendations about Canadian public policies. This book does not concentrate on describing policy, explaining its origins and the intricacies of its implementation, or predicting its future. The authors take what might be called the perspective of the citizen rather than that of the mere observer. Each chapter is meant to have implications for the terms of Canadian citizenship that extend beyond the topic it addresses.

This introductory chapter clarifies the notions of rights and democracy both individually and in their interrelationships. It is more explanatory and less controversial than the chapters that follow, but it makes no pretence of neutrality. In moral, legal, and political argument, one's conclusions depend partly on one's understanding of central concepts. For example, in the old dispute about whether driving a car is a right or a privilege, one's position depends partly on what one means by "right" and "privilege." That point holds true generally; the reader's critical guard should be up in this chapter as well as in later chapters.

Rights

This section discusses the nature of rights, their place in political arguments, and some of the difficult questions to which they give rise.

The Nature of Rights

Whatever else rights are, they are also entitlements. They are entitlements to *do* something (or refrain from doing it), such as an entitlement to run for public office, or entitlements to *have* something (or forego it), such as the repayment of a debt.

The distinctiveness of entitlements, and thereby of rights, may be illustrated by contrast. Most people believe that they should be charitable, or perhaps even that they have some kind of *duty* to be charitable. For example, suppose that A has fallen on hard times. He is a stranger in town, dead broke, hungry, unemployed, friendless, and homeless. A asks B for fifty dollars to tide him over so that he can look for work or welfare. Suppose further that B can afford to give A the money without seriously jeopardizing her own well-being or that of her dependants. It would certainly be charitable of B to give A the fifty dollars; it might even be wrong for her not to do so. But what cannot be said is that A is *entitled* to the money. Much as B believes in charity, she may have reasons that seem good to her for refusing

A. For example, B may believe that her charity should support worthy institutions, such as shelters for battered women, rather than particular unfortunates. Or B may believe that charity should be concentrated on the young, who still have some hope, rather than wasted on hopeless adults. Even if B's reasons are not good ones, A cannot claim that he is entitled to B's fifty dollars. B does not owe it to A, no matter how broadly "owe" is construed.

Consider a different situation. Several months ago, B borrowed fifty dollars from A on condition that the debt be repaid on a certain date. That date has now arrived. But now it is B who has fallen on hard times. Paying the debt will cause her serious hardship. Meanwhile, A doesn't need the money. He could easily forgive the debt entirely or give B ample time to repay it. But A is entitled to the money; he has a right to it. If A "stands on his right" and insists on collecting the debt, he may be despicable. Nevertheless, there is no denying that he does have the right.

But how can it be that one has a right to act badly, and perhaps even wrongly? To ask this question is to question the basis of rights. That is, it is to inquire about the sources of entitlements. The blunt answer to the question, "What is the basis of rights?" is rules or principles. To say that a person has a right means that there is a rule or principle that specifies that the person is entitled to do or refrain from doing something, or is entitled to have or forego something. It also means that another person may not prevent one from doing what one has a right to do and that another person must give one what one has a right to receive.[1]

Where are these rules or principles? There are different kinds of rights, and different kinds of rules or principles are appropriate to each.

Types of Rights

Rights can be classified in many ways. For present purposes, the crucial distinctions are between legal rights, moral rights, and natural or human rights. Lawyers hardly ever make these distinctions, and social scientists have usually been all too eager to follow their lead. Both groups usually assume that all rights are legal rights. The authors of this book reject that view, and many of the arguments presented in this book cannot be understood by those who reject the possibility of nonlegal rights.

Legal Rights
Everyone acknowledges that legal rights exist; for example, no one doubts that all Canadian citizens have the legal right to address complaints to members of Parliament or to receive medicare benefits. The basis of these legal rights is the law. This observation is easy to relate to the earlier, general account of rights, which emphasized the centrality of rules and principles. Some, but not all, laws are legal rules that affirm that some or all citizens are entitled to do certain acts or receive certain material goods, services, or forms of treatment. Among the exceptions are rules that simply

require certain acts such as paying taxes, or prohibit others such as jaywalking. The basis of legal rights, then, is simply valid legal rules that specify who has entitlements and who must respect them.

Moral Rights

Although some people deny it when they theorize about rights, most acknowledge that moral rights exist. When people maintain that black South Africans have a right to full participation in the government of their country, or that homosexuals in Alberta have a right to the same access to public facilities as heterosexuals do, they are not appealing to the laws of those jurisdictions—South African law does not recognize a right of full political participation for blacks, and Alberta's Human Rights Act does not extend its protection against discrimination to homosexuals. Maintaining that such rights "exist" does not mean that they are based on legal rules.

Does saying that such rights exist simply mean that it would be a good thing if blacks and homosexuals had those legal rights and that it is unfortunate they do not? It means more than that. It makes perfectly good sense to say that there are nonlegal rights. These *moral rights* are based on moral principles, which specify that certain people have moral entitlements, which others are morally bound to respect. The underlying logic of moral rights is no more complex or perplexing than that of legal rights. The fact that morality is, by and large, more controversial than law provides no grounds for scepticism about the existence of moral rights.

Natural or Human Rights

Natural or human rights are a subcategory of moral rights. For all practical purposes, the term "human right" is synonymous with the older term "natural right." These terms will be used interchangeably here. These rights are moral rights because their existence does not depend on their being enacted into law and because they are based on moral principles. However, although all human rights are moral rights, not all moral rights are human rights.

What differentiates the subcategory of natural or human rights from the broader category of moral rights? Richard Wasserstrom provides a clear and pertinent answer to this question. He maintains that a *human right* must have at least four general characteristics. It must: (i) be possessed by all human beings, as well as only by human beings; (ii) be possessed equally by all human beings; (iii) not be possessed as a result of having a particular status, such as that of parent, president, or promisee (because such rights are not possessed equally by all human beings); (iv) be a right that can be claimed equally against any and every other human being. (Wasserstrom's illuminating formulation is that human rights are "assertable, in a manner of speaking, 'against the whole world.' ")[2]

Following Wasserstrom's analysis, if A promises to meet B for coffee, B would have a moral right against A that A keep the promise, but this would not be a natural or human right. It would be a moral right rather than a legal one because, first, there is no law requiring the keeping of casual promises and because, second, B's entitlement that A show up for coffee is based on a moral principle, namely, the principle that promises should be kept. It would not be a human right, because it relates to a special relationship between A and B (that A made a promise to B); it is not a right that every human being holds in relationship to every other human being. A possible human right would be the right not to be tortured, a right that is conceivably "assertable against the whole world."

There was a time when virtually all Western thinkers believed that people had natural rights, but for well over a century this idea has been disputed. In a brilliant essay, H.L.A. Hart attempted to show that "there is at least one natural right, the equal right of all men to be free."[3] Many remain unconvinced of this; Alasdair MacIntyre, another eminent contemporary philosopher, remarks acidly that

> the best reason . . . for asserting that there are no [natural or human] rights is . . . of precisely the same type as the best reason which we possess for asserting that there are no witches and the best reason which we possess for asserting that there are no unicorns: every attempt to give good reasons for asserting that there *are* such rights has failed.[4]

Fortunately, the controversy need not be settled here, since none of the arguments presented in this book explicitly appeals to natural rights. Natural rights are discussed here for two reasons. First, Don Carmichael's critique of Tom Pocklington's essay on Native self-government (Chapter 7) may be thought to rest on an implicit appeal to natural rights, since he maintains that individuals have rights apart from the social groups to which they belong. Readers may wonder whether Carmichael is a natural-rights theorist. Second, many people believe that discussions of important issues of political ethics are incomplete or superficial if they do not invoke human rights. The preceding discussion should help readers to decide whether they share that outlook.

Rights and Obligations

The term "rights" is used in a variety of senses, none of which is improper or incorrect. However, in this book, it is used almost invariably in the strict or narrow sense. In the strict sense, a person has a right only if other people have a corresponding duty or obligation. In some contexts the terms "duty" and "obligation" have different meanings, but here they are used interchangeably.

Consider again A's promise to meet B for coffee. One effect of A's promise was to endow B with the right that A show up at the specified time and place. However, the promise had another effect: it imposed on A an obligation to keep the date. The right and the obligation are inseparable; they are, so to speak, two sides of the same coin. Looked at from one angle, the right implies the obligation; looked at from the other angle, the obligation implies the right. Rights in the strict sense are therefore sometimes defined as rights that are characterized by a "correlativity" between rights and obligations.[5]

Almost all the most cherished (and controversial) rights are rights in the strict sense, and several such rights are discussed in the following chapters. For example, if, as Carmichael argues in Chapter 4, Canadians have a right to a guaranteed annual income, governments have an obligation to enact and implement it. And if, as Pyrcz argues in Chapter 5, women's rights are regularly violated, men have an obligation to respect women's rights.

Rights in Political Argument: The Scope of Rights

Not until the seventeenth century did rights begin to play a very important part in moral and political discourse. Since that time, and especially in the present century, rights have come to occupy a more prominent place in the assessment of actions, practices, institutions, and public policies. Thomas Hobbes (1588–1679), the first great thinker to give rights a central place in Western thinking about morality, law, and politics, would have been surprised at the range of rights taken seriously nowadays. The list of rights Hobbes emphasized was sparse, to say the least. It concentrated above all, but certainly not exclusively, on people's inalienable right to preserve themselves.

The next generations of thinkers added to Hobbes's list mainly rights relating to the preservation of property. With the rise of democratic and liberal ideas, a considerably wider range of rights—to freedom of expression, to free and fair elections with universal suffrage, to fair treatment of people accused of crimes, and so on—became firmly established, at least as a matter of law, in the liberal democracies. By the end of the first quarter of the present century, a standard array of liberal and democratic rights was fully accepted in the official rhetoric, and to a considerable extent was embedded in the practice, of most Western countries.

After World War II, attention increasingly shifted to "social and economic" rights. More and more people came to believe that everyone should be protected from the vagaries of life, especially the "impersonal forces" of economic markets, as a matter of right, not through the hit-and-miss operation of charity. As a result, many countries now provide unemployment and medical insurance benefits, workers' compensation, old-age and disability pensions, and so on.

Recently there has been a trend to move beyond social welfare rights. Two principal manifestations of this trend have had some success. First, efforts have been made to establish rights that ensure that disadvantaged people are entitled not only to the means of survival, but also to the wherewithal to live a life of dignity. In this category are rights to schools for people with learning disabilities, wheelchair ramps, and job retraining for the unemployed who are technologically disadvantaged. Second, efforts have been made to combat types of systematic discrimination that were once thought to be purely private matters. For example, not long ago it was regarded as an employer's right to choose to hire men rather than women, a landlord's right to rent an apartment to people of Scottish but not Korean descent, and a nightclub owner's right to prohibit homosexuals but not heterosexuals from holding hands in the club. Many Canadians now regard such actions as violations of moral rights, and in some jurisdictions they are violations of legal rights. Chapter 4, on the welfare state, explores the trend to enhance the dignity of human life. Chapter 5, on gender and justice, addresses the attack on systematic discrimination.

Every extension of the scope of rights has resulted in controversy. Some people think that society should not offer more than the basic liberal–democratic rights or the minimum welfare rights. Others think that rights should be extended to animals, plants, and at least some inanimate objects. One's response to proposals to expand or shrink the scope of rights depends, in part, on one's general political outlook; but it also depends on one's view of the force of rights. If one thinks that warranted assertions of rights are so powerful that they prevent any further discussion, one is likely to be unsympathetic to an expansion of rights. If rights are as decisive as that, whenever they are relevant they exclude the possibility of political processes that most Canadians regard as quite important. In this view, bargaining, compromise, seeking a common good, struggling to achieve ideals, and rational persuasion have no place. If, on the other hand, one thinks that such assertions are not absolutely decisive, one is likely to be more sympathetic to appeals to rights, including newly invented rights.

Rights in Political Argument: The Force of Rights

This section makes three claims about rights. Each claim counters the widespread view that the warranted assertion of a right is conclusive, in the sense that it brings argument to an end.

Rights as Defeasible
It is sometimes thought that if someone has a right to do or receive something, he or she may do or receive that something, come hell or high water. In this view, all rights are absolute: nothing can override or undermine them. A moment's reflection reveals that this view is untenable. Recall once again the right B acquired by way of A's promise to meet her for coffee. Suppose now that, on the way to keeping the appointment, A encounters someone who has just had a heart attack. Suppose further that A is the only one present trained in cardiopulmonary resuscitation. What A should do in this situation is forget about coffee and render assistance to the heart-attack victim.

This conclusion does *not* mean that B's right and A's corresponding obligation magically disappear just because, all things considered, A was morally bound to assist the victim rather than drink coffee. The situation, rather, is that A violated B's right and failed to fulfil his obligation but was justified in doing so. The right and the obligation were overridden by a weightier consideration. Philosophers commonly describe the right and the obligation in cases like this as *defeasible*, that is, capable of being defeated by something more important.

Are all rights defeasible, or are some of them indefeasible, or *absolute*? Could *any* conditions override a right to fair trial? Would *any* conditions permit the violation of a person's right not to be the object of an unprovoked assault? Is anyone *ever* justified in violating another's right not to be tortured? It is tempting to say that these rights are absolute rights.

On the other hand, some people, including some proponents of human rights, maintain that it is irrational to commit oneself to a principle regardless of the circumstances (including unforeseen and unforeseeable circumstances) in which the principle must be applied. It is always possible, according to thinkers of this persuasion, that circumstances may arise in which it would be wrong to act on a principle that had once seemed inviolable. Such thinkers maintain, therefore, that there are no absolute rights.

The question whether there are any absolute rights is one about which reasonable people can and do disagree. However, they agree that if there are such rights, they are few and far between. Most rights are clearly defeasible; in most cases, people have to weigh the importance of respecting a right against competing considerations. The result of this conclusion is that someone's possession of a right is not always a justification for respecting it. Rights are not always such powerful considerations as they are sometimes supposed to be. This point plays a major role in Chapter 6's discussion of abortion and a minor one in Chapter 7's discussion of Native self-government.

Possessing Rights and Exercising Rights

The fact that one possesses a right does not mean that one would be well advised to exercise it or even that one may exercise it. Suppose that C reaches an intersection at the same time as D, an obviously drunk driver. D faces a stop sign and C doesn't, so C clearly has the right-of-way; C has the right to proceed but D doesn't. In this case it would be most imprudent of C to "stand on his rights." Or, recall the example in which B owed A fifty dollars but could ill afford to repay it, while A had no need of the money. There is surely a strong case to be made here that A would act wrongly in insisting on a right to repayment. This point plays a role in Chapter 2's essay on freedom of expression and pornography. While arguing that pornographers should be allowed to purvey their wares, the essayist maintains that the world would be a better place if most of them chose not to do so.

The practical point here, once again, is that moral rights are not as powerful as they are sometimes supposed to be. The fact that someone has a right does not prevent argument about whether he or she should exercise it. Exercising a right can be not only imprudent but even morally wrong.

Reasons for Enacting Legal Rights

The law sets out innumerable legal rights. Most laws do not enact moral let alone natural rights, and they are not intended to do so. They are enacted to achieve the commonplace objectives favoured by segments of the electorate, pressure groups, bureaucrats, politicians, or various combinations of these groups. When a provincial government passes a law giving farmers the right to form hog-marketing boards, or giving lawyers the right to form corporations, or giving oil companies the right to pay no taxes, no one supposes that this law implements moral rights. This is not to say that laws that neither implement nor violate moral rights are above moral criticism. There are many grounds on which enactments of legal rights can be applauded or condemned.

Not all legal rights are enacted to legalize moral rights, but some are. Human rights legislation, in prohibiting various forms of discrimination, has this purpose. For example, Sikhs had a moral right to the same treatment by landlords as Roman Catholics did before any legislature declared this a legal right. However, the fact that an individual or group has a moral right does not mean that this right should be enacted into law. Consider again the case of promises: the making of promises generates moral rights, but many people would oppose the enactment of this right as a legal right. Several good reasons exist for taking this view. They range from considerations of mere expediency, such as the difficulty and cost of enforcing such a law, to considerations of morality, such as principled opposition to unnecessary legal enforcement of morals. Once again, the conclusion is that moral rights are not as decisive as might be supposed.

The Importance of Rights

Although rights are not such decisive argumentative "weapons" as they are commonly believed to be, they remain very powerful considerations. The main reason for their great strength is that, however much one tries to undermine rights—by referring to their defeasibility, for example—possessors of rights are entitled to do or have certain things unless exceptionally pressing considerations justify overriding the entitlements.

Consider, one last time, the promise A made to meet B for coffee and the emergency situation in which B's right and A's corresponding obligation were overridden. Think now of the myriad considerations that would *not* override the right and the obligation. A would not be justified in breaking the date if he instead preferred to stare out the window, or chat with some friends, or browse in the record store, or write about rights, or even perform some act of great generosity. This point may not seem very impressive in regard to matters such as casual promises, but the same point holds, and is certainly not unimportant, with respect to more important issues.

Suppose that "pro-lifers" are right in claiming that fetuses have a right to life. This would make a great deal of difference, for it would mean that women should not have abortions except in rare circumstances. That conclusion would affect, directly and indirectly, the well-being of millions of people. Similarly, high stakes are involved if the dissemination of pornography is justified by the right to freedom of expression, or if Native people have a right to self-government, or if welfare-state rights should be strengthened and expanded. Close attention to rights, both real and alleged, is central to a serious assessment of Canadian public policies.

Democracy

Most citizens of the Western democracies believe that democracy is a good thing, not least because they believe that democracies are more likely than other kinds of political societies to pursue good policies. Most Canadians believe that Canada, though far from flawless, has excellent credentials as a democratic country. From these beliefs, many Canadians conclude that they have a duty to do their part in upholding existing Canadian political institutions and practices, and also to support—or at least to comply with— the policies that emerge from the present political process.

The authors of this book maintain that this conclusion is, to put it mildly, hasty. A more critical approach is called for; specifically, this book takes the view that an essential first step in assessing the democratic character of any association is to clarify the meaning of democracy. Only then will Canadians be in a position to judge the extent to which Canada is democratic and arrive at sound conclusions about their responsibilities as citizens. This book's discussion of democracy is briefer than its discussion of rights. It defines democracy largely, though not exclusively, in terms of rights.

Defining Democracy: The Centrality of Rights

The term "democracy" is derived from the Greek words *demos* (the people) and *kratein* (to rule). Historically, democracy means "rule by the people." Although there are many disagreements about the specific features of democracy, it retains that basic meaning. "Rule by the people," however, is a vague notion. To determine whether a particular institution, practice, rule, or law is democratic, more definite standards of democratic character must be formulated. This can be done by concentrating mainly on the rights associated with four general defining characteristics of democracy: popular sovereignty, political equality, popular consultation, and majority rule. The following discussion of these characteristics identifies some of the major disagreements about the nature of democracy.[6]

Popular Sovereignty

Popular sovereignty requires that, with reasonable exceptions, everyone have a right to participate in government. The phrase *"reasonable* exceptions" does not make this formulation unacceptably vague. Some exceptions are clearly unreasonable, such as excluding people because of their race, sex, religious persuasion, or social class. Other exceptions are clearly reasonable; for example, young children and the severely brain-injured. Genuinely dubious cases, such as inmates of prisons and mental institutions, are few in number.

A completely democratic polity would fully implement the principle of popular sovereignty. In such a polity, everyone except those excluded on reasonable grounds would have the right to participate in government. Actual polities, however, exclude people on both reasonable and unreasonable grounds. As far as the principle of popular sovereignty is concerned it makes no sense to draw a line between polities that are and are not democratic. There are gradations in the extent to which actual polities implement popular sovereignty, so in this respect, actual polities are either more or less democratic.

What holds for popular sovereignty holds also for the other principles of democracy. There is no clear distinction between polities that are democratic, because they fully implement the principles of democracy, and those that are undemocratic, because they do not. There are always gradations among those that implement the principles to a greater or lesser extent.

Political Equality

The members of a democratic association must be, in some important sense, political equals. It would be odd to maintain that an association embodying government by the people should allow some of its members (wealthy people, for example) a preponderant voice in decisions of the association. The principle of political equality can be understood as simply an implication of the principle of popular sovereignty.

The problem with political equality is that it can be construed in two quite different ways, both of which seem unsatisfactory. On the one hand, it can be construed as an equality of *rights*. According to this construction, political equality is achieved if everyone has the same rights of political participation, such as the right to vote, run for office, speak freely on political matters, and assemble for political purposes. The problem with this understanding of political equality is that it seems to sacrifice substance for form. Two citizens may have equal political rights, but if one is rich while the other is poor, or if one citizen's career provides plenty of opportunities to engage in political activities while the other citizen must work long hours to keep body and soul together, it is a tasteless joke to say that they are political equals.

The alternative is to say that people are political equals only if their *influence* on policy outcomes is equal. At first glance, this seems to be a more satisfactory way of defining political equality. Further reflection, however, reveals that this conception involves even greater difficulties than the first. Two problems are particularly acute. First, every society has standards, both of adequacy and of excellence. For a variety of reasons (including sheer luck), various members of a society will have greater or lesser success in meeting that society's standards. Some members will be unable to meet the standards at all; most will perform at an average level; and a few will excel. The few who excel will be admired, and in Canada admiration can be translated into political influence.

Although there are ways to diminish the connection between political influence and social standing, there is no reason to believe that this connection can be eliminated or even nearly eliminated. Since it is pointless to use a utopian standard of political equality, the notion of political equality as equality of political influence is not very useful. The second major problem with defining political equality as actual equality of political influence is that some people have good reasons for abstaining from political participation. Chapter 3's essay makes an argument to this effect. It would be odd to rely on a notion of political equality that required people to act irrationally.

This book opts, somewhat reluctantly, for the "rights" conception of political equality. It assumes, however, that the equal rights that constitute political equality must be *effective* rights, not merely formal legal provisions. Admittedly, a discussion of effective rights poses challenges to the liberal preconceptions that dominate Canadian politics. Some attention is paid to these challenges in the chapters on gender equality, freedom of the press, pornography, economic justice, and Native self-government. The notion of effective rights deserves fuller attention than it receives in this book.

Popular Consultation

Democracy is government *by* the people, not merely *of* the people or *for* the people. (*All* governments are governments *of* the people, and all *claim* to be governments *for* the people.) The peculiarity of democratic government is that the people themselves actually govern. However, in a large, economically complex, and culturally diverse country like Canada it is impossible for the people to govern themselves directly, as occurred in the ancient Athenian assembly or some early New England town meetings. Except within quite small associations, democracy in our time is necessarily *representative* democracy.

It is because democracy nowadays must be largely representative that the principle of popular consultation comes into play. This principle prescribes that citizens have a *right* to be consulted by their representatives and that representatives must be *responsive* and *accountable* to their constituents. It implies that citizens in a democracy have a number of specific rights that ensure the responsiveness and accountability of their representatives. Prime among these rights is the right to participate in free, fair, and reasonably frequent elections.

Popular consultation does not, however, merely consist of voters giving representatives a mandate every few years. Also essential to the responsiveness and accountability of representatives is a set of rights that operate between elections as well as during them. Most of these are well known: rights to speak and assemble freely, to pressure government officials, and to protest their actions or inactions.

A right—or, more accurately, a complex of rights—often ignored in connection with popular consultation concerns citizen education and information. If citizens do not understand how governments work, they are poorly placed to hold their representatives responsive and accountable. The same is true if citizens are poorly informed about the nature and implications of government policies. Popular consultation therefore involves rights to citizen education and information. Canada falls far short of excellence in satisfying these rights; shortcomings in political education at all levels of schooling and government secrecy come immediately to mind. The essay in Chapter 8 argues that the mass media have avoided bearing their share of the responsibility to provide information. The arguments advanced in that chapter should provoke readers to question the democratic character of the Canadian status quo.

Majority Rule

Ideally, rule by the people implies adherence to a principle of unanimity. Under this principle, measures would become public policies only if *all* members of a democratic collectivity agreed to them. One political theorist recently argued persuasively that a unanimity rule can be employed generally in some small communities and occasionally in larger jurisdictions.[7] However, on most important issues, unanimity is unattainable. In such cases, either the larger or the smaller group must have its way. Most people feel that rule by the smaller group is inconsistent with government by the people, and that is the pre-eminent justification of majority rule.

On the other hand, many people feel uncomfortable with the idea of unbridled majority rule. Two main considerations underlie this discomfort. First, it is clear that majorities can be wrong and evident that they sometimes are wrong. For example, some Nazi atrocities were authorized by a majority of the German people. Numbers, even overwhelming numbers, cannot make oppressive policies acceptable. Second, government by the people is impossible if certain minority rights are not respected.[8] If certain rights— such as freedom of speech, assembly, and public protest—are denied to segments of the populace, citizens cannot be certain that the *apparent* majority view really *is* the majority view. If the majority is given the opportunity to hear the views of a silenced minority, it might well adopt those views as its own. Thus, when certain rights are denied to minorities, people cannot be sure that a genuine majority view exists. In any case, the violation of minority political rights is contrary to the principle of political equality. Unqualified majority rule is simply inconsistent with democracy.

On these grounds one can justify such anti-majoritarian devices as constitutional provisions, including declarations of rights like the Canadian Charter of Rights and Freedoms, and court systems designed to protect rights. Also on these grounds one can dismiss as thoroughly disreputable a common tactic for evading serious discussion of the controversial issues discussed in this book. It is frequently maintained that in a democracy the only legitimate way to deal with issues like abortion, pornography, and the claims of Native people is to implement the views of the majority. Since majority rights are not the only democratic rights, this view is simply wrong.

Defining Democracy: Beyond Rights

So far, this chapter has emphasized the centrality of rights in democracy. Most people, however, find a definition of democracy that focuses narrowly on rights unsatisfactory. The authors share this view,[9] and that is why they define democracy largely, *though not exclusively*, in terms of rights. The trouble with characterizing democracy as merely a matter of respecting certain rights is that it simply does not do full justice to an understanding of government by the people. Even if the rights associated with the principles of popular sovereignty, political equality, popular consultation, and majority rule are deeply respected and carefully protected, the possibility remains that so few people will exercise these rights that it would be perverse to describe the polity as a system of government by the people. People who have the right to vote, to speak their mind on public issues, to organize opposition to proposed government policies, and so on may choose not to exercise these rights. When large numbers of people opt not to participate politically, even though their democratic rights are secure, government by the people is clearly diminished.

Popular control of government requires not only that people have the opportunity to participate in ruling, but also that they take advantage of this opportunity. An eminent American democratic theorist, Charles Hyneman, wrote the following words, which are fully applicable to Canada:

> The ideal in democratic government is obligatory response to the wishes of the people. Popular government, popular control of government, government by the people are short terms for instrumentalities and practices designed to achieve this goal. We can estimate the closeness of approach to this ideal by finding answers to these three questions: (a) how much of the population shares, (b) in how much of the critical decision making, (c) with how much impact or influence?[10]

Hyneman's three criteria for assessing the extent to which an association approximates the democratic ideal should give pause to those who award high grades to Canadian democracy.

Democratic Rights and Other Rights

The rights associated with popular sovereignty, political equality, popular consultation, and majority rule are the essential democratic rights. To the extent that a political system violates these rights, its right to be called "democracy" diminishes. Furthermore, any political system that violates these rights persistently and seriously loses any claim to be considered a democracy at all.

Not all rights are essential democratic rights. In some jurisdictions, the right to sunbathe nude, to have holidays with pay, and to deduct mortgage payments from one's taxable income are legal rights, but they are not essential democratic rights. The right of children to special consideration from their parents (and vice versa), the right of employees of the same economic enterprise to equal pay for equal work, and the right of members of religious sects to try to make converts are moral rights, but they are not essential democratic rights. Government by the people would not be destroyed or directly weakened by eliminating any of these rights.

Do the essential democratic rights always take precedence over other rights? The preceding discussion of majority rule concluded that "numbers, even overwhelming numbers, cannot make oppressive policies acceptable." This conclusion can be broadened. A process in which *all* the democratic rights (not just those of the majority) are respected may still produce policies that violate rights more important than democratic rights. A political system far more democratic than any the world has ever seen could engage in unjust wars, prohibit women from engaging in "unfeminine" activities like driving trucks and managing banks, or sterilize people with low IQs. Even a political system unparalleled in its respect for the essential democratic rights could pursue evil or unjust policies, including policies that persistently and seriously violate rights more deeply cherished than democratic rights.

What are conscientious citizens to do when thoroughly democratic processes generate policies that violate basic rights? They are then at least free, and perhaps even duty bound, to struggle for the recognition and protection of the more important rights. This raises one of the most difficult questions of political ethics. How far may citizens go in combating policies endorsed in a thoroughly democratic manner? Must they confine themselves to activities that are impeccably democratic, or may they resort to unconventional, perhaps even illegal, tactics? This question becomes even tougher in the real world of democracy.

In practice, *all* democratic associations, especially the state, are more or less flawed in their respect for the essential democratic rights. Not even its most enthusiastic boosters hold that the Canadian political system is faultless in its respect for the essential democratic rights. Canada's record,

though far from abominable, is marred by major disgraces like the proclamation of the War Measures Act in 1970[11] and the internment of Japanese
Canadians during World War II. Do these defects in the democratic process
provide justification for citizens to engage in acts of protest, dissent, or
resistance that would be unjustified if the essential democratic rights were
respected more fully? This question is addressed in part in Chapter 3.

The Importance of Democracy

We live in a society of people, not of angels. All our institutions are
imperfect; they could not be expected to be otherwise. Winston Churchill
once made a remark to the effect that democracy is the worst system of
government—except for all the others. That thought is worth pursuing.

A number of considerations, ranging from the highly pragmatic to the
highly moral, support the view that democracy is the best practicable political system. On the pragmatic end of the spectrum is the observation that
democracy encourages the peaceful settlement of disputes—the use of
ballots instead of bullets. Occupying a middle ground is the view that
democracy allows far more room than do other systems for people not only
to recognize but also to correct their mistakes. By legitimizing organized
opposition to the government, by opening channels for the expression of
grievances, and by providing regular opportunities to "throw the rascals
out," democracy institutionalizes the recognition that we are fallible beings
and allows for the correction of the errors of judgment that fallible beings
are bound to make. At the principled end of the spectrum is the claim that
the principles of democracy—or at least the most important of them—are
basic moral principles. In this view, the right of people to participate in
shaping their own destiny regardless of colour, gender, or creed; their right
to speak freely on public matters; and their right to hold leaders accountable
for their conduct are not mere expedients but fundamental moral rights.

The authors believe that all these considerations carry weight. At the
level of the state, representative democracy is the best practicable political
system available. If this conclusion is combined with the earlier conclusion
that human institutions are inescapably flawed, what does this combination
yield? It yields the precept that citizens should be wary of taking steps likely
to undermine democratic attitudes, beliefs, institutions, and practices. This
precept is prudent because representative democracy, although imperfect,
contributes to citizens' well-being better than other political systems do. It
is also morally sound, because people have a moral duty to support institutions and practices that are (compared to workable alternatives) relatively
just, humane, and beneficent.

The practical conclusion is that if a flawed democratic political system—
in this book, the Canadian democratic system—were in serious peril, its
citizens should give it the benefit of the doubt. In other words, if the survival

of democracy were in doubt, citizens should be unusually forgiving of its flaws and unusually hesitant about demanding speedy redress of grievances.

But Canadian democracy is not a frail flower; its survival in the foreseeable future is not in doubt. Graver dangers to the vitality of Canadian democracy are posed by too great a willingness to tolerate its flaws rather than too little, and by too much reticence in demanding better public policies rather than by excessive reforming zeal. The following chapters give expression to the authors' belief that Canadians have far more to fear from smug complacency than from critical reflection about their democracy and their rights.

Notes

1. The account in this paragraph, as well as the subsequent discussion of the role of rules and principles in the definition of rights, is simplified. Fuller discussions may be found in David Braybrooke, *Three Tests for Democracy* (New York: Random House, 1968), Part One; and Richard E. Flathman, *The Practice of Rights* (Cambridge: Cambridge University Press, 1976).
2. Richard Wasserstrom, "Rights, Human Rights, and Racial Discrimination," in *Rights*, ed. David Lyons (Belmont, California: Wadsworth, 1979), pp. 49–50. Although the exposition in the text is not, strictly speaking, a direct quotation, it does largely repeat Wasserstrom's own words.
3. H.L.A. Hart, "Are There Any Natural Rights?", *Philosophical Review* (1955), p. 175.
4. Alasdair MacIntyre, *After Virtue* (Notre Dame: University of Notre Dame Press, 1981), p. 67.
5. Although all rights in the strict sense imply correlative obligations, it is not the case that all obligations imply corresponding rights. Thus, there may be a duty to be charitable without anyone having a right to the charity of anyone else.
6. These terms are taken from Austin Ranney and Willmoore Kendall, *Democracy and the American Party System* (New York: Harcourt, Brace & World, 1956). Although the elaboration of these notions is indebted to Ranney and Kendall, the discussion in this book is not meant to be a summary of their views and it should not be assumed that they would agree with what is said here.
7. See Jane J. Mansbridge, *Beyond Adversary Democracy* (New York: Basic Books, 1980).
8. Strictly speaking, this emphasis on minority rights is inappropriate. Because the rights in question pertain as much to members of majorities as of minorities, they would be more appropriately designated as essential democratic rights, as they are later in this chapter. As a practical matter, however, a focus on minority rights is apt here because minority rights are the ones most likely to be infringed.
9. Greg Pyrcz is particularly dubious about conceptions of democracy that place an unduly heavy emphasis on rights. His conception of healthy political life is strongly influenced by the Rousseauian vision of co-operative, highly participatory endeavours to find mutually satisfactory

solutions to practical political problems. Although he is somewhat more prudent in his aspirations, he is sympathetic to the highly participatory "strong democracy" commended by Benjamin R. Barber in *Strong Democracy* (Berkeley: University of California Press, 1984). Pyrcz's contributions to this book place less emphasis on rights than do Pocklington's and far less than Carmichael's.

10. Charles S. Hyneman, *Popular Government in America* (New York: Atherton Press, 1968), p. 9.
11. See Denis Smith, *Bleeding Hearts, Bleeding Country* (Edmonton: Hurtig, 1971), and Thomas R. Berger, *Fragile Freedoms* (Toronto/Vancouver: Clarke, Irwin, 1982), Chapter 7.

CHAPTER 2

Pornography and the Problem of Rights

This chapter explores the controversy over the censorship of pornography and treats it as a test case of freedom of expression. In the essay, Don Carmichael reviews the leading arguments used by each side of the issue. The case against censorship is based primarily on the grounds that it violates the freedom of individuals, the press, and artists. The case for censorship is argued on the grounds that pornography is immoral, or promotes sexual assaults, or violates the rights of women to be treated with respect.

In Carmichael's view, a free society must respect the right of individuals to live and amuse themselves on their own terms. This is crucial because, although there are several excellent reasons for objecting to pornography in certain forms, they do not quite justify censorship because they do not override the right of individuals to live on their own terms. It has not been shown that pornographic materials directly incite sexual assault, and although they portray women in demeaning and offensive terms, this does not violate women's rights. Indeed he suggests that censorship based on women's rights may simply be a version of traditional moral conservatism "born again" in the language of human rights. The "bottom line" is that while pornography cannot be defended as genuine freedom of expression, what can be defended is the right of individuals to use it if they choose.

Greg Pyrcz disputes this in his critique. He argues that pornography directly and substantially harms women, and that this is a sufficient ground for censorship. Pyrcz develops this through the parallel case of hate literature by arguing that pornography heightens the fear and insecurity that many women already feel in Canadian society. He concludes that if this insecurity could be eliminated by censoring pornography, then pornography should be censored.

||E||S||S||A||Y||

Should pornography be censored? This question has become the subject of considerable controversy. It is said that pornography is immoral, vulgar, and offensive; that it violates women's rights; and that it endangers their security by legitimizing sexual aggression. These are strong reasons for censorship. It is also argued, however, that the enjoyment of pornography by mature adults is essentially a private matter; since it does not affect others directly, it should be none of their business. To censor pornography is therefore to violate the freedom of individual expression and publication. The question, therefore, is whether the reasons for censoring pornography are strong enough to justify restrictions on individual freedom.

Traditionally, conservatives objected to pornography primarily on moral grounds, because of their opposition to explicit or permissive sexuality, while "liberals" and radicals on the left objected to censorship in the name of free expression. Today, however, the issue is more complex. The traditional conservative view has been joined by the different claim, which is argued on the left and by many feminists, that pornography harms women. Together the two groups make a formidable political force, but they have little in common. Those who oppose pornography because it harms women do not object in principle to permissive sexuality; they usually hold views about the rights of women, and their rights in society, that are rejected entirely by traditional moral conservatives. Thus, while the two groups agree in opposing pornography, their reasons are antithetical: one groups seeks to prevent sin, while the other wants to protect human rights. An examination of the opposition to pornography, both from the "right" and from the "left," will show that some calls for censorship from the left may simply be a new, inverted form of moral conservatism, disguised in the language of human rights.

Preliminary Considerations

There has been a recent, major change in the nature of pornography in Canada and in public attitudes toward it. Twenty years ago, pornography was a relatively insignificant issue, confined to a handful of "girlie" magazines and seedy strip shows. It portrayed primarily adult sexual titillation. Opinions were divided about whether it should be permitted, but few people cared deeply about the issue, one way or the other.

Today, however, pornography is a major industry in the main-stream of society. Prime-time television commercials routinely use sexually suggestive material that would have been prosecuted twenty years ago. Once-deviant sexuality has become legitimate, and pornography now portrays violence, degradation, and the sexual abuse of children and animals. This material is widely accessible through magazines, videocassettes, and cable television, and much of it is readily available to children.

It is now conventional to distinguish "soft-core" pornography, which intends to portray and produce mild sexual titillation, from "hard-core" versions that feature violence, degradation, and bestiality.[1] This distinction is somewhat arbitrary. Another distinction, made particularly by some feminists, is between erotica, or "genuine" sexual expression, and pornography (from the Greek word for "harlot"), which degrades women.

Although widespread agreement exists on the need for censorship, intense disagreement exists about the kinds of pornography that should be restricted and the reasons for doing so. Most people agree that pornography featuring children should be banned, especially when it involves incest or violence, but some want to make exceptions for works of artistic merit. Similarly, although there is considerable pressure to ban hard-core pornography, there is also disagreement about what this entails. Among those who want to ban it because it degrades women and those who want to do so because of its sexual content, there are divisions over whether to exempt works of artistic merit and also over how much soft-core pornography to permit.

However the issue is decided, the principles that are legislated will be put into practice by the police, in deciding whether to prosecute, and by the courts, in deciding whether to convict. Vague principles give wider powers of interpretation to these agencies, and the result may very easily be that the principles on which citizens agree will be applied in terms they dislike. Consider the proposal to censor pornography that degrades women but to allow pornography that celebrates sexual expression. What does this mean? Some people argue that women cannot be degraded by any material, however offensive it may be, so long as they are not forced to view it. On this basis, nothing would be banned by the proposal. Others take the view that any presentation of the female body as a sexual object degrades women. This view would result in the banning of many television commercials. Thus, the proposal can be interpreted to ban either everything or nothing.

The Law

Pornography is subject to legal controls primarily through the obscenity provisions of the Criminal Code of Canada. Until 1958, the courts understood "obscenity" as it was defined by the Hicklin test of 1868:

> [T]he test of obscenity is this, whether the tendency of the matter charged as obscenity is to deprave and to corrupt those whose minds are open to such immoral influences, and into whose hands a publication of this sort may fall.[2]

By current standards, there are three problems with the Hicklin test: it focuses on the immorality of sexual expression, it says nothing about violence or degradation; and it does not permit a defence based on artistic or intellectual merit. In 1958, the Hicklin test was replaced by a statutory definition. Section 163(8)[3] of the Criminal Code stipulates that

> [f]or purposes of this Act, any publication a dominant characteristic of which is the undue exploitation of sex, or of sex and any one or more of the following subjects, namely, crime, horror, cruelty and violence, shall be deemed to be obscene.

This definition is not very clear. Whether any work can be judged obscene by it depends upon how "dominant" and "undue exploitation" are interpreted. The courts have interpreted them very liberally. "Dominant" has been held to mean that the exploitation of sex or sex-related themes must characterize the work as a whole, not just parts of it; and claims that this exploitation is "undue" may be offset by evidence of artistic merit. In effect, this interpretation exempts works in which sex is a subordinate theme.

Even works that are highly erotic may be defended on the grounds that sex is not exploited unduly in relation to the artistry of the treatment or the seriousness of the subject matter. More generally, the test of "undue" exploitation is whether the accepted standards of tolerance in the contemporary Canadian community have been exceeded. These standards do not refer to what members of the community themselves want to see or think it is right to see, but rather to what they would not abide being seen by others.

Section 163(8) of the Criminal Code is now more than thirty years old. It does not expressly address any of the problems raised by the more recent flood of pornography, such as material featuring children and the degradation of women, concerns that such material may prompt or legitimize sexual assaults, and the ready availability of such material to children. As a result, there is considerable support for tougher restrictions on pornography, but it tends to break down when specific proposals are made. In its first term of office, the Mulroney government introduced two bills on pornography. Both received initial support, then intense criticism, and finally were allowed to die.

A final legal issue is raised by the Canadian Charter of Rights and Freedoms. Section 2(b) guarantees "freedom of thought, belief, opinion and expression, including freedom of the press and other media of communication." This might invalidate legal restrictions on pornography, either through section 163(8) of the Criminal Code or any amendments. On the other hand, section 1 of the Charter asserts that the freedoms of section 2 are subject "to such reasonable limits prescribed by law as can be demonstrably justified in a free and democratic society." Thus, restrictions on pornography might be justified by section 1, even if they violate section 2. As a result, two questions arise: (i) can pornography be covered by section 2, as a legitimate case of freedom of expression; if so, (ii) can the freedom in this case reasonably be limited by the values of a "free and democratic" society?

There is very little case law dealing with these issues, and there is no way of telling how the Supreme Court of Canada will eventually decide them. However it decides, the court will have to answer the question that is the focus of this chapter: can restrictions upon freedom in the name of controlling pornography be "demonstrably justified" in "a free and democratic society"?

Should pornography be censored? The arguments on each side of this issue fall into three categories. The main argument against censorship is:
(i)   the freedom of individuals to read or view what they choose; to this may be added, as subordinate principles,
(ii) the freedom of the press and other media of communication; and
(iii) the freedom of artists.
The main arguments in favour of censoring pornography are that:
(i)   it is immoral, vulgar, or offensive;
(ii) it harms women by inciting or legitimizing acts of assault; and
(iii) it violates the rights of women to be treated with dignity and respect.
The following discussion considers these issues separately.[4]

Freedom

The primary value of liberty is that it permits individuals to live on their own terms. This is a fundamental commitment of a liberal–democratic society. Thus, although section 2(b) of the Charter guarantees freedom equally to individuals and to the press, the freedom of individuals should be more important than that of the press. Freedom of the press might reasonably be restricted to protect the security and effective freedom of individuals; such a society would still be "free and democratic" as required by section 1. But the society would not be "free and democratic" if individual thought and expression were restricted.

Freedom of thought and expression, in turn, can be exercised fully only in a society that allows extensive freedom of the press and other media of communication. Freedom of the press therefore, is not a fundamental value in its own right, but rather the means of protecting and promoting the freedom of individuals. It follows that freedom of the press must depend upon how it affects individuals. The freedom to publish pornography may be defended to protect the freedom of individuals to read it; conversely, it may be restricted if it violates other rights and liberties.

This argument leaves little to be said in support of the freedom of the press to disseminate pornography. Most pornography is without artistic or intellectual merit; it does not inform people about the world, develop their faculties, or offer different vistas to their imaginations. It is produced simply as commercial titillation, and increasingly in forms that feature and endorse violence, degradation, and abuse. The freedom to consume such material[5] cannot plausibly be defended as a fundamental liberal issue, as if it were like the right to read the Bible or Karl Marx. Thus, since pornography is produced and consumed simply as commercial amusement, it may be regulated by the same restrictions that apply elsewhere in the marketplace. "Freedom of the press" in this context has no special value.

This does not mean that pornography may be regulated without restriction. However vulgar it may be, it is an expression of individual taste. Endorsement of the general principle that individuals ought to be free to live on their own terms means that amusement through pornography should be protected by the "freedom of thought" provision of section 2(b), and that only very strong reasons should be allowed under section 1 to restrict it.

Should special exceptions be made for works of artistic or intellectual merit? If pornography is protected in the name of freedom of thought, then this protection must be correspondingly stronger for works of an intellectual or artistic nature that genuinely involve this value. Moreover, this special protection should cover all works that truly aspire to protect freedom of thought, regardless of their merit or their success in achieving it. Protection based on merit may protect only the best and—in the name of freedom of thought—ban all the rest. Hence, *any* work should be given special protection to the extent that it seeks to inform, develop capacities, or enlarge the imagination.

However, this special protection has limits. Some people wave the banner of artistic freedom over the issue as an absolute principle, as if works of artistic and intellectual distinction should never be censored.[6] There are, however, reasons for restricting freedom of expression in other cases that might also apply to artistic works.

Suppose someone is defamed by two works, crudely in one case but with great power and artistry in the other. Would anyone suggest that the artistic work was not defamatory or that it should be exempted from liability on this account? On the contrary, its defamation might be all the more effective and enduring because of its artistry. Similarly, if a film were of such power that it provoked viewers to acts of sexual assault, would its artistic quality be a reason to exempt it from censorship? No; the film might be more dangerous precisely because of its artistry, and therefore more deserving of censorship on this account. It might be said that such works do not corrupt because of their artistic quality. But this is to say that such works are unsuccessful, that they fail to affect those who view them. This "defends" artists by insulting them! The same applies to all other reasons for censorship. Although works of artistic or intellectual merit deserve special protection, this protection is qualified. The idea of absolute freedom for artistic or intellectual works is nonsense.

The Value and Limits of Liberty

Thus far a strong case has been made for individual freedom. But do the reasons for censoring pornography justify limitations of this freedom? To answer this, the reasons for censorship must be weighed against the value of the freedom they would limit. This is a daunting task, but it can be simplified by considering why liberty is valuable. Two views may be distinguished here.

The most common view is that the value of any liberty depends upon the morality of the conduct it permits. If the conduct is morally acceptable, then it should be permitted by law as a liberty, and in important cases, such as freedom of religion, this liberty should be protected as a fundamental right. If the conduct is morally wrong, it should not be permitted. In short, liberty is based on, and limited by, morality. No fundamental value is assigned to the freedom of individuals to decide for themselves how best to live. What matters is that they should live in ways that are morally right.

The second view is more individualistic. Society is understood as consisting of a number of individuals, each with their own lives to lead. As a result, the authority of the society derives from the more basic rights of the individuals who, in principle, are mature adults capable of governing themselves.[6] All of them are presumed to be responsible for deciding how to live and for acting accordingly. The result is a conception of justice and law that places a high value on individual freedom. Insofar as individuals are the proper custodians of their own lives, they ought to be as free as possible to live on their own terms, and this freedom should be limited only to protect the equal freedom of others.

These are sharply contrasting positions. One holds that liberty depends upon morality; the other holds that morality is something individuals should be free to determine for themselves. This does not mean that what individuals think is therefore true—as if all possible views were equally true—but merely that adults are competent to determine such views for themselves.[7] They may not do so wisely or well; their views of life may be well or poorly founded, concerned for others or narrowly self-absorbed, and so on. They are, however, presumed to be competent, and therefore entitled, to determine such views for themselves. In this respect, individuals should be free not because there is no truth about morality, but rather because one basic truth is that individuals are entitled to decide such issues for themselves.

The "moralistic model" denies this. By restricting liberty to morally correct conduct, it limits the freedom of individuals to determine for themselves how to live and treats them like creatures who are not capable of governing themselves. Although some individuals may need to be governed by others, it is unreasonable to assume that all do, by imposing a morality of correct choices upon them. This is a definite weakness of the moralist model, and in what follows the individualist approach is assumed.

This approach answers the question posed by section 1 of the Charter. Freedom of expression is guaranteed by section 2(b), subject to restrictions under section 1 that are reasonable "in a free and democratic society." In situations concerning the ability of individuals to decide for themselves how to live, this freedom should be as extensive as possible and should be limited only to ensure the equal freedom and security of others. With reference to the Charter, it follows that freedom of expression as guaranteed by section 2(b) may be limited under section 1 by only one kind of consideration, that is, where it is necessary to protect the equal freedom and security of others. In all other cases, freedom of expression should be unlimited. What happens when this is applied to the reasons for censoring pornography?

Morality, Vulgarity, and Offensiveness

Pornography has been claimed to be immoral, vulgar, and offensive. While all of these are reasons for objecting to pornography, none of them is a reason for censoring it. Even if pornography is immoral, this does not mean that those who indulge in it are incapable of governing themselves. They must be allowed to be immoral in this way if they choose. Conversely, to censor pornography because of its immorality is to treat those who consume it as if they were incapable of directing their own lives.

It may be also objected that pornography corrupts those who consume it. If this were correct, those who like pornography are corrupted and unable to make a "free" decision about it; hence pornography must be restricted to protect them from corruption. It is not clear, however, that there is any "corruption" here, other than the fact that many people apparently enjoy pornography. Nor is there any reason to treat this enjoyment as evidence that such persons are incapable of deciding the terms of their own lives.

Does the enjoyment of murder mysteries indicate corruption? Are those who spend their leisure time reading thrillers instead of poetry necessarily unable to make a free choice between the two? Should thrillers be banned to protect readers from corruption? Clearly, it is absurd to try to protect individuals by requiring that they read what they don't enjoy. The more fundamental issue, however, is this: if individuals want to corrupt their taste or character by reading thrillers or pornography instead of poetry, this is a personal matter.

In a free society, individuals must be allowed to act in ways that are imprudent or corrupting. They may be urged to act more wisely, but they cannot be required to act as others think best. To respect them as competent adults is to recognize that they are able to decide for themselves how to live, and so long as they do not infringe the equal freedom and security of others, this is their right. Similar considerations apply to the vulgarity and offensiveness[8] of pornography. If an individual chooses to be vulgar, so what? If this vulgarity does not directly harm others, it should be none of their business. However despicable an individual's taste, others must respect that person's right to decide it for himself or herself.

Many feel that society must have the right to legislate standards of acceptable behaviour, and consequently that fundamentally immoral, indecent, or offensive acts should be forbidden. But what is "society"? It does not exist in its own right, as a separate entity, but only as a set of individuals. Its authority derives from, and must respect, the more fundamental rights of its members. When any society violates these rights, its authority is illegitimate. Moralistic legislation and censorship violate one of the most basic of these rights, that of individual self-determination. Society cannot legislate on this basis, therefore, without violating its own legitimacy.

Yet the objection may persist: "Surely the majority must have the right to decide what is best for society, and to legislate standards on this basis." The question now arises, "What is the majority?" There is no magic power or secret authority in a majority that somehow makes its decisions correct, wise, or inherently right. The majority, like the minority, is only a group of individuals; the only difference is that there are more of them. Each, however, is a separate individual, and taken together they constitute the society on an equal basis.

Thus the majority may legitimately legislate standards of behaviour in the name of society so long as it does not oppress the minority or use the authority of society in a way that would violate it. In any society that considers itself free and democratic, therefore, the democratic principle of the right of the majority must be limited by a respect for the right of individuals to govern themselves, subject only to restrictions that protect the equal freedom and security of others. Each individual has this right. It cannot legitimately be infringed by other individuals, not even when they add up to a majority.

The Problem of Harm

The claim that pornography incites sexual assaults is a powerful objection. No one in a civilized society can be permitted to harm others, and proof that pornography causes assaults would be sufficient reason to restrict it. But does pornography cause sexual assault? Although it seems inconceivable that anyone could consume hard-core pornography without being affected by it, causality is difficult to establish.

Any claim of causality hinges upon the strength of the correlation between the supposed cause and effect, and the correlation must include both positive and negative factors. This is a problem in the case of pornography because the instances that confirm its causality vastly out number those that negate it. If it were shown, for example, that every male convicted of sexual assault was a pornography consumer, what would this prove? Virtually all men have read or viewed pornography at some point. If pornography caused sexual assault, then it should do so in all cases. The correlation would be no better than that between sexual assault and being male; there would be no more reason to conclude causality in one case than in the other.

One can get better correlations by specifying the variables more precisely. For example, it might be objected that many more men are guilty of sexual assault than are ever convicted. But even if we suppose that one male in five is guilty of sexual assault, there are still four cases counting against the alleged causality for every case that confirms it. As a claim of direct causality, this is weak.

As a result, it is difficult to prove that pornography directly causes sexual assault. However the variables are juggled, the instances confirming causality are overwhelmed by those contradicting it. This is clearest in the case of soft-core pornography. Any claim of direct causality for it is quite implausible, given the large numbers of people who read and view such material without being driven to violence by it. The same may be true of hard-core pornography. Although this material is far more offensive, it is not clear that it directly provokes those who consume it to violence. Here again, claims of direct causality are imperilled by a majority of negative cases.

What, exactly, is the nature of this supposed direct causality? One possibility is that pornography is sexually stimulating, so much so that it overpowers the individual's will and provokes immediate acts of assault. However, evidence suggests that pornography is simply not that provocative or interesting. An alternative view is that the causality of pornography exists in establishing attitudes toward women—as objects of sexual prey—that lead to assaults. This view is more credible, because it focuses attention on the assailant's attitudes and the determinants of those attitudes. But it alters the primary causal relation to one between assaults and attitudes. The causality of pornography, because it influences the attitudes, is now indirect. This suggests that the difficulty of proving direct causality may be due to the fact that it does not exist, and that the causality of pornography is instead secondary and indirect.[9]

Why do individuals enjoy pornography in the first place? They must already have held certain attitudes, such as regarding women as objects of sexual prey, before consuming the pornography, or they would not have acquired or enjoyed it. Thus pornography alone cannot be the cause of such attitudes. It might reinforce or legitimize them, but these attitudes must exist before, and to some extent as causes of, the interest in pornography. The enjoyment of pornography must be as much the effect of such attitudes as their cause; so its causality cannot be direct.

This does not mean that pornography is irrelevant to sexual assault. Its causality is probably secondary and indirect, as it is in the case of alcohol, in reducing inhibitions and legitimizing and reinforcing sexually violent and aggressive attitudes toward women. Although this remains to be proven, it is a real possibility. For example, the indirect causality of soft-core pornography and mainstream entertainment may be insidious. Although hard-core pornography is more offensive; it is not ubiquitous. The presentation of women in other media, however, has an extensive audience and might have more insidious effects because it appears to be legitimate.

The analogy with alcohol suggests that if the causality of pornography is indirect, the case for censorship is weakened.[10] Alcohol is not banned because of its violent effects; why should we treat pornography any differently? It might be said that alcohol and pornography are morally different. There is nothing intrinsically wrong with alcohol, so it would be wrong to deny it to those who enjoy it simply because some abuse it. It would be difficult to make the same claim about pornography, as though it were a good thing that a few misuse. On the contrary, pornography is considered either neutral or offensive. But although this moral distinction claims that alcohol may be good in a way that pornography is not, it does not show that the effects of the two are different. It does not establish any causal basis for treating pornography differently. Since alcohol is allowed, pornography should be permitted.

It might be replied, however, that there is a major difference between the two, with respect to the effects of their enjoyment. One might say, "There is nothing wrong in the enjoyment of alcohol, nor is there any necessary connection between drinking and sexual violence. But there is such a connection in the case of pornography. Hard-core pornography revels in sexual assault and humiliation. It invites the enjoyment in fantasy of acts and attitudes that are morally hideous in reality."

This, however, does not prove causality. Although it explains why the enjoyment of hard-core pornography is morally offensive, it does not show that this enjoyment is causally dangerous. Granted, it is difficult to see how individuals could enjoy such material without being affected by it, and it is tempting to suppose that such enjoyment in fantasy establishes attitudes toward women that lead to assaults in reality. Yet it is apparent that this causality is difficult to establish, that it is probably of a weak and indirect nature, and that an interest in pornography must to some extent be the effect of the very attitudes it is said to cause. What remains is an assertion of strong causality that on analysis is reduced to a possible claim of indirect causality, or reinforcement, and a very strong moral objection. By itself, the moral objection does not establish causality. Therefore, the claim that pornography ought to be censored because it incites assault appears to be a claim of morality dressed up as though it were a claim of causality.

Sufficient grounds would exist for censoring pornography if, and to the extent that, it were shown to incite sexual assault. The problem is that direct causality is difficult to establish, while indirect causality is easier to establish but does not provide a sufficient ground for censorship. In discussing censorship, it is particularly important to beware of moral objections masquerading as causal claims. This awareness does not negate moral objections, but it does mean that they should be assessed for what they are. Although one may believe that the enjoyment of sexual assault is morally offensive and an insult to the dignity of all women, in itself this is not a sufficient ground for censorship.

Self-Respect, Dignity, and Human Rights

Can a stronger case for censorship be made on the grounds that pornography violates women's rights? Pornography expressly presents women as subordinate and inferior, as creatures who may be used and abused as objects of pleasure, degradation, and violence. It may therefore be argued that pornography violates the right of women to be treated with dignity and respect, the essential right of every human being in a civilized society.

This is a complex claim. It uses the apparently liberal considerations of human rights to argue the apparently illiberal conclusion of censorship. At the same time, there is no reason in principle why liberalism cannot justify censorship, as long as it is in the name of extending effective human freedom. Traditional nineteenth-century liberalism took a more restrictive view, namely that individual freedom could be limited only to protect others from direct and immediate harm. This was typically advocated in the belief that liberty has an essential role in permitting individuals to live autonomously, on their own terms. A major development in liberalism over the past century has been a change in the way this autonomy has been understood. Today, most liberals believe that liberty will be effective in realizing individual autonomy only if it is accompanied by certain measures of material security and self-respect. These must be guaranteed to individuals, even at the cost of limiting other liberties. Whether and to what extent this should be done depends upon what will establish the most effective freedom for all individuals. Thus there is no objection in principle to the idea of censoring in the name of human rights; nor is there any reason why liberals cannot insist upon this. It all depends upon whether such censorship extends or diminishes freedom. This principle, however, allows the justification of censorship *only* in the name of freedom and not on any other basis, such as morality or public policy. Hence if pornography is censored to protect human rights, these rights must be shown to be essential for autonomy, that is, for individuals to be able to live on their own terms.

This point needs emphasis because of a current tendency to treat all of the ways in which individuals ought to be treated as their rights.[11] This is incorrect. Although one ought to give money to those in need, this does not mean that they have a right to it, or, that it belongs to them, not to the owner, in any sense that would justify them in taking it. On the contrary, the owner has the right to dispose of it as he or she chooses; and while the owner ought to donate it to those in need, it is his or her right not to do so. By contrast, if the owner had promised the money to the needy, they would have a right to it; they might then demand it from the owner, and he or she would have no right to refuse because it would belong to them. Thus "rights" claims are stronger than "ought" claims. If A ought to be treated with respect, then other persons have a duty to do so, but they cannot be required to act upon it. Hence they remain free to decide for themselves what their duty is and how to act.

But if A has a right to such respect, then other persons are required to give this respect, and they may be required to do so by A. In this case, they have no freedom to decide otherwise, because their freedom is limited by A's right. Because rights claims are so much stronger, therefore, it should take more evidence to establish them. It is not enough to show merely that A ought to be treated in a certain way; it must also be shown that the reasons that establish this duty also entitle A to limit the freedom of others in requiring such treatment from them.

An important conclusion follows from this. Because a right entitles the individual to limit the freedom of others, it follows that in legislating rights we establish the freedom of some individuals to limit the freedom of others. In the extreme case, if "ought" claims automatically established claims of right, then each person would have the right to require morally correct behaviour from all others; but by gaining this right, people would also lose the right to decide for themselves how to act in relation to one another. Independence and autonomy would be eviscerated in the name of individual rights!

As this suggests, much of the program of traditional moral conservatism may be restated in the language of individual rights. If the claim that all individuals ought to be treated with respect is taken to mean that all individuals have a right to be treated in this way, behaviour that offends any individuals could be said to violate their right, since it fails to treat them with respect. On this basis, all behaviour that appears immoral or offensive might be forbidden in the name of human rights.

This would be a parody of human rights. It is, however, a real danger, especially when legislating human rights in matters of dignity and self-respect. This is not to say that these rights should not be guaranteed, but simply that efforts to do so should ensure that any such right truly extends effective freedom and is not merely a pretext for legislating morally correct behaviour. The test is whether the right is required specifically to protect the autonomy of the individual. If, instead, it is advocated only because that is how people ought to be treated, then it is not a matter of right but of morality.

Which kind of claim is involved in the assertion that pornography violates womens' rights? Although pornography demeans women and in this respect is morally offensive, moral offensiveness alone does not establish claims of right, so it cannot be used to limit the freedom of others. The question, therefore, is whether anything stronger can be said. Can it be shown that pornography in some respect violates women's autonomy?

Since pornography systematically portrays women as inferior and subordinate, the public expression or institutional endorsement of this attitude violates the right of each woman to be considered in public on her own merits, as an individual. It does not follow, however, that anyone's rights are violated by the private expression of such attitudes. In permitting individuals to amuse themselves in private as they choose, the community does not endorse such amusements; rather, it takes the view that, being private, they are not a matter for public scrutiny. The fact that pornography is permitted by law does not mean that it is endorsed any more than ethnic jokes are endorsed by the fact that the law does not forbid them. Hence the private enjoyment of pornography cannot be said to violate anyone's rights in the same sense as would community endorsement of the same attitudes.

In what sense, then, can the private production or consumption of pornography violate women's rights? Consider a case: A produces a pornographic film; B (female) "stars" in it; C rents it; and D objects. Whose rights are violated? So long as there is no question of community endorsement of this material, the only rights at stake are those of the individuals involved. Thus it is B's right to act in the film if she chooses; others, in producing or viewing it, cannot violate her rights if she consents. So far as B is concerned, her rights are violated by the film only if her consent is not given or is abused. Failing this, is it correct to say that B cannot be in the film because doing so would violate her rights? This would be nonsense. If she has any rights at all, it is up to her to decide whether and how to exercise them. Although the film demeans her dignity, therefore, it must also be her right to waive this dignity if she chooses. To say that she cannot do so because it would violate her rights is merely to use the pretext of her rights as an excuse to violate them.

It might be said that no self-respecting woman would allow herself to be used in such a film. But this is something individuals must decide for themselves; it is B's right to decide whether she wants this kind of self-respect, and how much it is worth to her. Others are not entitled—in the name of B's rights—to impose their version of self-respect upon her. In this case B's rights are not violated by the film. They would be violated only if she were prevented (by D's objections) from appearing in it.[12]

Does pornography violate the rights of other women? Those who make such claims are quite rightly offended by pornography, but it is not clear whether pornography violates their rights. Is the question of rights and self-respect perhaps only a liberal (or "emancipated") version of moral conservatism, which the previous discussion showed was an insufficient basis for censorship? This question arises because there is a major problem with the idea that it could violate women's rights. Pornography demeans women only if their sense of dignity and self-worth is actually reduced by it. How could the fact that someone enjoys pornography diminish any woman's sense of self-respect, or have anything at all to do with the way in which she understands herself?

One would think that the views of those who enjoy pornography would be dismissed by women as absolutely without consequence; hence these views could not demean women because they would have no effect upon how women regard themselves. The converse is also true: a woman's sense of self-respect could be diminished by pornography only if she first allowed her sense of herself to be defined by it or by those who enjoy it. She can be demeaned only through her own consent; hence her rights are not violated. So, although pornography may offend women's sense of self-respect, it cannot do so in any way that violates their rights because the terms of self-respect are determined by individuals for themselves.

It follows that the way to stop pornography from demeaning women is not to censor it, but rather for women to dismiss it and those who enjoy it as irrelevant. Conversely, to censor pornography because it demeans women is to treat women as though they were incapable of determining their own terms of self-respect. This approach determines that women must be shielded from offensive views because, like children, they are not capable of autonomy. In effect, it denies women's rights in the name of protecting them. It appears to be traditional moral conservatism dressed up in the language of human rights.

Autonomy and Censorship

It might be said that this analysis is unrealistic in supposing that all adults are fully autonomous, that it ignores the difficulties involved in becoming autonomous in Western society. Individual autonomy and self-respect are dependent to some extent on the terms in which one understands oneself, and gender is basic in each child's self-definition. If women are systematically presented in subordinate terms, a sense of subordination will be instilled into each young woman's developing sense of herself. It would therefore be naive to suggest that women are free to ignore the attitudes conveyed by pornography and those who enjoy it.

There should be no doubt about where my own sympathies lie on this point. The presentation of women in pornography is offensive, and the idea that individuals can be entertained by hard-core pornography is truly disturbing. As one student put it, "They're not playing with a full deck." In these respects, the pornography issue reflects and symbolizes the vulnerabilities of women in our society. But censorship is a mistaken response. The presentation of women as subordinate is not confined to pornography or to the fringes of society. Similar attitudes are conveyed more systematically through mainstream entertainment and may be more insidious because they are viewed more widely, especially by youngsters, and under conditions that appear to condone them.

If its concern is to promote autonomy, society should focus on the material viewed by young women and men; but any kind of censorship in this case is beside the point. It does nothing to correct current attitudes toward women; it merely silences unpopular views. As an exercise in developing autonomy, therefore, it is counterproductive. In the final analysis, autonomy—being one's own person and responsible for one's own destiny—is a value that each individual must produce for herself or himself. It can only be produced the "hard way," by confronting obstacles directly. On this point, perhaps, men and women in our society have much in common.

Notes

Earlier versions of this paper have been read at meetings of the Atlantic Provinces Political Science Association at Acadia University on October 26, 1985, and a symposium at the University of Calgary on March 13, 1986. The author is grateful to those present on each occasion for their lively comments, especially to Greg Pyrcz, Tom Pocklington, and a number of students for their generous criticisms on the earliest version, notwithstanding their disagreement with some of its claims.

1. See *Pornography and Prostitution in Canada: Report of the Special Committee on Pornography and Prostitution* (the Fraser Commission), Vol. 1 (Ottawa: Supply and Services Canada, 1985), p. 59.
2. R. v. Hicklin, L.R. 3 Q.B., 369 at 371.
3. This section was numbered 159 until December 1988.
4. This analysis deals only with adults. The consumption of pornography by or involving minors is best treated as a special case.
5. Reference here is to the "bulk" of pornography, not to special cases of artistic or intellectual merit, which are considered later in the essay.
6. See, for example, the Fraser Commission *Report*, pp. 274 ff., and recommendation 7.
7. A common defence of liberty today is that "each person's opinion is as valid as any other's" and that "there are no moral truths"; hence there is no basis for moralistic legislation. The problem with such claims is that they allow no basis for freedom either, because there could be no reason for any point of value. The argument here, however, is that certain moral claims are more firmly based than others and that there is a better moral basis for liberty, grounded in the competence and entitlement of mature adults, than against it.
8. An excellent account of why offence can be subject to restriction and of the limits of doing so is Joel Feinberg's *Offense to Others* (New York: Oxford University Press, 1985).
9. The Fraser Commission *Report*, p. 99, stated emphatically that, on the basis of the evidence and research it considered, it could not conclude that pornography was a "significant causal factor" in the commission of violent crime.
10. Arguments for censorship based on indirect causality can cut both ways.

It has been argued that the emancipation of women in western societies has led to increases in criminal activity by women. This claim may be disputed but even if it were true it would not be a reason to oppose the freedom of women. This is discussed by Joel Feinberg in *Offense to Others* (New York: Oxford University Press, 1985) at p. 155, quoting an unpublished paper by Fred Berger.

11. Thus, the evil of child abuse is construed as though it were a violation of the child's rights; similarly, the fact that pornography demeans women is automatically treated as though it were a violation of women's rights. This is mistaken. Surely the evil of child abuse is independent of, and logically prior to, questions about whether the child has rights that are violated.

12. Similar considerations apply to A and C in producing and viewing the film. So long as those directly involved consent, there is no violation of a right. In this case, then, rights would be violated only if D's objection prevented the other individuals from doing what they wanted to do.

CRITIQUE

In his essay, Don Carmichael provocatively challenges those who would like to prohibit pornography in the name of morality. In doing so, he presents one stream of contemporary feminism as moralism in disguise. His argument rests upon a specific notion of individual autonomy: adult human beings are capable of making the best decisions for themselves by themselves. Accordingly, they ought to be left free to make these decisions as long as they do not harm or restrict others in the process. The most important decisions people make are those that define the kind of persons they are or seek to become. Defining themselves, without the interference of others, is here the principal means by which people achieve and maintain individual identity and self-respect.

Censorship of opinion is inconsistent with this notion of personal integrity. At the very least, it is an affront to those who understand themselves in this way. In Carmichael's view, to treat anyone as incapable of maintaining integrity of personality, even in the face of the vilest, most demeaning opinions of others, is to treat that person as a child. This is what, in his view, some feminists and all conservatives do to persons in general when they support the censorship of pornography.

Although I share Carmichael's commitment to human autonomy, this however, does not mean that pornography must be tolerated by law. Freedom of expression need not be such a comprehensive right, not even in a liberal democratic regime. The censorship of some pornography can expand human freedom and self-respect, rather than impede it. This contention relies on the concept of *effective degradation*.

The effective degradation of an individual or a group constitutes direct and substantial harm to these persons. To degrade persons is to treat them as if they belonged to a lower order of beings. *Effective* degradation undermines the psychological resources available to such persons. It denies them the powers crucial to choosing, achieving, and maintaining an autonomous identity. In its debilitating and sometimes crippling effect upon a person's inner resources, effective degradation undermines a self-respect in which everyone has an interest, that is, the positive self-regard that Carmichael *assumes* in his defence of freedom of expression.

The disagreement with Carmichael can be summarized as follows. Many, if not most, people (women *and* men) are vulnerable to psychological weakness when they exist in a social context in which they are systematically and contemptuously regarded as belonging to a lower order of beings. Moreover, they are not, as a consequence of this simple and general human vulnerability, children housed in adult bodies. Carmichael holds that such vulnerability is simply not a characteristic of adult human beings. To assert it as a characteristic of women, he contends, is to degrade the very persons whom censorship of pornography would principally seek to protect.

It is largely irrelevant to this defence of limited censorship whether or not pornography is immoral, though it appears that part of pornography's appeal to those who consume it is that it regards women as objects of often violent desire and domination. Still, there are practices in this society that, while immoral, have no debilitating effect upon its members' psychological or inner powers. Indeed, most immorality is of this nature: while it may offend people, exposure to it does not undermine the inner resources they need to govern their own lives. This does not mean that there is no general connection between what people take to be immoral and their internal sense of well-being. Whatever morally offends people can psychologically discomfort or, *hurt* them, but the hurt of some as a sufficient ground to censor the expression of others only occurs in the most oppressive of regimes.

Censorship is not warranted even if it were to be shown that those who produce pornography and those who consume it have "tarnished souls." The purpose of law in liberal societies is not to determine moral character, but rather to protect individuals' freedom to define it for themselves. As such, questions of individual moral development are simply not open to public determination. This commitment separates moral paternalism (conservativism on the issue of pornography) from feminism, a distinction that the essay blurs. Conservatives focus on the immorality of pornography to seek a role for the community in guiding the moral development of individual citizens. Feminists are largely disinterested in the morality of pornography. They are concerned instead with the real harm pornography does to the power of women to act freely in their communities.

It is also irrelevant to the issue—though Carmichael provides a powerful critique of behaviourist attempts to fashion public policy in matters of morality—that no empirical evidence has sustained the conclusion that exposure to pornography leads men to assault or otherwise abuse women. If such a causal connection could be sustained, the case for censorship of pornography would be a strong one. But even if it can't, this does not imply that censorship is wholly unwarranted.

The effective harm done to women by pornography is not indirect, through the potentially violent and discriminatory actions of others who are predisposed and ill-disposed against them, but direct. It undermines the inner confidence of some women and harms the psychological resources necessary to exercise the freedom of choice enjoyed by other human beings.

Carmichael points tellingly to the fact that the pornographer's hostile disposition toward women exists before, not after, the consumption of pornography; it is a predisposition. But this discovery too is largely irrelevant to the real justification of pornography. Society may not be able to purge itself of hostile predispositions toward women, short of inciting a cultural revolution, but it can forbid the expression of this hostility if the attitude is shown to be harmful. The feminist need not believe that censoring pornography will cure a society of sexism, but simply that it will prevent some psychological harm being done to some women.

The assertion that the practice of pornography significantly lessens the inner resources of some women is a bold one. However, this critique does not try to prove such harm; it seeks to persuade the reader that the assertion of pornography's direct harm to women is a strongly plausible one and that the essay's defence of freedom of expression is much less persuasive in the light of this strong plausibility.

The first step in this direction is to draw the reader's attention to the difficulty most individuals seem to have in expressing a personality that doesn't merely mimic or surrender to the expectations of others. It seems that living a life that doesn't just imitate one's role models or peers or play out Hollywood's symbols or stock roles is a struggle for many. So, too, is moving beyond the aspirations of one's family, class, church, or fraternity. The real struggle for authenticity, for defining one's own aspirations, is well catalogued both in philosophical works and in creative literature. Moreover, psychological texts are rich with accounts of the various stages in the challenging process of individuation in contemporary liberal democratic culture, a political culture in which individual autonomy is among the most important goals of human development.

Nor need one have many courses in sociology to see that a strong current of conformity operates in most of society's groups and subgroups. It is the push and pull on the individual by significant reference groups that makes the elements of political organization, such as leadership, party and pressure-group politics, and campaigning, relatively easy matters. While people are not born sheep, neither are they born rebels. The ability to define and maintain one's chosen identity, especially in the face of social consensus and convention, is a difficult task even for adults. Adult individuality is an achievement that requires inner resources that are active, well-honed, and secure. To disregard this, as I believe Carmichael's argument must if it is to succeed, is to misread the concrete human context in which freedom functions.

The discussion concerning the relative infirmity of adult confidence—that individuals are not easily the powerful creatures the essay assumes them to be—raises a related point. While it is plausible that human beings are capable of defining their own character, no human beings do so alone. The human identity that people will for themselves (through choice) is brought into being by reference to or in the light of the opinions of others. What others expect of individuals, what the culture and social context tease out in their nature, what the aims are of their closest communities, are not merely hurdles to be jumped over on the way to an autonomous identity. They are also among the most important means by which human lives are defined. It seems that as social beings, people require the reference points, the hurdles, provided by the acknowledgments and assessments of others. What others think of them is among the most important data people rely upon, if only to deny it, in making even radically autonomous choices.

The heart of this critique's argument for the censorship of some pornography is that some hurdles—those assessments provided by others that degrade individuals or groups—are in fact obstacles too great for many people to surmount. Instead of dismissing the expression of racism or sexism, its victims often give in to it. To expect them to do otherwise is to expect the unreasonable, to expect that they act not as human beings, but as heroes. This is unreasonable.

What is it about the expression of degrading opinion that makes it too unreasonable a hurdle in human development for a liberal democracy legally to tolerate? It has been asserted that some degradation is effective, that it undermines the confidence necessary for individuals to choose for themselves, as they ought to, within communities of opinion. But more than this seems to be required. How is this confidence undermined in the self-regard of those who are members of a group degraded by pornography? What is it that some pornography does to some women that effectively and unjustly undermines their psychological powers?

Here it may be helpful to ask whether or not legally to tolerate the practice of ethnic–racial hate literature. Hate literature seems to constitute effective degradation when it evokes fear in the members of the group it degrades. Were it not for the past persecution of some ethnic–racial minorities, attempts to degrade members of such groups might be viewed by them as mere offence or hurt, not harm. Almost everyone has had an experience of being referred to as less than fully human, but unless he or she believes that the name-caller intends harm, such opinions are rather easy to dismiss. However, where the person in question does harm and has the potential to harm further, the language this person employs is not easily disregarded. Harm experienced by members of a group degraded by others is, like that experience by the individual, central to the effect of subsequent degradation.

It is the fear of proven harm from others, a sense of victimization, that triggers the crisis of confidence in those who belong to the group at whom expressed hatred or degradation is directed. A hostile attitude toward women does not depend upon exposure to pornography. Rather, pornography is the result of the hostile predisposition against women in those who produce and consume it. Thus, women harmed by pornography are not at risk of any more subsequent harm than they would be if pornography were banned. Similarly, ethnic–racial minorities may not be in jeopardy of more harm as a consequence of the hate literature directed at them. So why forbid its expression?

Carmichael misses the point here: while pornography and hate literature may cause no more harm to those they victimize, they confirm and heighten the real fears of members of the groups they depict. This effect is harmful because it further restricts the fearful individual. All members of a society face the prospect that harm may be done to them in their everyday lives. They may be struck down by a drunken driver, mugged by a cocaine addict, denied a job for which they are best qualified, perhaps even manipulated by their friends. However, the prospect of such harm, real as it is, prevents few of them from acting with confidence in their lives. They continue to go about their lives, to relate to and define themselves by reference to others as if they were not the intended victims of such harm. Those who do not do so are thought to be neurotic, to suffer phobias, to be imagining the likelihood of harm to be far greater than it actually is. In most communities, if individuals do not have the confidence to walk to the corner store for a litre of milk because they fear that "coke fiends" will rob them, that fear is irrational. The odds, and therefore the rationality, of the choice might be different if one lived in Miami.

However, the harm done to women by assault and discrimination is different from the harm discussed above in three important ways. First, some harm done to women is done simply because they are women. This is quite unlike the sort of harm to which males are vulnerable, whether they live in Wolfville or Miami. This would be true, of course, unless I were to be pursued by a person after *me*, or a group of "me", say a group of "professor torturers". It may be that I heighten the likelihood of personal harm if I appear well-to-do in Miami or professorial in a professor hating town, but these are qualities that I can do something about and perhaps ought to if it doesn't compromise my chosen identity. This is quite *unlike* the quality of gender. The fear (or the "victimization") some women know would be more like my "fear" of violent or discriminatory "professor haters", were such a group to exist and where being a professor was inescapably a matter of my identity, than it is like my general terror of life in Miami.

Second, the harm done to women is suffered irrespective of the community in which they live. Although some forms of sexual assault are more likely to occur in some communities, the overall likelihood of assault and especially discrimination against women is not as geographically variable as are the general threats to males. Third, the harm done to women as women is harm *celebrated*, both subtly and clearly, in visual and written pornography. The generalized harm to which males are vulnerable is not celebrated in the same way. Even where violence is portrayed as falling upon unsuspecting and unknowing male victims, there is less cause for them to associate their prospects with such portrayals (and therefore to feel more fearful and less confident) than there is for a woman to identify herself with portrayals of violence against women.

Is, then, this special fear of harm experienced by a woman, the corresponding loss of inner resources, and the confidence to act in society and to govern herself irrational when it is heightened by pornography in her community? No. Although it may be true, as Carmichael holds, that pornography does not alter the likelihood of harm done to women, it does change the way these odds are assessed by them. This difference in the assessment is totally justified. Everyone acts somewhat irrationally or courageously when making decisions about the type of life that is, for them, worth living. These actions and choices require that individuals go forward in the face of some danger and social consensus. But their courage to do so is a function of *their* assessment of the risk of harm. Seldom are these assessments objectively sound.

Most males, when they walk to the store for a litre of milk, believe that they will not be mugged, partially because they are males. Every time they seek an opportunity or a job they assume they will be given a fair chance. But if they know that a sizable group of "male-haters" were viewing films in which people very much like them were seized, contemptuously degraded, and tortured, *even if the odds of harm to them were not shown to have been altered*, their confidence would be shaken. Their assessments of the rationality of pursuing their chosen plans would be altered; their choice of action would be a different, more restricted, one. Were they to think and act otherwise, they would be foolhardy.

Professor Carmichael is wrong to ask for so strict a criterion of rationality, so brave a requirement of adulthood. Such a postulate of adulthood, in the face of effective degradation, is too perfect and demanding an ideal, not a plausible working assumption for defending freedom of expression. Censorship of at least some expression, that which increases the fearfulness of degraded persons or groups of persons, would expand human freedom, not limit it. The price paid in the loss of the pornographer's delight pales by comparison.

Notes

The author is indebted to Herbert Lewis and David Braybrooke, who read an earlier draft of this critique, and wishes to acknowledge the critical and helpful comments of members of Acadia's Philosophy and Public Affairs Group.

Discussion Questions

1. Should pornography be censored? Indicate which types, if any, should be banned, and whether an exception should be made for works possessing artistic merit or genuine "erotic" expression.

2. Is there anything wrong with censoring on moral grounds? Imagine a film that shows women being brutalized unremittingly. Could anyone reasonably disagree with the statement that it would be wrong to enjoy such a film? If enjoying it is wrong, why shouldn't the film be censored?

3. Are the arguments for the causality of pornography convincing? Even if it has not been established that pornography directly causes sexual assault, isn't the suggestion that pornography reinforces or legitimizes aggressive attitudes plausible enough to justify censorship?

4. Some feminists argue that it is misleading to treat pornography as an issue of freedom of expression. They argue that this puts it in a "liberal" perspective, when pornography is actually an issue of power: that of men over women. Does this view affect the argument about censorship?

5. In this chapter, who is right: Carmichael or Pyrcz? If Pyrcz is correct, where should the line be drawn?

6. Greg Pyrcz suggests that pornography can be treated in terms that parallel the response to racism. Suppose a movie is produced that features the brutalization of a particular visible minority, and that a great many people enjoy this. Would there be a case here for censorship on any of the grounds discussed by Carmichael or Pyrcz?

7. A related issue concerns the public portrayal of the female body as a sex object in, for example, beer commercials and wall posters. When this is done, is there a case for censorship?

Further Readings

A good account of the legal and political background of the pornography controversy in Canada up to 1988 appears in Chapter 3 of Robert M. Campbell and Leslie A. Pal, *The Real Worlds of Canadian Politics* (Peterborough: Broadview Press, 1989). More specific information, especially on the controversy over the effects of pornography, can be found in two works:

The Report of the Committee on Obscenity and Pornography (New York: Bantam Books, 1970), especially Part Three, section II; and the report of the Fraser Commission, *Pornography and Prostitution in Canada: Report of The Special Committee on Pornography and Prostitution*, Volume 1 (Ottawa: Supply and Services Canada, 1985).

A good collection of essays has been edited by David Copp and Susan Wendell: *Pornography and Censorship* (Buffalo: Prometheus Books, 1983).

On the general issue of freedom of expression, the classic and still unsurpassed account is John Stuart Mill's *On Liberty*, especially Chapters 1, 3, and 4. More recently, society's right to legislate morality has been justified by Lord Patrick Devlin in *The Enforcement of Morals* (Oxford: Oxford University Press, 1965). His account has been criticized by H.L.A. Hart in *Law, Liberty and Morality* (New York: Vintage Books, 1966). An excellent brief overview of the value of liberty and the main arguments that might be used to support restrictions of liberty can be found in Joel Feinberg, *Social Philosophy* (Englewood Cliffs: N.J.: Prentice-Hall, 1973), Chapters 1–3.

Many feminist writers regard the pornography issue as a particular instance of the general oppression of women in contemporary society. This is argued by Catharine A. MacKinnon in Chapters 11–16 of *Feminism Unmodified: Discourses on Life and Law* (Cambridge, Mass.: Harvard University Press, 1987). The broadly "liberal" perspective on the issue adopted in this text is challenged by MacKinnon in Chapters 8 and 11 of a more recent work, *Toward a Feminist Theory of the State* (Cambridge, Mass.: Harvard University Press, 1989). Feminist perspectives are surveyed more generally in a superb account by Rosemarie Tong, *Feminist Thought: A Comprehensive Introduction* (Boulder, Colo.: Westview Press, 1989). Further readings are suggested in Chapter 5 of this book.

CHAPTER 3

Democracy and Political Participation

Greg Pyrcz's essay in this chapter illustrates his contention that conventional wisdom on the issues of democracy and rights in Canada is less compelling than it first appears. The conventional wisdom in Canadian political science is that citizens ought to become more fully involved in political life to achieve a civic culture.[1] They ought to vote even more regularly than they now do, join political parties and support pressure groups, occasionally seek office, protest when annoyed, and generally incite other citizens to follow their lead. Canadians do vote regularly—one is tempted to say religiously—especially in national and provincial elections. But, beyond this, their political participation is uneven. Some contend that Canada suffers from a spectator–participant political culture.[2]: Canadians vote in significant numbers but mainly sit back, typically in front of the television set, happy to cheer for their political teams. Many believe that this posture indicates a weakness in Canadian democracy, just as the non-participation of the poor and disadvantaged minorities in the United States is seen to be a weakness in theirs.

Pyrcz argues against greater political participation. He contends that most of those who now refrain from participation in politics, the "politically aloof,"[3] are wiser than they appear, and certainly wiser than those who participate routinely. He contends that apathy is not often what it appears to be, that it is laudable, and that more of it is justified.

The essay surveys a number of reasons that support greater political participation. The author begins by denying the popular notion that Canadians have a duty to participate because they have a right to do so. He then distinguishes between two camps that have formed around the issue of greater political participation—gladiators and realists—to highlight and develop the issues in the debate. The essay attacks gladiators, who favour greater participation in politics, by contending that their arguments are compelling only in a specific social context that is unavailable to Canadian citizens. It attempts to persuade the reader that only when the conditions of social justice and nonmanipulatory political relations are actually met should the gladiators' call to action compel citizens. It contends that in the context of political participation, these conditions are not now satisfied in Canada. Nor could they be without resulting in political martyrdom, which for the citizen of a democracy is above and well beyond the call of duty.

Tom Pocklington defends greater political participation in his critique. He notes that despite its appearance, Pyrcz's argument against political participation proceeds from assumptions that essentially, though quietly, favour it. Moreover, he contends that the conditions of political life in Canada are not really so incorrigible as to warrant the passivity of the citizen. The context of politics, Pocklington maintains, is never ideal. Not even widespread political aloofness (the essay's "call *from* arms") will improve the quality of politics in Canadian democracy. Though far from a perfect game, political participation is the only means to social justice.

Few propositions in democratic political culture are more deeply entrenched than the assertion that citizens ought to participate more fully in the political life of their communities. This conventional wisdom is striking, because there are few political matters upon which citizens so widely agree and because so little participation of real consequence stems from these citizens. This essay probes the citizen's relationship to the democratic state by considering whether or not the citizen ought to become more politically active. Two schools of thought are critically surveyed and developed: one favours greater participation in politics; the other defends the status quo. Then arguments that lend greater support to those citizens who now refrain from participating in politics, the "politically aloof," are given. In these arguments, the apathetic citizen, the beer-in-hand, sitcom-watching couch potato, by steadfastly avoiding political activity, is both rebel and saint.

Is There a Duty to Participate in Politics?

Most citizens believe they have a duty to participate in politics. Many of them think this duty is established by their right to do so. Although this belief is popular, it is nonetheless mistaken. Citizens of a democracy do indeed enjoy the right to participate in public affairs. Recognition of the right of citizens to participate in government and politics is one of democracy's defining characteristics, and it provides one of the reasons for democracy's value as a superior form of political regime.

It is also true that nearly all rights imply correlative duties. For example, A's right to freedom of expression means that B has a correlative duty not to restrict A's freedom to speak. One might be teased by this correlativity into believing that possessing the right to participate in public decisions implies that one has a duty faithfully to exercise the right by regularly participating in decision-making. But the duties correlative to rights are those that fall upon others, as does B's duty to refrain from restricting A's freedom of expression. They are not the duties of those who possess the right. One's right to vote, to join political groups, to lobby, and to seek public office implies that others are duty-bound not to prevent one from doing so nor to coerce or manipulate one's political purposes and preferences. It may also imply that governments have a duty to provide some of the means for citizens fairly to exercise their participatory rights. However, possessing the right to vote does not imply that the citizen has a duty, nor even that he or she ought, to vote. To maintain that it does is to misrepresent the correlativity thesis of rights.

Although a duty to participate in politics is not entailed by the right to do so, it might be argued that this duty stems instead from the need to protect the practice of voting, to guarantee that the right to vote continues to be recognized by those in power in order to preserve democracy. To understand why this second strategy for securing a duty to participate is not much more promising than the first, it is important to realize that democratic elections, referenda, and policy battles between parties and between representative groups are typically the means to legitimize majority rule in a democratic regime.

Democratic political activity achieves two goals simultaneously. It determines which party or platform has the support of the majority (or, in multi-party contests, the plurality) of citizens. This is commonly acknowledged. But it also is the means whereby citizens grant authority to the winning party, platform, or policy, to govern citizens and extract obedience from even those citizens who have expressed a preference for another party, platform, or policy. Those who express dissenting views and preferences are understood in a democracy to have bound themselves *morally* to live with the outcome of democratic decisions, by virtue of their participation.[4]

The obligation of dissenters to acquiesce in the implementation of the majority decision stems from a commitment each citizen is assumed to make when forming and continuing to animate a democratic regime. Their willing participation is the source of a moral bond to democratic governments and law. The same is true of the obligation to obey the rules of a game that one has freely and knowingly undertaken to play. In both cases, the decision to play according to certain known rules constitutes an acceptance of the rules, even though they may come to be applied to the players in ways not to their liking.

If the desire to protect the right to participate is understood as the reasoning for a duty to participate, this second goal of democratic participation would be unmet, the general authority special to the democratic regime would be undermined, and the moral bond of dissenters to the majority would disintegrate. This is what is wrong with compulsory voting. Coerced participation, such as is found in Australia, where it is against the law not to vote, does not indicate whether dissenters have, by virtue of their coerced participation, authorized the implementation of majority preference.[5]

This is also why political apathy appears to be so disturbing. To what authority, if any, are the "apathetic" in a democratic regime bound? Not only have they failed to express an interest or preference in the outcome of democratic contests, they have refused to "play." The state undeniably has the power to coerce such citizens to obey, but by what authority is this power legitimately employed? The answer appears to be that the citizen is bound by no such authority. For these reasons it is problematic to hold, for instance, that citizens must vote to protect their right to vote. This claim undermines the democratic significance of such participation.

Still, the right to participate is fully respected only in democratic regimes, and a regime that fails to respect the right to participate cannot be considered democratic. Does not this alone imply a duty to participate? Again, it seems not. The right to vote does not gain its moral quality from the popularity it enjoys in a particular society. Citizens do not possess the right to participate simply because they favour democratic politics, even though they must favour democratic politics if the conditions for *enjoying* the right to vote, such as the constitutional protection of the right, are likely to be assured. The moral right to participate in politics is totally independent of its legal recognition. It is grounded elsewhere, typically discovered in the kind of creatures humans are, that is, creatures capable of and fulfilled only when governing themselves. This is why it is meaningful and important to say that those who now suffer from political tyranny, such as South African blacks, possess the moral right fully to participate in government even when this right is not respected in their land.

Threats to the right to vote could generate a moral obligation to participate only if those threats were real. It might be that during critical times in a democracy's evolution, getting the vote out would be necessary to preserve legal recognition of the right to vote. But these crises in democracy are rare, even though they are regularly conjured by those anxious to receive political support.

That citizens are not bound by a duty to participate, however, does not really settle the matter of whether they ought ever to participate in politics or even whether they ought to participate more than they do. Fortunately, more relevant and compelling considerations exist to determine these questions.

The Realist's Case Against Greater Participation

Two schools of thought have dominated debate on the value of political participation.[6] The realist school maintains that the current levels of political participation in Canada are acceptable and that attempts to induce higher levels might damage the stability and responsiveness of government.[7] Realists contend that greater political participation is both unnecessary for the polity and burdensome for the citizen. They argue that from the point of view of the whole population, high electoral participation rates provide little if any more authority to a democratic outcome than do moderate rates.

They contend that a moderate electoral turnout captures the preferences of citizens just as efficiently as a public opinion poll sample surveys a population.

A sample must be representative of the population it seeks to survey. The realist might acknowledge that more of Canada's poor than now do so must participate if the outcomes of democratic contests are to represent majority preference and that less middle-class participation may be required than at present. The middle class is over-represented in actual participation rates and could be replaced by more participation from the poor, who are under-represented. If this were done, the required overall participation rate, if citizens' preferred party or policy is to be discerned, remains roughly the same as, or even lower, than it is.

The realist is not especially hostile to greater participation, but regards it as a superfluous and sometimes expensive way to induce the activity of poorly motivated and thus poorly informed citizens. If establishing the preferences of the majority is the goal of electoral participation, then less is as good as more, at least from the point of view of the society as a whole.

The realist also contends that from the individual's perspective, greater participation in electoral politics is largely unnecessary. For example, where a constituency's population is large and the likely outcome *within that constituency* is known by the citizen, the individual's participation, as one mere vote, contributes virtually nothing to the outcome of an electoral contest. Voting for a likely winner is superfluous, and voting for a likely loser is usually pointless. The citizen who votes in these circumstances displays either a herdlike mentality or an unhealthy taste for carrying unnecessary burdens.

Undeniably there are occasions when one vote may affect an outcome. The realist contends that when the probability of such an occurrence is high, the citizen is indeed wise to vote. But the publication of ever more public opinion polls and the ubiquity of the mass media make these opportunities increasingly scarce, at least within constituencies and for all but the least perceptive citizen.

It might be said that the realist's view underestimates the personal pleasure one may find in electoral participation. Even herdlike activity—being on the winning side or supporting the "moral victory" of the losing side—is not without charm. But for the realist much of this pleasure appears to emanate from the mistaken belief that one's vote has made a difference and from the wholesome feeling some get from performing a perceived duty. These, the realist contends, are a fool's pleasures. Those voters are little different from hockey fans who derive pleasure from attending games in the belief that their *individual* attendance will contribute to the outcome of the game.

The realist is interested not only in assessing the pleasures more realistically but also in acknowledging some of the burdens of participation, especially the burden of extra-electoral political participation. Admittedly, voting takes little time and effort, but it is time and effort that could be spent otherwise. More pressing is the time and effort required to prepare oneself to identify policies that one genuinely supports, the discomfort felt in being at odds with one's friends even when one's vote is truly secret, and the nagging and unpleasant sense that one's participation was unnecessary to the outcome. The pain of defeat is often palpable, and the pleasure of victory, for the perceptive individual voting on the side of a majority, is tinged with irony.

But what if everyone were to act in the manner advocated by the realist? If followed by all citizens, the realist's advice might threaten democracy. This dire consequence is, however, preventable and is usually prevented, even by a jaded citizenry. Where democratic contests within a constituency are too close to call, where the number of participants in a race is very low, where one's interest is traditionally under-represented, where the constituency is small, or where democratic politics appears really to be in danger, it is certainly rational to vote. Here, one vote has the promise of truly affecting the outcome, and the pleasure of this "threshold involvement" is genuine.

The realist's case is especially compelling because it assesses the value of extra-electoral participation. Urging others to support a favoured candidate or policy, serving in pressure groups or political parties, community organizing, and political activism are all accepted by the realist as the terms of democracy. However, the realist believes that only a small proportion of citizens in any society is willing to participate in these kinds of public activities. To urge most citizens to do so is to ask them to carry a heavier burden of citizenship than is carried by others more at ease with a public life.

Realists contend that in a diverse democratic system, government can accommodate only some demands and effectively satisfy only a few of these. Greater demands upon government create expectations that cannot be met and frustrate the aspirations of citizens left unserved. This frustration contributes either to political instability—motivating ever greater and more divisive political action and eventually revolt—or to political alienation. The conclusion is that greater extra-electoral participation is not only a burden for the ill-disposed citizen but may lead eventually to a decline in the quality of democracy.

The realist regards participation in political parties, pressure groups, political movements, and protest as being governed by a logic of collective action.[8] In this logic, it is irrational for an individual in a group to work for the success of that group if others are likely to do so. The impact of one more person at a rally is negligible if the rally is already well served by the participation of others. Alternatively, if most citizens remain aloof, one citizen's participation is insufficient to have any real impact; few one-person campaigns ever succeed. Thus, the rational protester scans a rally before joining it and joins in only if the attendance is large enough for an impact to be felt. This is also true of political parties, pressure groups, and political movements, where membership numbers are more easily known by the citizen than is the likely turnout at a political rally.

Readers sympathetic to greater political participation, especially those who religiously attend poorly supported parties, groups, and rallies, will point to a number of apparent flaws in the realist's case. They might contend that democracy, by definition, requires an active citizenry; it is not defined solely by the right to participate but by actual participation. Thus the participation thresholds the realist identifies, while real enough politically, do not characterize a true democratic polity.

Critics of the realist position also contend that extra-electoral participation provides a unique sense of fulfilment available only to the citizens of a democracy, a sense badly misunderstood and underrated by realists. They may also assert that participation, far from being peripheral to the life of a democratic citizen, constitutes instead a fundamental element of personal identity. To be active in politics is to be a happier and more fully developed human being; it is simply necessary to the integrity and development of human character.

Realists respond to this criticism by acknowledging that it may well be true that political participation is pleasurable, fulfilling, and necessary to the identities of *some* citizens of a democracy. But actual democracies are often quite diverse. They consist of citizens who understand themselves and value politics differently. Indeed, it is one of the remarkable virtues of a democracy that it seeks to accommodate various conceptions of good citizenship and diverse ways of living. It makes sense to realists that some citizens would not fit the realists' picture of rationality, that the pleasure some citizens take in political participation is not tied to affecting the outcome. These citizens may enjoy the "edifying" effect political participation has upon their sensibilities. They think differently about their lives, even when their participation has proven superfluous. In the hockey metaphor, they are real fans.

Realists, however, contend that the fact that participation is enjoyable for and important to some citizens works in favour of their case, not against it. Realist arguments are not meant to defend widespread passivity in the electorate, but only to justify currently moderate levels of participation. The fact that some citizens are driven to participate achieves these levels. Activist citizens are good for the polity. They keep governments honest, keep the agenda of public debate and policy open, and speak for citizens not disposed to do so. Active citizens generate the thresholds necessary for democratic politics, just as the core of a community organization keeps the organization afloat by doing more than its share.

For most people, though, political participation is often unpleasant, inefficient, frustrating, fruitless, and disruptive of their emotional and psychological well-being. To lose politically when one's contribution was superfluous and detracted from one's personal life colours a citizen's life with pathos. That some may feel an aloofness from politics augers in favour of it being respected by the democratic theorist. Realists conclude that more political participation is neither likely nor justifiable, given the rationality and sensibilities of citizens.

The Gladiator's Case for Participatory Democracy

Gladiators think that more political participation is a good thing for everyone. They face a genuine challenge in meeting the arguments of the realists. Lamentably, their strategy has too often been merely to extol the virtues of greater political participation both to other gladiators and to the uncommitted, in a spirit simply contemptuous of the realist perspective.

The gladiator is not impressed by the realist's pursuit of stability or efficiency in democratic representation. A democratic regime, the gladiator contends, must leave no stone of political opinion unturned, no voice unheard, no discussion avoided, in its search for political consensus. Tolerating less than this leaves a polity vulnerable to individuals and groups who are bent on undermining true consensus by discouraging or repressing those who hold dissenting opinions. Realism also tolerates the exclusion from democratic politics of the poorly educated, the powerless, and the poor. Gladiators are quick to notice that "the apathetic" have traditionally belonged to "the underclasses." Is the nonparticipation of these citizens really a matter of their individual personalities and their exercise of free choice, as realists contend? Gladiators believe that such a view tragically rationalizes rather than justifies nonparticipation.

Gladiators contend that the political aloofness of people alienated from the political system reinforces the social injustices they suffer and worsens the alienation they feel. The poor fail to participate as fully as they might partly because of their poverty and partly because of their domination by others. This failure is one of the means by which others effectively avoid redressing the poverty or the domination suffered by the disadvantaged. In the gladiator's eyes, poverty and domination are reinforced by apathy, generation after generation. Only if disadvantaged citizens courageously break free to participate in politics, primarily to change society, is there any real prospect for alleviating the social conditions that sustain both their suffering and their apathy. Only massive political participation will achieve and protect social justice.[9]

Gladiators also maintain that electoral and other democratic contests are not only the "winner take all" games portrayed by realists. Although minority opinion suffers the ignominy of defeat in particular contests, the positive effect of the minority's participation, according to the gladiator, occurs in the outcomes of *subsequent* contests. A participant's activity on the losing side of a political contest can induce others to alter their opinions and activities. Merely one vote can help to temper the subsequent zeal of the majority and intensify the verve of dissenters. Even participation on the majority side is warranted to cement the resolve of majority opinion.

The gladiator's logic, in which political participation is a continuing and developing "event," is most compelling when used to justify extra-electoral participation.[10] While acknowledging that a single vote may not create even a future tide of support for a preferred opinion or interest, the gladiator contends that even one citizen's activism in a pressure group, political party, or protest is consequential. Every citizen's participation counts not only for its own sake, but for the effect it can have upon the likelihood that others will join in. Political activism also uniquely provides for political martyrdom, in which the effects of a single act can travel far. The gladiator contends that the realist misreads the nature and underrates the potential of political activity.

In democratic theory, supporting the gladiator's argument is a complex proposition. In the gladiator's vision, democracy does not consist merely of contests between competing parties and ideas or the recognition of democratic rights. It is a type of relationship that exists between the members of a community, one in which reasoned discourse achieves public consensus. Citizens must engage one another in discourse if the exercise of their democratic rights is to be genuinely democratic. Allowing some individuals to bow out of this exercise disconnects a citizenry, and in doing so it undermines the completeness and vibrancy of democratic decision-making. Modest rates of political participation, even when the opinions of a citizenry are statistically well represented, are understood by the gladiator to indicate a diminished democracy.[11]

This point is often advanced metaphysically: a citizenry has qualities that are not reducible to those of individual citizens or to the relationships between them. Gladiators hold that diminishing the extent of democratic discourse in a population, even when it has no political effect, affects not only the lives of those left out but the quality of the citizenry as a whole. But it is not necessary to put the point so abstractly. If democratic citizenship is defined even partly by the exercise of reasoned political discourse, then the extent of this activity is a measure of a society's democratic quality. The more citizens exercise their democratic right to participate, the greater is the democratic quality of the society they animate.

Thus far the gladiator's argument has focused on the effect of participation on the polity as a whole and on the advancement of group interests, such as the interests of the poor. But the realist's case is strongest when asserting that the burdens of individual participation are greater on the citizen than its benefits are to the polity or the favoured group. What do gladiators make of this assessment?

It is here that gladiators find realist views most perplexing. Political participation may be difficult, frustrating, and even discouraging, but for gladiators it is not burdensome. It is like ice time for a hockey player; only in active political participation are one's capacities as a social being completely exercised. While it may be difficult at times to exercise these distinctly human capacities, only by doing so can citizens experience the fulfilment available to them as human beings. Moreover, this fulfilment is the stuff of which happiness is made complete. Although gladiators recognize that not all citizens experience this pleasure of participation, they do not see this as being due to different personalities. They hold that the pleasure of reasoned discourse about public life arises from one's membership in a species, not the idiosyncrasies of individual psychology.

By analogy, those who do not keep fit because exercise is painful have failed to discover in themselves the qualities that make exercise fulfilling. So too with the politically passive. The qualities and fulfilment experienced by the gladiator exist in the passive personality as well, but they are masked by poverty or repression. Gladiators hold that political participation is not only profoundly fulfilling for themselves but would be for others when they discovered this source of personal fulfilment. Realists are simply too preoccupied with winning and losing political contests. This focus blinds them to the real potential of political participation. It is the process of politics that is lost in the realist's focus on the product of participation.

At stake in this disagreement are competing visions of the nature of human well-being. Realists hold to a formal conception in which happiness stems from the satisfaction of desires, whatever they might be. Gladiators consider this conception one-dimensional. Indulging only one aspect of one's being in this way leaves other potential sources of happiness underdeveloped. The happiness that emanates from activity requires nurturing and may require some prodding. However, this does not mean that activism is foreign to the passive individual; it simply means that such a source of pleasure is not always obvious or initially easy to experience. Gladiators find in political activity a special quality of interaction that yields a distinct quality of pleasure.

The appeal to the aloof goes further than this. Gladiators believe that citizens who participate in politics develop as human beings in ways that nonparticipants don't, in three significant ways. The first relates to the idea of reasoned discourse as the means of arriving at public decisions. Political argument, the gladiator contends, is a unique and demanding human activity. Contributing to public decisions is one way in which people govern themselves. To do so they must continuously exercise their capacity to think clearly, reflectively, and critically about their lives, an exercise that produces increasingly sophisticated skills and abilities. Democratic political participation, in the gladiator's view, is unique in this respect. Unlike the process by which individuals make life decisions involving private deliberation (for example, choosing the type of literature to read), public decision-making requires the agreement of others. Arriving at this agreement calls upon the capacities to persuade, respect, and tolerate others, which if not exercised, quickly atrophy.

A second achievement claimed to be unique to political participation is the citizen's development of a sense of justice. Making public decisions together requires the acknowledgement and comprehension of other people's life situations, cultural commitments and individuality. To truly persuade others of something, one must confront and respect them as they are. It would be nearly impossible to conduct an election on the issue of poverty without involving the poor, those who seek to redress poverty, and those who find it quite tolerable (typically the wealthy). This engagement enables access to the reality of poverty that otherwise can be avoided by the citizen. In the process, the gladiator contends, citizens are morally sensitized and politically awakened in a way that they might not otherwise be. Political participation seldom yields a unified public morality or a universal sense of justice; nor may it alone create moral sensitivity. However, for gladiators, it is an effective and unique antidote to moral numbness and political naivete. It makes concrete what otherwise remains tragically abstract.

The third way in which political participation may enhance the development of citizens involves the commitment to values or interests that political participation requires. When citizens participate in politics, they act either to advance the values they wish to see reflected in public decisions or to protect the interests they or others have in such decisions. Acting on values or interests, it is argued by gladiators, produces a firmer commitment to them than does merely holding them. It is one thing for a man to favour women's rights. But when he speaks out in their defence, his sense of their significance is qualitatively heightened.

What is altered by political activity, in this respect, is captured in the concept of character. When one speaks out on women's rights, others see one as committed to them. If one persists, one develops a reputation for such a commitment, a reputation that distinguishes one from others and identifies one with a community of like-minded others. This process occurs by the expression to others of qualities in one's personality, namely values and interests, which form part of what is best described as character. To the extent that the image one has of oneself is a product of others' perceptions of one, one's sense of one's own character is revealed and reaffirmed by those who have observed, shared, or opposed one's political activity.

If, on the other hand, one chooses to mask one's cherished values and interests by remaining politically aloof, one leaves others' sense of one's character opaque. As a result, one cannot draw upon others' sense of one's character to clarify and confirm one's own sense of it. This disability may not be fatal to one's personality but it does serve a lack of resolve in one's self-understanding. Without interaction with others, one can become opaque even to oneself. Moreover, it is likely that the sharper one's understanding is of one's own character, the more productive will be one's attempts to alter it, should one choose to, by altering and then acting upon new values and interests. While political activity is not unique in this respect, it provides a special means both for grasping a better sense of oneself and for one's development as an individual. In the process, as an added bonus, one achieves the self-confidence that can emanate from identifying oneself as a member of a like-minded community and the sense of personal integrity that emanates from opposing others whose views and interests one finds abhorrent.

Gladiators reject the realist definition of politics as consisting principally of the effective representation of citizens' interests. Instead, they define democracy as a distinct form of political inter-action between citizens (reasoned discourse leading to public deci-sions), the scope of which measures the democratic quality of a society. Gladiators reject the "burdensome" qualities of individual participation. They challenge the realist conception of human fulfil-ment, arguing that well-being is achieved not through passivity but through exercising capacities. They contend that political partici-pation provides three developmental processes not afforded to the nonparticipant: the skills of political dialogue, a sense of justice, and the self-understanding, integrity, and community that emanate from a publicly expressed character.

The Realist's Case Revisited

The arguments presented by realists and gladiators don't quite meet each other because they present different definitions of democracy and contrasting conceptions of human well-being. Must one then simply choose between the two views? Perhaps not. This section of the essay develops further the realist's case on one major point to make it more relevant to the gladiator's argument. The intention is not to make a realist out of the reader but to close the gap between the two views, to show how the question of political participation is resolved best when it is considered in context. This chapter considers two variables in the context of political participation: the dominance or relative absence of manipulation in the politics of a society, and the likelihood that a society can be significantly reformed by political participation in one generation. Although there are other variables to consider, these two currently work in the minds of the politically aloof.

Imagine two towns. In the first, Backwaters, all participants in politics fully understand their political interaction with others. They are not deceived by those with whom they have direct political contact, nor by third persons practising deception through them. Few of them believe much of the television news they see and hear. The citizens of Backwaters suffer no unfounded ideas of duty, nor do they depend upon ritual nor myth. They are little moved by rhetoric or charisma and are seldom, if ever, teased to serve the interests of those who aggrandize their own status through the exploitation of others.[12] Political life in Backwaters is not perfect, but when political problems arise they are resolved by the citizens of the town in one generation.

In the second imagined town, Mercedes Hill, the social, political, and economic relations of the citizenry are manipulative. To the outsider, the townsfolk seem unable to resist the appeal of contrived duties, majority consensus, ritual, rhetoric, and so on. But not all political contact on "the Hill" is manipulative; attempted deception sometimes fails, myths are occasionally unmasked, and some contacts are manipulation-free. However, enough interactions are manipulative to make most contacts between citizens uncertain. To make matters worse, manipulation occurs even among the reformers. The prospects of citizens who try significantly to reform Mercedes Hill are bleak. An intergenerational strategy is necessary to right the current wrongs in the town's political life. Thus those who might reform the town are not in a position to determine the eventual terms of this reform.

One reason given by gladiators for justifying greater participation in politics is that it develops and exercises the capacity to reason with others in making public decisions. This capacity is a complex one, consisting in skills of both deliberation and argument. But public discourse involves the competitive engagement of others' wills as well; politics is in part the activity of some persons seeking to affect the preferences and actions of others. It is not a matter merely of collecting and representing the preferences of a society, but also includes shaping the preferences of others. It is a dynamic process, in which individuals and groups have their subsequent preferences altered or strengthened by their wilful engagement of others. But not only are one's values shaped in political activity; one's future political conduct as well is shaped by earlier engagements. Participants pursue strategies and define goals that they wouldn't have otherwise, were it not for the intervening goals and strategies pursued by other "players." How Gretzky proceeds down the ice in the face of an opposing team is qualitatively different from the way he proceeds when skating alone.

The engagement of others' wills is inherent in politics.[13] This is so because politics seems always to involve the direct or indirect distribution of goods and opportunities in society. It is essentially concerned with issues of justice. Is there a public issue that does not in some way alter or reinforce the distribution of goods or opportunities enjoyed by citizens? Because all citizens have a stake in distributional decisions and all prefer some distributions to others, their desire to alter or strengthen the preferences of other citizens is simply a function of their stake in "who gets what, when, where, and how." The distributional dynamic in politics transforms public discourse. The move from the seminar room to the town hall significantly affects the skills required by the citizen.

The gladiator contends that political participation uniquely develops the capacities of human beings to "reason with and secure the agreement of others." This is a compelling proposition. Totally passive citizens, just like silent students in a seminar, plainly miss something in the development of their skills to deliberate and especially to persuade others when they remain aloof. Their loss is a direct consequence of their practised tacitness. But does it follow that participation would therefore be beneficial to them? This conclusion is less certain than it may appear. Instead, it seems that the benefit of political participation to the participant is determined by both the context and the terms of this participation. It is not found in all political activity.

To see how this may be so, contrast the skills that would be useful in influencing public decisions in Backwaters and in Mercedes Hill. In Mercedes Hill, a central skill in public activity is that of manipulating the opinions and conduct of others without being found out. Perhaps some citizens of this town resist the dominant manipulatory mode of politics by choosing courageously to be direct and to unmask the manipulatory strategies of others. But since the dominant form of "discourse" in the town is at odds with their efforts, this strategy appears doomed. It would be naive to maintain that in a game of manipulatory power the noble citizen would thrive, even when frankness may at times be an advantage.[14]

This does not mean that citizens could not resist such "politics." However, if they were to do so, it is difficult to see how they could develop the skills they might have developed if they were acting in Backwaters. In Mercedes Hill, other players would simply not be playing according to rules that require the very skills citizens seek to develop in themselves, those of deliberation and argument. More-over, persisting in the effort would not defend their stake in the distributional decisions being taken by the manipulatory politics of others. For these reasons, wise citizens would choose either to partici-pate in the manner required to succeed in the town or to remain aloof from politics, seeking their development elsewhere.

To see how a life of manipulatory politics might threaten the well-being of a person, consider again what it means to develop a capacity. That newly found skill becomes part of the individual. The most obvious instances of this phenomenon are the capacities chil-dren develop, especially the capacity to communicate. This capacity profoundly affects their development; but even lesser capacities have this quality, from the capacity to appreciate music to that of an effective backhand in tennis. Once it is developed, it becomes part of what individuals can do, and accordingly it becomes part of who they are, at least in their own minds.[15]

Developing a capacity as a part of an individual's self-identity can create a need for its exercise. This is especially so of athletic capacities. No one needs to do much physically beyond what is neces-sary to see the day through, but once an athletic capacity has been developed it becomes unpleasant not to continue exercising it. People begin to "need to work out" in much the same way as they need to communicate with someone after a period of silence. The capacities exercised in politics, if they are like physical and linguistic skills, are not donned and removed like clothing, at the wearer's pleasure. Manipulating and being manipulated by others is not something that can be turned on and off. Part of the habit of exercising athletic, musical, and linguistic capacities is physiological. But a measure of the desire to exercise even these developed capacities comes from the way in which their exercise adds to one's self-esteem, self-confidence, and sense of power.

Habits can be altered, but an initial habit may be all that is required to challenge the gladiator. Once a person uses manipula-tion to succeed in a town that requires this kind of politics, it may be difficult to give up its exercise in other relationships or other towns. This is both because other skills requisite to the manipulative rela-tionship have been acquired and because they are seen to be useful in influencing "who gets what, where, and when."

One might contend that manipulating and being manipulated by others develops an identity tied to this kind of politics and eventually develops the habit of such politics. One might also assert that if manipulating and being manipulated by others is not unpleasant to the citizen, then it should be. If citizens experience no discomfort in blindly deferring to others or in having others blindly submit to them, then they have lost or never really enjoyed the human experience of relating to others more openly. They are poorer in personal well-being for their loss.

This conclusion rests on two contentions: first, that being aware of the influences upon one produces a greater sense of well-being than does blind submission to others' wills, even when one gives in to them; and second, that relating to others openly, even when they knowingly surrender to one's influence, is more conducive to one's well-being than having others blindly surrender to one's manipulation.[16] It is difficult not to accept these claims. Or, to be more judicious, they are more plausible than the gladiator's contention that individuals will be improved, through the development of their capacities, by any and all participation in politics.

A related feature of life in Mercedes Hill is the effect of manipulation in the town's politics. Manipulation compromises the development of friendships among those who participate and who thereby develop political skills. Friendships require trust, some degree of predictability and openness, even when conflicts arise. To call someone who manipulates one without one's knowing it a friend is to misunderstand what it is to be a friend; it is like the friendship enjoyed by a puppet and puppeteer. The expansion of civic friendship is cited by many gladiators as an extra benefit enjoyed by political participants. But while expanding friendship may be the result of greater political participation in Backwaters, it appears unlikely in Mercedes Hill. In Backwaters, friendships may survive even sharp political battles on public policy. But in Mercedes Hill, staying out of politics appears to be a wiser choice for those seeking the well-being of "true" civic friendship.

It seems that the effect of participating in the politics of Mercedes Hill is not the same as it is in Backwaters. To participate in Mercedes Hill is to develop the capacity both to manipulate others to be deceived by others. These capacities become part of the citizen's self-identity and may be difficult to set aside; this moderates the appeal of the gladiator's call to action. Gladiators hold that the capacities developed by political participation are required for public deliberation and discourse, and are thus pleasurably exercised. While this may be true of participation in Backwaters, however, it is not, at least in the same way, true of participation in Mercedes Hill.[14]

All this has shown only how the personal development of political participants may be different and far less appealing when the participants exist in a context of manipulative politics than they are when politics is conceived more ideally. The strategy has been to accept the developmental terms of the gladiator's argument, but to challenge the way in which they characterize both the political experience and the skills and abilities essential to successful political practice. This is a different strategy from that pursued by realists, who reject the developmental terms of participation in politics.

But what about the other acclaimed virtues of political participation: the greater sense of justice and the self-understanding, integrity, and sense of community that emanates from a publicly expressed character? It seems that political activity in Mercedes Hill would develop a poorer sense of justice and a weaker sense of character than would simple aloofness or, for that matter, political participation in Backwaters. Three responses to this line of analysis spring to mind. The first is to claim that only participation in the politics of Mercedes Hill holds any prospect of political reform. It may involve a sort of political martyrdom, a sacrifice of personal well-being now for the happiness of future generations, but it may nonetheless be warranted. Second, one might contend that only by participating in the town's politics can citizens influence the distribution of goods and opportunities. This too is a sort of political sacrifice; it abandons the ideal of developing one's capacities as a human being in favour of protecting one's share of the society's goods. Finally it might be conceded that in very few societies are the terms of politics as bad as those in Mercedes Hill. Political life in Canada is not so demented; if anything, Canadians are more like the citizens of Backwaters than of Mercedes Hill.

It is not possible to address these responses in full, but some aspects of them must be considered. In Mercedes Hill, reform required intergenerational strategies. A life of political martyrdom there would produce political and social change well beyond one's control. If one was certain that political participation in Mercedes Hill would one day transform the politics of this town, then political martyrdom might be called for. But this is far from certain. For those who want to serve future generations, a much more certain and more rewarding strategy of community service exists. Contributions to education, family life, literature, and the economy may also serve future generations, while developing the human capacities of the martyr.

More telling though, is the point that political aloofness may be as effective in reforming Mercedes Hill as would an intergenerational strategy of political activity. Earlier it was contended both that political participation defined democracy for gladiators and that the only way of concluding that citizens had a duty to obey majority decisions is that they had participated in forming them, even if they held a minority view. Widespread political aloofness might undermine the confidence of the majority in applying public decisions to those who hold minority views, because aloofness frees citizens from any moral bond to majority decisions. If reform is sought by citizens, then pulling the "rug of legitimacy" out from under the feet of those who determine the dominant form of politics may be preferable to activism. From this point of view, the current moderate rates of participation are not too low, but too high! What is required is more apathy.

The argument that political participation, even in bad politics, is necessary to defend citizens' interests is undeniably compelling. It has a realism not usually found in the gladiators' more lofty view of politics. But it too falls short; its appeal for greater participation would govern individual citizens only when their preferred interests are enhanced by their participation. Thus, a logic of collective action similar to that advanced by realists applies. It may indeed be wise to participate in Mercedes Hill to protect an interest, even if doing so means that one must sacrifice some personal well-being. But why participate in this way when one's interests will be advanced anyway or when one is not likely to succeed in advancing an interest? Why not go along with or simply passively acquiesce in the majority's decision and preserve the integrity of one's private life.

It is difficult to deal with the question of whether or not real societies, like Canada's, suffer from the political viruses found in Mercedes Hill. This is not because there is too little but rather because there is simply too much to say. Is Canadian politics plagued by an insidious and intractable dependency upon myth, ritual, duty, and other forms of manipulation? Do Canadians play their politics face-to-face, directly, and honestly? Do they know when they are being influenced, when they are blindly surrendering to the preferences of others? If not, how likely is it that their participation in politics will reform the terms of citizenship?

These are not easy questions. They involve ambiguous evidence and inconclusive examples. Still, they must be answered by every citizen, and they are best answered critically. Until satisfactory answers are given, the wisdom of the aloof citizen is as compelling as the wisdom of the activist.

Notes

The author would like to express his gratitude to David Braybrooke for critically reading and suggesting improvements to both this essay and his critique in Chapter 1. He has also profited from criticism of an earlier draft of this essay from numerous colleagues, especially Duff Spafford and Fred Barnard.
1. Gabriel Almond and Sydney Verba, *The Civic Culture: Political Attitudes and Democracy in Five Nations* (Boston: Little Brown, 1963). This kind of political culture is highly valued in American society.
2. Richard Van Loon and Michael Whittington, *The Canadian Political System: Environment, Structure and Process*, 4th ed. (Toronto: McGraw Hill Ryerson, 1987).
3. J. Roland Pennock and John W. Chapman eds. *Participation in Politics: Nomos XVI*, (New York: Lieber-Atherton, 1975).

4. See Peter Singer's *Democracy and Disobedience* (New York: Oxford University Press, 1974). This argument is developed further in the essay in Chapter 9 of this book. Here the authorization of law in democracy is held not to be obtained by tacit consent to political authority but only by participation in political life and democratic "contests." It should also be pointed out that citizens are not understood to be bound, by their participation in democratic politics, to morally abhorrent outcomes, especially those that undermine the rights or basic well-being of themselves or other citizens.

5. It is possible to conduct separate plebiscites authorizing the implementation of majority rule. Such plebiscites would need to be regularly held, however, because there is no good reason to believe that the choice of a regime to which one is committed is lifelong or even week-long.

6. This essay distinguishes two schools of thought on the value of political participation: the realist school and the gladiator school. For a definition of the gladiator in politics, see L.W. Milbrath and M.L. Goel, *Political Participation: How and Why Do People Get Involved in Politics*. (Chicago: Rand McNally, 1965 and 1977), p. 11. For a broad introduction to realism in political participation, see the books cited in the "Further Readings" at the end of this chapter.

7. This attempt broadly to characterize a school of thought may not state the views of each of its adherents to their full satisfaction, but it will serve as an umbrella characterization. The reader will find this view espoused in numerous introductory political science textbooks, even those that call for marginally higher levels of participation. However, in characterizing these arguments, the author has extended them, in some cases by adding to them and in others by seeking to render them more explicit.

8. For an extended discussion of the logic of collective action, see Mancur Olson's *Logic of Collective Action* (Cambridge, Mass.: Harvard University Press, 1965). Olson argues that the rationality for group membership in large groups seeking public effects is so little as to require either incentives or coercion to maintain it.

9. There are, of course, disaffected groups on all sides of political issues. For example, the participation of the "religious right" in recent American politics can be seen as a courageous break with the political alienation they have suffered and as being motivated by a desire to redress the injustices they perceive.

10. See David Gautier's work for how this logic works in co-operation games.

11. See Christian Bay's "Political and Pseudo Politics," *American Political Science Review*, Vol. LIX, No. 2 (1963), pp. 39–51.

12. Manipulatory politics are defined by Robert Goodin in *Manipulatory Politics* (New Haven: Yale University Press, 1980). In this and subsequent discussions in this chapter, the author is indebted to this splendid work by Goodin.

13. It may seem to the reader that the author is establishing a key point definitionally here. This is partly right; however, the point about the dynamic, competitive, and engaging quality of politics is one that must be conceded by gladiators if their doctrine is to be intelligible. Were it not conceded, political participation, as a means of developing the skills of deliberation and rhetoric, could be replaced by good discussions in

political philosophy classes or by those around a kitchen or barroom table, with nothing lost. This the gladiator can't concede.

14. The suggestion that frankness might be of value even in manipulatory political relations is David Braybrooke's.

15. Accepting this point should be easy for the gladiator, for it is a lasting effect upon the person and his or her conduct that the gladiator hopes to achieve in the citizen's participation.

16. The underlying contention here is that acting autonomously is more conducive to one's well-being than is blindly acting on the influence of others. Blindly surrendering to others may yield pleasurable consequences for the individual; this is part of the story of the fairy godmother, who does her "good work" without presenting herself. Indeed, the pleasures of blind submission may have to be weighed against the pleasure lost in not acting autonomously. Such considerations might well figure in the decision of whether to choose to "play the game" in Mercedes Hill.

CRITIQUE

Greg Pyrcz's essay challenges the view—perhaps it would be better to say article of faith—that, at least in liberal democracies, the higher the level of political participation, the healthier the body politic and the individuals who compose it. Pyrcz would challenge the "public service" announcements that urge, "Vote as you like, but please vote."

His case has three main parts, each of which deserves attention. First, the right to vote and exercise other participatory rights does not entail a duty to vote; in fact, there is no duty to vote. Second, the arguments of gladiators, who maintain that increased political participation is an unmitigated good, are much less compelling than is commonly believed, while the reasoning of realists, who hold that the present level of political activity is sufficient, has much to commend it. Finally, under certain circumstances, political aloofness is not only defensible but wiser than political participation.

I hope to establish two main points. First, Pyrcz's case is not nearly as daring and unconventional as it seems. Appearances to the contrary, he is very close to the gladiators in his political outlook. Second, he underemphasizes or ignores considerations that favour increased political participation.

The Right and the Duty to Vote

Pyrcz affirms that citizens have a moral right to vote but that this does not entail a moral duty to do so. Is this right? Surely it is; the right to vote seems to be thoroughly analogous to the right to whistle while one works. It is entirely up to the individual to decide whether to exercise either of these rights. In general, Pyrcz finds no reason to accept the view that there is a duty to vote. He does allow, rather tentatively, for one exception, namely, a situation in which so few people were exercising the right to vote that the effectiveness of this right was genuinely threatened. It may be, he says, "that during critical times in a democracy's evolution, getting the vote out would be necessary to preserve the recognition of the right to vote." This may be taken as an irresolute endorsement of a duty to vote that is applicable only in unusual circumstances. But even if a duty to vote occasionally does come into play, it is still not entailed by the right to vote. If there is such a duty, it would have to be based on a more basic duty, such as the duty to do one's part in upholding the most just—or least unjust—political institutions and practices, namely, democratic ones. Therefore, Pyrcz is right in maintaining that, except in unusual circumstances, there is no duty to vote.

But is this a radically unconventional conclusion, strongly at variance with the prevailing view? Probably not. Neither the public and private organizations that urge citizens to vote nor the political theorists (Pyrcz's gladiators) who commend increased political participation rest their case on the citizen's duties. They extol the personal and social benefits derived from participation. Accordingly, I think Pyrcz shows good judgement when he chooses to concentrate mainly on the question whether, in the absence of a duty or obligation to do so, citizens ought to participate in the politics of their communities. The central question is not about a duty to participate; it is about the value of participation.

Realists and Gladiators

The central sections of Pyrcz's essay describe and evaluate the arguments of those who favour significantly higher levels of political participation (the gladiators) and those who maintain that current levels are satisfactory, if not excessive (the realists). If these two sections are isolated from the crucial section that follows them ("The Realist's Case Revisited"), it is apparent that Pyrcz sees the gladiators as carrying the day by a decisive margin. This is not to say that he fails to give the realists their due; he presents their case fairly and makes it clear that they make some telling points that are too often ignored by the gladiators. However, in the end, realists emerge as proponents of a decidedly impoverished conception of democratic politics. In regard to both the individual and the social costs and benefits of political participation, realists are portrayed as partisans of a constricted, myopic understanding of human rationality and sensibility.

Gladiators certainly do not emerge unscathed. For example, they are shown to have an unbecoming propensity to preach to the converted and to underrate the personal and social benefits of non-political pursuits. Nevertheless, they are portrayed as upholding a conception of democratic politics that is incomparably richer than that of the realists. The contrast is revealed vividly in Pyrcz's summary of the gladiators' case for political participation, which I quote at length:

> [T]he gladiator rejects the realist's definition of politics as consisting principally in the effective representation of citizens' interests. She defines democracy instead as a distinct form of political interaction between citizens (reasoned discourse leading to public decisions) the scope of which measures the democratic quality of a society. From the point of view of the individual the gladiator rejects the claimed "burdensome" qual-

ities of participation. She challenges the conception of human fulfillment accepted by realists, arguing that well-being is achieved not through passivity but instead through the exercise of capacities. She contends that political participation provides for three developmental processes that are not afforded the non-participant: the skills requisite to political dialogue, a sense of justice, and the self-understanding, integrity, and community which emanates from a publicly expressed character.

If this were all that is to be said, readers would be left with the conclusion that the gladiators make a far stronger case than the realists do, that political participation is indeed A Good Thing, and that Pyrcz does not boldly challenge the proposition that increased political activity is desirable. But he does not think that this is all that is to be said. The most important section of his essay, "The Realist's Case Revisited," advances some highly imaginative arguments to show that, under certain circumstances, political aloofness is wiser than political participation.

Manipulation, Martyrdom, and Political Aloofness

To understand the case for political aloofness, Pyrcz asks readers to imagine a political collectivity, the town of Mercedes Hill, which is characterized by two main features. First, the social, political, and economic relationships among the townspeople of Mercedes Hill are predominantly, but not exclusively, manipulative. No political objectives in this town, including the reform of its politics, can be achieved without misleading rhetoric, deception, and appeals to myths. Second, a significant reform of the town's politics cannot be achieved within the lifetimes of the current reformers. The nature of any reform will be decided by a future generation.

Under these circumstances, Pyrcz maintains, the arguments of the gladiators are undermined and those of the realists are strengthened. The manipulative character of politics in Mercedes Hill subverts the gladiators' claim that political activity is both pleasurable and conducive to self-improvement. Acting manipulatively is not something that one can turn on and off while retaining one's personal integrity. Inescapably, the character of the manipulator is corroded. To the extent that the case for political participation rests on its contribution to the happiness and self-fulfilment of the political activist, its corrupting effect in a manipulative environment surely speaks in favour of political *dis*engagement.

The second feature of political life in Mercedes Hill that commends political aloofness over political activism is that no citizen can have any confidence that his or her efforts at reform will bear fruit, since the terms of any reform cannot be determined by that citizen. Both the success and failure of reform and the nature of any successful reform will be determined by a future generation, but there is no guarantee that *any* reform will succeed.

Accordingly, there is a very real possibility that a citizen of Mercedes Hill who opts for a life of intense political participation is opting for a life of futile martyrdom. As a result, Pyrcz argues, the citizen would be wiser to turn his or her zeal to activities with a greater prospect for success: "contributions to education, family life, literature, and the economy may also serve future generations, while developing the human capacities of the martyr."

Pyrcz finds an additional, important justification for political aloofness in Mercedes Hill. Widespread refusal to participate in the manipulative politics of the town could "undermine the confidence of the majority in applying public decisions to those who hold minority views," so that "pulling the 'rug of legitimacy' out from under the feet of those who determine the dominant form of politics may be preferable to activism."

Here, at last, is a case against political participation that is truly daring and unconventional. But it is also unconvincing, because it is, ironically, parasitical on Pyrcz's preference for the gladiators' case over the realists'. As he acknowledges, his argument for political aloofness is contextual. His goal is to show that "the question of political participation is resolved best when it is considered in context." The case for political aloofness in Mercedes Hill depends on a context in which political life is degenerate and corrupting. But this presupposes that under better circumstances, political participation is desirable. Thus Pyrcz remains firmly in the camp of the gladiators. He shows, at most, that "apathy" is a lamentable response to lamentable circumstances.

But perhaps all citizens live in Mercedes Hill. Perhaps the politics of the liberal democracies in general and of Canada in particular is *characteristically* degenerative and corrupting. If so, the essay's case for political aloofness might be thought still to be a powerful one. But two of its features exclude this possibility. First, Pyrcz holds that reformist activity in a corrupt polity makes sense only when success is certain: "If one was certain that political participation in Mercedes Hill would one day transform the politics of this town, then political martyrdom might be called for. But this is far from certain." Mercedes Hill is not unique in that the success of the long-range projects of its citizens is uncertain; long-range political projects invariably risk failure. If people were to act politically only when their success was guaranteed, they would never act. The value of political participation is not undermined by the prospect of failure, for the risk is inseparable from the activity.

Second, Pyrcz's suggestion that widespread political aloofness would undermine the confidence of the politically dominant in imposing their will on nonparticipators is belied by experience. Consider the assurance with which public policies are enforced by Canadian city councils, even though it is rare for more than one-third of the eligible voters to cast ballots in municipal elections. Significant reform may never be achieved. It is certain, however, that if it is achieved, it will be through the intensification of political activity, not through withdrawal from the fray.

Discussion Questions

1. Who is right about the current qualities of political life in Canada? What kind of evidence, if any, might be cited in favour of either author? Is Pyrcz's contention that context is important to the morality of participation naive?

2. What kind of personal qualities must be assumed of citizens if the gladiator's argument in favour of greater political participation is to withstand Pyrcz's concern about context? Are these reasonable qualities to assume?

3. Realism, as Pyrcz construes it, seems to favour the status quo with regard to levels of political participation. But do his arguments against the gladiator permit the status quo?

4. Does the critique really undermine Pyrcz's defence of the politically aloof?

Further Readings

The most accessible and interesting work for those interested in political participation in a democracy is C.B. Macpherson's *The Life and Times of Liberal Democracy* (Toronto and New York: Oxford University Press, 1977). Macpherson discusses a number of competing conceptions of democracy and offers an interesting proposition about participatory politics in North America. He also offers a provocative proposal for restructuring Canadian political parties and processes to permit greater participation.

Carol Pateman's *Participation and Democratic Theory* (Cambridge: Cambridge University Press, 1970), especially in its first two chapters, discusses traditional arguments for greater participation and advances a proposal for greater "political" participation in the workplace, a proposal that served as much of the focus for the democracy movements in Eastern Europe and the student movement in the 1960s.

Ben Barber's book, *Strong Democracy: Participatory Politics for a New Age* (Berkeley and Los Angeles: University of California Press, 1984), is a treatment of the basic call to greater participatory politics heralded by the American and French New Left. A very interesting study of participation in consensus politics is provided in Jane Mansbridges's *Beyond Adversary Democracy* (New York: Basic Books, 1980).

To pursue arguments on the realist side of the debate, see Joseph Schumpeter's *Capitalism, Socialism and Democracy* (New York and London: Allen and Unwin, 1976) and Anthony Down's *An Economic Theory of Democracy* (New York: Harper and Row, 1957).

CHAPTER 4

Justice, Rights, and the Welfare State

The welfare state guarantees the means of a decent life for all, irrespective of their financial ability. Two generations of Canadians have grown up with this security established in the fabric of their society. But the welfare state is expensive, and some of its programs (especially in the area of health care) promise to become even more expensive in the next decade. At the same time, it is expected that more people will claim these benefits and fewer people will pay for them. As a result, a debate is now developing about the justification of the welfare state.

Virtually everyone engaged in this debate accepts the need for some kind of welfare state—in principle. But there is disagreement over two broad issues: the extent of the benefits to be offered, and the terms of the benefits. The minimal view is that benefits should be provided only for those in genuine need, as a kind of charity, and that these benefits should be policed to prevent "scroungers." The maximal view is that the welfare state should ensure the means of a decent life for all, and that this should be guaranteed equally, as a right of community membership.

Both the essay and the critique in this chapter support the maximal position, but for very different reasons. In the essay, Don Carmichael tries to show how a maximal version of the welfare state can be established from the premises of the minimal position. The thrust of his argument is that the welfare state can be justified on the grounds of self-interest and fairness, as a comprehensive and collective insurance package in which basic material security is supplemented by guarantees for autonomy and self-respect. This defends a strong version of the welfare state in terms that give it a strikingly individualistic slant.

Tom Pocklington challenges this. He also supports a strong welfare state, but he does not think that it can be established adequately on an individualistic basis. He argues that Carmichael's individualism is deceptive, in that it rests upon—and perhaps conceals—a moral view. This is important, because a welfare state based only on individualistic values would result in an impoverished society, one that promoted individual autonomy at the cost of social values such as friendship and community.

ESSAY

This essay explores the justification of the welfare state and focuses on the rights of individuals. Are the benefits of the welfare state required by justice, as the entitlements of individuals, or do such benefits violate the rights of those who must pay for them?

The welfare state in Canada provides "cradle to grave" security for all citizens by guaranteeing provision for the basic needs of life, irrespective of the recipients' ability to pay for it. The programs of the welfare state include medical care, education (including technical training), child support, assistance for those with special needs (for example, people with disabilities), and income supplements for the unemployed, the poor, and the elderly to support a minimum standard of life. In effect, the welfare state operates as a system of collective insurance: all contribute within their abilities, so that each may benefit as needed.

Most Canadians accept the need for some kind of welfare state,[1] but there is disagreement about both its benefits and its terms. One question concerns the proper extent of the welfare state. Which benefits should be provided, and to what extent? A second question arises about their terms. Should benefits be provided as assistance for those in need, or instead be guaranteed as the rights of their recipients?

The importance of the welfare state in Canada's institutional fabric means that these questions inevitably raise basic issues of justice. Fundamentally, justice is a matter of giving individuals their "due," of respecting their rights, and of establishing a justifiable distribution of benefits and burdens in the social structure. Thus, questions about the welfare state, especially those concerning the proper extent and terms of its benefits, also raise issues about justice in society and the rights of individuals.

Two positions may be distinguished on these issues. The minimal view is that community assistance should be provided only for the barest and most basic of needs, and only for those who are genuinely unable to provide for themselves. It must also be policed and kept somewhat unattractive in order to discourage "scroungers." This was the view of laissez faire liberals[2] in the nineteenth century, and it has been resurrected more recently by neoconservatives.[3] At the other extreme, the maximal view is that the means of a decent life should be guaranteed for all, in terms that protect each person's self-respect and as a right of community membership. Although this position cannot be identified with any particular ideology, it will be designated somewhat roughly as social democratic.[4]

These positions are each informed by rival principles of social justice. For neoconservatives, the just society is one that protects the liberty of its members to make their own choices and to live on their own terms. Hence, each individual should have a right to the widest possible liberty. From this perspective, the welfare state is unjust in two respects. First, its programs are mandatory: individuals are forced to participate in state-determined insurance, such as medicare and pensions, instead of choosing their own coverage. Second, these programs are redistributive: individuals with higher incomes are forced to provide benefits for others, whether they want to or not.

For social democrats, on the other hand, the just society is one that promotes the well-being of its members. In an affluent society, the means of a decent life should be guaranteed for all individuals, irrespective of their ability to pay. This should be guaranteed as a right, in terms that respect the individual's dignity.

In short, views about the justice of the welfare state seem to fall between two extreme positions:

	Neoconservative	Social Democratic
Benefits:	minimum	maximum
	(bare necessities)	(decent life)
Terms:	assistance	right
	(unattractive)	(protect self-respect)
Ideal:	liberty and autonomy	well-being

Although these positions are stated as extremes, few people propose either to dismantle the welfare state entirely (the neoconservative minimum) or to guarantee the means of life completely (the social democratic maximum). Rather, questions about the welfare state usually focus more narrowly on whether to increase or reduce particular benefits. Even so, it is clear that the two extreme positions state the principles and tendencies that underlie more practical controversies. Every proposal for new or increased benefits is a step toward the social democratic maximum. Equally, the first objection to every such proposal is its cost, that is, that taxpayers should not be expected to pay for it; and this is a step back toward the neoconservative minimum.

Thus, although most Canadians reject these positions in their extreme forms, they accept the underlying principles. It might be more accurate to say that what they reject in the extreme positions is their one-sidedness. Canadians are unwilling to hold either position to the exclusion of the other because they agree with the principles underlying both of them. They want the basic needs of all individuals to be met, but they also want individuals to do this for themselves so far as is possible because they believe that society should be organized to promote both liberty and well-being, with respect for all the rights of all individuals. From this perspective, Canadians may prefer some combination of the positions—a liberal society, in which individuals are responsible for looking after themselves, but with the welfare state as a safety net for those who cannot do so adequately. Put in these terms, the problem of justice is to find the best compromise between these opposing positions.

There is a problem here, however. Precisely because these positions are opposed, they cannot be combined without creating injustice. Any compromise between them will inevitably violate one position or the other. If it is true that mandatory and redistributive programs violate the rights of those who are made to pay for them, then any form of welfare state will be unjust. Conversely, if individuals are truly entitled to the means of a decent life, then anything less than this (and current programs fall far short of it) will violate their rights. In either case, the compromise position will be unjust.

The Problem of Benefits versus Entitlements

A further problem arises about the nature of the welfare state itself. Support for the welfare state is usually based upon one of three principles:

(i)   *Morality*: It would be wrong to allow any individual to suffer for want of the means to meet basic needs.
(ii) *Public Policy*: It is in the public interest that no one be allowed to die (or languish) because of inability to provide for basic needs.
(iii) *Human Rights*: Individuals have a right to the means of a decent life.

These principles can be used to justify specific benefits of the welfare state. The question, however, is whether these benefits can be justified in terms that also provide any degree of entitlement and protection for the self-respect of those who receive them. This combination—benefits as entitlements—is difficult to justify.

For example, a moral principle, such as charity, can be used to show why help should be provided to those in need; but it does not show that assistance is owed to those who need it or that they have any right to it. Instead, with this justification, the right lies with those who give, not with those who receive. Suppose that someone supports the United Way as a charity because of a sense of duty to help others. Does this entitle the United Way to demand help from that person as its right? On the contrary; it is the contributor's right to determine which causes they will support, and by how much. It is also their right to terminate this support if they feel it is being abused, or if they can think of a better use for it, or if they just feel like doing so. That is, the causes one supports have no claims upon the donor; they must appeal for one's help and be grateful for it. Similarly with the welfare state: it can be justified on moral grounds, but not in terms that allow individuals any right to its benefits or security in their continuation.

Similar considerations apply to justifications based on public policy. Higher education might be supported in this way, because of the benefits to the community of having well-educated citizens. But this does not give anyone a right to an education. It is for the state to decide whom to educate, and in what way; and the assistance can be changed or ended at any time. Even though this might disrupt students' hopes and lives, it does not violate their rights because they have none in this area. The point of the education program, from this perspective, is not to benefit students but merely to use them as the means of serving the community.

To put this point more generally, the welfare state can be justified on grounds of morality or public policy, but not in terms that establish that individuals have any rights to its benefits. This makes recipients dependent upon the judgement and power of those who administer the programs. The benefits might be revised, withheld, or suspended in ways that decisively affect the recipients, but over which they are powerless.

This problem is avoided by the third type of justification, human rights, but in a way that creates a different problem. Clearly, if the benefits of the welfare state are justified as human rights, then recipients will be entitled to them. The problem is the "*if*", because claims of human rights are more problematic than they seem. Such claims are often merely ways of asserting what "ought" to be done; for example, a "human right to higher education" is sometimes just a way of saying that it ought to be provided. This would merely be another version of a moral justification, with the difficulties already considered. It might show that the benefit should be provided, but not (despite its rhetoric) in terms that would establish any rights of the recipients.

If, however, "human rights" are asserted in a stronger sense, as genuine entitlements, different problems arise. First, it is difficult to see where these rights come from, or how they might be proven. How does the fact that someone is human give him or her the right to demand the means of life from others?[5] Moreover, if the benefits of the welfare state are justified on the grounds of "human rights," then the same benefits are owed to *all* human beings, not just to those in one's own society. This means that any benefits of the welfare state can be established on a human rights justification only if the same benefits are provided for all human beings. Few benefits could be guaranteed so broadly. The result of such a justification, therefore, would be a strong sense of entitlement but very few benefits.

Justifying the Welfare State

The problem of justification is further complicated by a conflict between two distinct issues raised by the welfare state: its benefits and its terms. Benefits can be justified by principles of morality or public policy, but not in terms that establish any entitlement to these benefits. Or, entitlements can be established on the grounds of human rights, but not in terms that permit many benefits to be justified. The problem, then, is whether the welfare state can be justified at all, at least in any sense that protects the entitlements of recipients.

The task of this essay is to argue that the welfare state can be justified as a comprehensive and collective insurance package in which basic material benefits are supplemented by protections for autonomy and self-respect. This justification bases the welfare state on grounds of general self-interest and fairness and bypasses appeals to public policy, morality, or human rights. Although it establishes a strong version of the social democratic principle, it does so in terms that capture what is morally appealing in the neoconservative position and that imply that a fundamental element of individual well-being is control over the terms of one's life. What this "establishes" is a liberal socialism, or a welfare state with a strongly individualistic slant.

The argument will be presented in three stages. First, the welfare state is justified in general terms. Then, it is argued that the benefits of the welfare state should be established as entitlements. Finally, some practical implications of the analysis are considered by referring to issues of work, equality, guaranteed income, and the idea of autonomy.

In Defence of the Welfare State

There are two images of the welfare state. One is the image of "welfare," of state-administered assistance for those who cannot provide for themselves. Only a small proportion of citizens are beneficiaries of the welfare state in this sense. However, almost all Canadians benefit from the welfare state in its second sense, as a collectively funded health and education insurance program. Everyone who uses the health-care system is a beneficiary of the welfare state; so is anyone who receives any formal education. These benefits are not understood as "welfare" in the first sense; rather, they are regarded by their recipients as entitlements. Those who visit a doctor do not see themselves as receiving a benefit charitably provided by others. They feel themselves entitled to the benefit because they or their families have paid for it through health-care contributions and taxes. The benefit is regarded as a *right* in the social democrat sense.

If *all* the benefits of the welfare state were paid for in this way, the social democratic version of the welfare state could be justified on the straightforward grounds of individual entitlement. But this is not true; many benefits are not paid for by their recipients. These benefits seem to be "welfare" rather than "entitlements," because they are provided by others. Even so, they can be construed as "entitlements," purchased through a special and somewhat abstract insurance system.

Consider health care. Individuals are entitled to this when they need it, because it has been paid for. But do individuals pay for the health care they use? No. Strictly speaking, the provincial health insurance system pays for it. Individuals are entitled to it because they have purchased insurance through health plan contributions, and this obliges the system to pay for the care when the individual needs it.

But why purchase insurance? The reason is that medical treatment can be very expensive; hence, without insurance, individuals might need treatment that costs more than they can afford. For example, few can afford lengthy treatment in an intensive care unit for injuries suffered in a car crash. They might try to borrow the money, but there are serious problems with this approach: (i) those who require intensive care are not in a position to negotiate a bank loan; (ii) even if they were able to borrow the money, the costs of repayment would cripple them financially; (iii) they might be unable to borrow money just because, in view of their injuries, no one would believe they would be able to repay it; and (iv) they would not want their medical treatment held up at any stage by doubts about their ability to pay for it.[6]

Insurance guarantees treatment when people need it. It might not be necessary; in the course of a lifetime, they may never need expensive medical treatment, in which case they will pay more in premiums than they receive in benefits. But no one can be certain of this. Even the vigorously healthy may sometime need expensive medical treatment as the result of an accident. Without insurance, they risk death through their inability to afford treatment. Thus, even if the insurance costs more than the medical benefits it pays over one's lifetime, it would not be rational to forego insurance because the savings would not justify the risk. The protection guaranteed by the insurance justifies its cost.

Insurance systems provide this protection by "spreading the risk." Suppose an illness that costs $100,000 to treat strikes only one person in ten thousand. Although an individual would need $100,000 to pay for such treatment, in an insurance system this risk can be spread around, so that with an insured group of one hundred thousand the protection might cost each person only $10. The size of the insured group is important. If the group has only one hundred members, the cost must be spread more narrowly (at a rate of $1,000 per person). Even in a group of one hundred thousand, the underwriters must insure themselves against the possibility that more than one person might develop the illness, and the costs of this secondary insurance will be passed onto each of their clients as a higher premium. This problem disappears when the group is large enough. If the group has twenty-five million members, there is no need for secondary insurance and the risks can be averaged over the membership. In large groups, then, risks can be averaged across the members and guarantee protection for each member at low cost.

Although only one illness has been considered as an example, there are hundreds of similar cases. The same principle applies; individuals in a large group can insure themselves against all medical needs in a comprehensive package. This averages the risks among all individuals and for all medical conditions. However, this approach also ignores certain differences among individuals. Men have a zero probability of breast cancer and women a zero probability of prostate cancer, so men and women might be insured separately in these categories. Would this lower anyone's insurance rates? The result would be that men pay nothing for coverage for breast cancer but more in premiums for prostate cancer insurance, and women would pay nothing for coverage for prostate cancer but more in premiums for breast cancer insurance. If the insurance costs of the two cancers are similar, then men and women would save nothing from this procedure. The savings would be cancelled by the costs. Therefore, instead of insuring men and women separately for the two illnesses, it is more efficient to have a single policy that insures everyone for both.

This point can be taken further. In developing health insurance, individuals might be covered selectively, a separate rate could be calculated for each illness, and specific risk discriminations could be made for each category. The result would be an infinite variety of insurance plans. However, since everyone needs insurance against all possible medical conditions, a comprehensive health policy could be developed. In this case, many of the differences among the specific health plans would cancel one another out. However, not all of the differences would cancel out. For example, the costs for lung cancer insurance are higher for continuing smokers than for nonsmokers, so the insurance rates for individuals in these categories might reflect this difference. Even here, though, the simplest procedure is to charge everyone the same rate and to collect the costs of treating lung cancer from smokers in the form of taxes on tobacco.

In other cases, however, differences among individuals disappear within a comprehensive coverage program. An above-average susceptibility to heart disease may be offset by lower risks of diabetes, kidney disease, and so on. The result is that most differences among individuals become insignificant in relation to their total health needs.

Instead of developing a mass of separate policies, it would be better to establish a single and comprehensive policy, with coverage for all medical needs averaged among all individuals.

This scheme does not describe the welfare state, but it takes some steps toward it in two respects. First, it assumes mandatory participation; individuals are required to participate in many programs. In the case of medicare, it appears rational for the state to have a comprehensive insurance policy. In making this mandatory, then, the welfare state only requires what it would be rational to want in any case.[7] The same can be said of any other program, as long as (i) it is one that would be rational for every individual to want, (ii) it provides quality service,[8] and (iii) it allows scope for individual choice within its programs.

Second, although the previous examples assume that benefits are limited to contributors, the system could absorb a certain number of noncontributors, that is, people who are covered even though they cannot afford it. If the proportion of noncontributors is kept small, say 5 percent, it would not be against the interests of the contributors to include them in the protections of the system. It might seem that this would increase each contributor's premium by 5 percent, but this cost might be unavoidable in any case. If coverage is denied to those who cannot afford it, contributors would incur the extra costs of policing the system, such as determining whether individuals have paid, and also, more importantly, of settling disputes that ensue when individuals were denied medical coverage. For both humanitarian and administrative reasons these people would not be denied medical care when they needed it, so, one way or another, the care would be provided and its costs would eventually be passed on to the contributors. As a result, the choice for the contributor is not whether to accept an additional 5 percent cost for the sake of guaranteeing universal coverage; a good part of this 5 percent will be paid anyway. The question is only how it will be paid; by a dispute-ridden system or by one that guarantees care for all.[9]

Thus the provision of health care for noncontributors might be an unavoidable cost. But something stronger can now be said. Thus far, this essay has argued that comprehensive medical insurance is desirable as a protection against all possible medical needs. Now, for similar reasons, it can be argued that it would be rational to prefer a society that guaranteed such coverage universally to one in which coverage was limited to contributors.

Imagine two societies, in each of which about 5 percent of the populace is unable to afford health care.[10] The difference is that in society A, health care is limited to the 95 percent who are able to pay for it, while in society B it is provided universally at the cost of an extra 5 percent in premiums. Now suppose that one had to choose which society to live in, but without knowing anything further about one's place in it. Which society is the best choice?[11] Statistically, there is a 5 percent chance that one will wind up in the lowest group in either society. Hence, the choice is whether to save 5 percent in premiums, but at a 5 percent risk of being unable to afford medical treatment (society A) or instead to pay the extra 5 percent to guarantee coverage in the lowest group (society B).

Put in this way, society B is the rational choice, for all the reasons that make insurance rational in the first place. Indeed, society B is simply an extended form of insurance. Just as comprehensive insurance guarantees coverage for all possible medical conditions, in case an individual suffers from any of them, the choice of society B insures the same coverage for all social positions in case one occupies any of them. It costs more, just as insurance does; but the extra charge is justified by the protection it guarantees. Such insurance is comprehensive, in covering all needs, and universal, in covering all social positions.

The same argument applies to all other basic needs and also to any "special" needs (such as those of the disabled) that impose particular burdens upon individuals' abilities to care for themselves. That is, *if* one had the choice, and *if* one did not know one's place or condition in society, it would be rational to consider a society that guaranteed provision for such needs as preferable to a society that did not. Guaranteed provision would cost more for those able to pay, but the extra charge would be worthwhile as a form of insurance. In every case, it would be rational to insure all basic needs for all social positions, so it would be rational to prefer a society that guaranteed such coverage universally. This, in principle, is the welfare state.

Some important implications flow from this argument. Before considering them, however, some objections will be considered.

Objections

First, it might be objected that in a hypothetical choice between societies, individuals might gamble on being well off,[12] so that they would not need the protections of society B. But it is difficult to see how such a gamble could be rational. Assuming a 95–5 percent split in the society, the gamble incurs a 5 percent chance of being unable to meet basic needs for the sake, at best, of a 5 percent reduction in insurance premiums. The risk is enormous, and the payoff is insignificant.

Next, one might object that "I would have no reason to insure the worst position, because I know I would never wind up there. In our society, there is enough opportunity for individuals to succeed if they want to, if they have the right determination, character, and drive. Those who are poor lack this drive. But I don't, so I will never need the protections of the welfare state."

This claim—that poverty is the result of poor character—is mistaken. Even if it were true, it would not invalidate the argument for the welfare state. It does not apply to special needs, such as mental or physical disabilities and special health problems. Whatever one's views about poverty in general, these are all conditions against which it would be rational to insure if one could. Further, even if poverty were the product of weak character, there remains a 5 percent chance that in any society the objector might be such a person. Of course the objector believes this is impossible: "Poverty results from weak character; I do not have a weak character; therefore I would not be poor." But this misunderstands the point. *If* there is a 5 percent chance that one might be poor, then there is a 5 percent chance that one would be a person who has the weak character and attitudes that allegedly go with it. Whatever one thinks about such people, it would be in one's interests to protect their position because one might belong to that group.

Further, the claim that poverty is "one's own fault" cannot apply to children. In our hypothetical society, 5 percent of children will not receive adequate sustenance, medical care, or education because their parents are unable to afford it. So it might be said to the objector: "Wouldn't you want to insure yourself against being one of those children, if you could?"[13] Even if the parents were poor through their own fault, there is no reason why their children should pay for this. Children do not deserve to be in need; they were simply unlucky to be born into poor families. In view of this, wouldn't it be prudent to remove the role of luck by guaranteeing basic needs for all children?

Thus, even those who regard poverty as the result of a character defect would have sufficient reason to prefer a society with the safety net of a welfare state, if only to protect their interests as children. But a special feature of this insurance argument is that, normally, people pay premiums first and receive benefits later, if needed. Using the approach here, however, they would agree to insure social positions so that they could receive benefits when they need them, as children, before they can pay for them. This is one of the main features of the welfare state: it protects people at times of vulnerability, when they are young (or ill, or elderly) and are unable to provide for themselves. In effect, people receive the benefits when they need them, as children, and pay for them later, as adults.

Consequently, the welfare state must be seen in slightly different terms. Normally, its costs are thought of as being paid for by adults, as premiums for themselves and their children. On this basis, it may seem wrong (as neoconservatives argue) to make those with no children pay for the education of others. Using the insurance argument, however, this is not true. Education taxes should not be seen as purchasing education for children. Rather, the taxes are deferred insurance premiums. They ensure quality education for all, especially for those born into families that cannot afford it. The beneficiary of the tax, accordingly, is the person paying it. It is simply that he or she has already received the benefit and now is paying for it.

The same is true of many other benefits of the welfare state. If taxes are understood as payments for benefits, then it may seem unfair that some people pay more than others (because of their higher tax bracket); and it may also seem unfair that people in need should get benefits without paying for them. Strictly speaking, however, the benefits are not purchased. What is purchased is protection in the form of an insurance system, and in many cases the tax is a retrospective premium for protection already received. This is justified on the ground that everyone—*if* they had the choice, and *if* they did not know their actual social positions—would prefer a society with these protections to a society without them.

This raises a final objection. In reality, people *do* know their social positions. An individual might object as follows: "Although I would have agreed to this system if I didn't know my actual social position, I know that my family was able to provide for all basic needs. Hence, there is no need to provide these universally in order to guarantee them for myself; so I see no reason why I should pay the extra costs of providing such goods for others."

The point of the insurance argument, however, has not been that it is in everyone's greatest interests to have a welfare state. Rather, it has been to show that the welfare state is *fair*. In reality, the welfare state, like any other fair policy, will be needed more by some than by others. Some, indeed, might be marginally better off without it, but this does not affect its fairness. Thus the reason for supporting the welfare state even if one does not need its protections as much as others do is because doing so is fair. It is the policy all people would accept if they did not know their actual social positions.

This idea of choosing without knowing one's own position seems bizarre, but it has elements of fairness and impartiality. In one sense, a policy or rule is fair if everyone can agree to it. On the issues raised by the welfare state, however, there is no policy on which all people would agree if they knew their actual social positions, because there is no policy that maximizes the interests of all positions. So the next step is to devise a policy that is fair in a further sense, namely, one that everyone would accept if they were impartial. This is the point of choosing without knowing one's social position. To decide the justice of the welfare state in this way means that one must approach the question as if one might be anyone in the society, and thence in terms of how it affects everyone. Thus the insurance argument shows that the welfare state is fair in the sense that it is the policy that everyone would accept under conditions of impartiality. In reality, some people will need the protections of the welfare state more than will others; but it is only fair to support the system, because it is an agreement that all people would have made if they could.

Finally, this is not against one's interests. Although one may not need some of the provisions of the welfare state, they are still in one's interests in the abstract sense that they would protect one if one needed them, just as car insurance continues to be in one's interest even if one never claims on it. Indeed, paying car insurance for several years without claiming it does not mean that one has wasted one's money, or that one has received nothing for it.[14] By the same token, for those fortunate enough not to need many protections of the welfare state, it is still in their general interest as members of the society that those protections exist. Consequently, it is only fair that all members pay their share of the costs.

The Goods of the Welfare State: Benefits versus Entitlements

How should the benefits be established? This question can be considered in the same way as before: if one didn't know one's place in society, what kind and amount of protection would it be rational to ensure?

Presumably, one would hope to be a self-supporting adult, able to look after oneself, but sometimes this is not possible. The aim of the welfare state is to protect against this by guaranteeing that one would be able to meet one's basic needs, live a decent life, and look after oneself as well as one can. On this basis, it would be sensible to guarantee the following:

(i)   health and education (including vocational training), because these services are needed by everyone but beyond the ability of almost everyone to pay for directly;

(ii) sufficient income to support a decent life for those unable to work or unable to earn enough, such as the ill, the unemployed, the elderly, and those with disabilities; and

(iii) facilities to enable those with mental or physical disabilities to live a full life.

Thus the insurance argument broadly justifies the welfare state as it exists today in Canada, Britain, and Western Europe. But this list of benefits is incomplete. Although it covers an impressive range of material benefits, it does not include two other goods that are highly valued: namely, autonomy, or control over one's life, and self-respect. It would be wise to guarantee these goods as well, by requiring that benefits be provided in terms that protect the individual's sense of autonomy and self-respect.

Consider, for example, the provision of facilities for people with disabilities. On the basis of the insurance argument, which contemplates physical disabilities as conditions that might happen to oneself, it would be in each person's interests to protect the opportunities of people with disabilities to live as full a life as possible, including appropriate care and facilities for housing and recreation. But it should also include measures to help them lead regular lives as members of the community. They should be given opportunities to attend university classes, run for public office, hold regular jobs, do their own shopping, and so on. This requires special transport, guaranteed jobs, wheelchair-accessible buildings, and generally the co-operation of everyone in the community. It might be objected that this is too costly, that help for people with disabilities should be limited to basic care in treatment centres. But this would not be said by people who thought they might become disabled. They would want to ensure that their lives were as rich and complete as possible. Considering it in this way, no one would accept only basic care confined to a treatment centre; on the contrary, people would insist upon additional facilities to permit people with disabilities to lead the kinds of lives they would have chosen in the absence of the disability. What is crucial here is autonomy, that is, being able to live on one's own terms.

This emphasis upon autonomy and self-respect suggests an important distinction. Broadly speaking, the benefits of the welfare state are intended to protect the ability of individuals to live a good life. But there are two ways to view these benefits, because there are two ways to understand the good life itself. The standard view is that such benefits protect each individual's ability to live a happy life, the life that satisfies his or her desires. According to this approach, the welfare state should protect each individual's "happiness package" by guaranteeing the basic ingredients of a happy life whenever individuals are unable to do so for themselves.

An alternative view is that the good life is the life lived on one's own terms. In this approach, the welfare state should protect each individual's "autonomy package," not by guaranteeing the ingredients of happiness but rather by protecting the abilities of individuals to decide the terms of their own lives. This seems crucial. No one would choose a life, however "happy," that denied all opportunities for self-determination or squashed the individual's sense of self-respect.[15] Hence, the autonomy package is an essential ingredient of the welfare state.[16]

Rights and Entitlements
It follows that the benefits of the welfare state should be established as the entitlements of those who receive them.[17] These benefits are not the expressions of charity or public benevolence. Rather, individuals are entitled to them in the same sense that they have a right to medical care if they have paid their medicare premiums.

There are two reasons for this. First, the benefits have been insured and paid for; therefore, those who need them are entitled to them. Neoconservatives will object that the poor are not entitled to such benefits because they have not paid for them, but this is false. Entitlement does not depend upon who pays for the benefits, but upon who qualifies for them. The fact that the poor themselves may not have paid for the benefits is irrelevant to their entitlement, in the same way that one's right to medical attention as a child was not invalidated by the fact that one did not pay for it oneself. Where benefits have been paid for, eligible recipients are entitled to them. Hence, the poor are entitled to the protection of the welfare state because the protection has been paid for and because they qualify for it. If a society guarantees comprehensive coverage for all social positions, there is no reason not to establish such coverage in the same way for all, as an entitlement.

The second reason for establishing the protections of the welfare state as entitlements, is to protect each recipient's sense of self-respect and autonomy. To be "entitled" to something is to have a right to it; this means that one is justified in claiming it and that others have a duty to provide it. By establishing the benefits of the welfare state as entitlements, therefore, society protects the recipients' sense of self-respect and autonomy by reducing their dependence on the power of supervising state officials.

The Importance of Entitlements

The entitlement principle is particularly important because, in Canadian society, money is a form of power and control. Those with money are able to control those who need it; conversely, those in need are dependent to that extent upon the power and control of those who might help them. Thus, by helping individuals, the welfare state may replace one form of dependence (need) with another (dependence upon the continuation of the benefit); and in receiving benefits, individuals may escape from one form of subjection (of need) only to be caught in another (control by the state).

This is not an imaginary concern. Many Canadians believe that the poor are not entitled to assistance and that "welfare" should be treated as charity. They believe it must be made unattractive to minimize freeloaders (or "welfare bums") and that if it is not policed, recipients will drink it away. Clearly, this is demeaning. Instead of promoting autonomy and self-respect, it degrades and controls recipients as dependents. No one, expecting to need such "help," would want it to be established on such terms. To stop this, the idea of welfare as charity must be eliminated and the principle of entitlement must be established in its place. The problem, however, is not confined to those who regard welfare as charity. It is built into the structure of the welfare state. Many persons are simply and absolutely dependent upon the welfare state; they have no alternatives. As a result, they are dependent upon the power of supervising officials in ways that reduce their control over their own lives. This dependence can be offset only by establishing benefits as entitlements.

Consider the following incident, reported by a leading British newspaper:

> A one-legged man seeking a state mobility allowance had to struggle up four flights of stairs to the room where a tribunal was to decide his claim. When he got there the tribunal ruled that he could not have the allowance because he had managed to make it up the stairs.[18]

Such incidents might be humorous if they were not real; but they are inexcusable. To make a one-legged man climb four flights of stairs to claim a mobility allowance is abusive, then to treat the ability to do as disproving the disability is ridiculous. It seems to be a "catch-22" situation: one can't have a disabled allowance unless one applies, but if one is able to apply, one isn't disabled. This abuse merely flaunts a power that is inherent in the situation: the tribunal can make the applicant climb four flights of stairs, and do much else in addition, because it controls what he needs.

Suppose, however, that the tribunal was an insurance agency, and that the one-legged man was claiming a benefit under his coverage. Would it treat him in this way? Clearly not, if it wanted to stay in business. Even if it rejected his claim, it would treat him courteously because, as a client, he would be entitled to it.[19]

By way of comparison, consider a different case. Suppose that a fully insured stereo is stolen, and that a claim is made for it. The insurance company refuses payment on the grounds that:

(i)   since establishing the policy, it has changed its mind about what the policy covers;

Surely this is irrelevant. If the coverage is valid, then the claimant is entitled to payment. The company cannot change its mind about the coverage because it gave up the right to do so in establishing the policy. Similar considerations would apply if the company refused to pay on the grounds that:

(ii) it is not sure the claimant will use the money in the "right" way; or

(iii) it knows the claimant will use the money for a stereo, but it disapproves of the claimant's taste in music.

Does it matter whether these views are true? Is it reasonable for the company to require proof that the claimant will use the money in the right way before it pays? Surely not. If the claim is valid, the company is obliged to pay. Its views about how the money will be spent, or the claimant's musical taste, are simply irrelevant. It gave up the right to impose such conditions when it established the policy. Having done so, it is now bound by the claimant's right.[20]

Similar considerations ought to apply to the welfare state, but they do not. Here is endorsed what would be opposed in any other system. At present, there is no entitlement attached to its benefits. Indeed, each of the three "reasons" rejected out of hand in an insurance system are routinely cited in the welfare state as grounds for policing, altering, and withdrawing benefits. Recipients have no rights; their benefits are constantly at risk; and they are dependent upon supervising officials. No one would subscribe to insurance along such lines. Nor, therefore, should this be tolerated in the welfare state. Its benefits should be established as entitlements in the same way, and for the same reason, as those of any other insurance system.

Problem: The "Welfare Bum"

An objection may be raised at this point. Establishing benefits as entitlements has the virtue of freeing individuals from the absolute control of state officials. But what about the so-called "welfare bums," those who drink their benefits away or waste them on drugs or gambling? Isn't supervision necessary to prevent this?

This is a real problem. Some individuals will drink away their benefits if they can, and it is difficult to see why the society should pay for this. But monitoring policies are not very effective. If individuals are determined to drink, they will find a way to do so, despite the vigilance of supervising social workers. Further, those who abuse benefits are a small minority among the beneficiaries of the welfare state. It does not make sense to consider them the norm in determining the terms of benefits for everyone else, that is, to regard everyone else as a potential "welfare bum" and therefore as needing supervision. It would be better to regard the majority of beneficiaries who are entitled to their benefits as the norm and to recognize that there are only a small number of "hard cases."

But what really is the force of the "welfare bum" objection? It is the concern that community assistance should not be given to individuals if they are going to abuse it and that the reasons for establishing such assistance should be protected by supervising its use. These concerns are reasonable, but they ignore a major consideration on the other side of the issue, namely, the need to establish benefits as entitlements to protect the recipients' autonomy and self-respect. There will inevitably be cases in which benefits are used in unpopular ways, but that is precisely why it is important to establish them as entitlements: to protect the recipients' ability to live on their own, rather than the terms the state (or the social majority) might impose upon them. It may be that the recipient drinks; but it might instead be that he or she is irreligious, sexually promiscuous, or unpatriotic. These are qualities that, from some point of view, can be judged wrong, but they are not illegal or criminal. Individuals are entitled by law to live in these ways if they choose. Thus if the benefits of the welfare state are established as entitlements, the recipients should be entitled to use them as they choose, just like other people do.

Suppose, from this point of view, that a "welfare bum" goes to the bar with some friends who are working and they all get drunk. Does the fact that the friends drink their money away show that they are not entitled to it? On the contrary, it is their own money. They earned it themselves, so they are entitled to spend it as they choose. The welfare bum is in the same situation. Since there are sufficient grounds for establishing welfare benefits as entitlements, it is the recipient's money to spend as he or she chooses. Restrictions and supervision are no more justifiable for the recipient than for the friends.

But what if one drinks away money that is needed by one's family? Clearly, this would be a tragedy and an injustice to the family members, but it has nothing to do with the drunk being a welfare recipient. A wage-earner who drinks away the family income leaves the family in the same condition. At some point, in each case, the rights and needs of the children might require their removal from the family; but this outcome is not significantly affected by whether the money the drunk wastes is earned or a welfare entitlement.

In short, the fact that an individual abuses a benefit does not mean that he or she is not entitled to it, so it does not provide any reason for not establishing the benefit as an entitlement. And this example was taken up only as an objection. The great majority of recipients do not abuse their benefits. Their entitlement should be respected.[21]

Practical Implications for Social Justice

This section considers some practical implications of the preceeding argument. A great many topics might be covered here, but this section focuses on issues of work, equality, guaranteed income, and the idea of autonomy.

Work

If the concern for autonomy and self-respect is taken seriously, then the same considerations that favour regarding the material benefits of the welfare state as entitlements indicate that these benefits should also include opportunities for meaningful work.

Work is potentially important as a measure and expression of one's control over one's life. The income derived from work is desirable in this respect, because it can be spent as one chooses. Work also involves "changing the world," exerting one's powers, and acting in ways that "make a difference." This can be a vital ingredient in a person's sense of control over his or her life.

Work, however, is also important to one's self-respect. People's sense of themselves as individuals is largely conditioned by how they are regarded (or think they are regarded) by others. In Canada, rightly or wrongly,[22] economic success is widely regarded as the mark of human worth. This is because the amount one earns is the measure of how much one is needed by others. As a result, economic independence (through paid work) is almost essential as a condition of self-respect, whereas to be dependent upon another is to feel subordinate and inferior.

For reasons both of autonomy and self-respect, therefore, opportunities for meaningful work should be included in the benefits of the welfare state. This may seem surprising. Work is generally regarded as unpleasant, as something people will do only if they are paid. But while this is true of many jobs, it is false as a general principle.[23] Expending effort and energy is not necessarily unpleasant; skiing, lovemaking, or working hard at something one really wants to do are pleasant pastimes. Of course, most jobs are not like this; they can be unpleasant precisely because they do not have the features that make other activities "fun."

What is unpleasant about work is not that it involves the expenditure of energy, but rather how it is organized. Typically, a job involves working for others, at their direction, and often doing things they don't want to do for themselves. The sense of autonomy that is so essential to the enjoyability of other activities is either absent or assaulted in organized labour. In addition, unpleasant jobs often involve work that is regarded as unworthy or demeaning, and in such cases, self-respect is diminished rather than enhanced. This does not mean that work itself is unpleasant. It can be beneficial as an opportunity to express autonomy and self-respect. It is unpleasant when it is organized in ways that deny these values instead of expressing them.

This difference is important. The standard view, that work is unpleasant in principle, implies that people will work only if paid. This view assumes that (i) working conditions don't matter much, because the work itself (rather than the way it is organized) is unpleasant; (ii) people will not work unless they need the income; hence, welfare benefits undermine the need to work, so they must be policed and kept unattractive; and (iii) with developing technology it would be desirable to minimize work and to maximize its products, that is, material goods and the income to purchase them.

But these views are false or, at best, distortions of a more complex reality. If properly organized work is a potential benefit, then any policy of minimizing the number of jobs would be a disaster. Instead of minimizing jobs, society should eliminate the features that make work unpleasant and, conversely, increase opportunities for more meaningful work. Consider whether anyone would choose to work if they were guaranteed a basic income without it. For most people, the answer would depend upon the job involved; they would prefer to work if the job were interesting. Consequently, it is not true that welfare benefits as such undermine the incentive to work. This is true only for jobs that combine low incomes and oppressive working conditions. People must be paid to do such jobs, not because they are lazy, but because the jobs are unattractive. The jobs have no internal rewards that will make people to want to work in them. Thus, it does not follow that welfare benefits should be made unattractive to keep people in such jobs. Quite the reverse: since it would be rational to ensure everyone's opportunities for meaningful work as part of the protections of the welfare state, it follows that unattractive jobs should be eliminated, or improved, or better paid.

Guaranteed Basic Income
A practical way to realize the principles enunciated in this essay is to guarantee a minimum income for every citizen. It would be the same for each citizen, and just enough to secure a minimal standard of living (something like the income of many students). In addition, provision would be made automatically for health care, education, and special needs. But that would be all; there would be no unemployment insurance, pensions, welfare, family allowance, child care programs, student loans, or anything else. There would be no need for them. Instead of child-care assistance, for example, parents would be guaranteed a basic income for themselves and for each of their children. Single parents would be able to afford child care, so that they could work, and if there were several children, it would be possible to stay home and raise one's children oneself. This would be a choice that parents could make for themselves.

The main advantage of this proposal is that it guarantees a basic standard of living for everyone as a basic right of community membership. It would free individuals to decide for themselves how to live, without entangling them in paperwork and supervision by a social worker bureaucracy. Nothing, however, is perfect, and it must be admitted that this proposal is open to criticisms from both the left and the right.

The left may object that a guaranteed income would do too little to promote economic redistribution and equalization. In particular, it may be said that the proposal does not reduce the immense inequalities of wealth, income, and power in this society. It may even legitimize them. However, although inequalities are undesirable, they are hardly the fault of a guaranteed income, so they should not be a reason for opposing it. It is true that this proposal would allow a wide range of inequality in the society, but why should this matter so long as every individual has enough to be able to decide freely how to live and is not trapped by constraints into submitting to the control of others?[24]

It may be asked, is it right that the income of various groups, such as the elderly, should be so low? Of course this is not desirable, but again perhaps the concern should be less about equalizing and more about liberating. Guarantee basic needs, such as health and education, along with a minimum standard of living, and then leave individuals free to earn more if they choose. Questions about how hard to work, how much to save, and what to buy should be left to individuals to answer for themselves. Fundamentally, these are issues of how to organize one's life.

On the other side, the proposal may be criticized by the right because of its cost and its effects on wage rates. It should be remembered, however, that the guaranteed income is a minimum, enough only for subsistence. Most people will want to earn more, so they will continue to work.[25] In such cases, the basic income will simply be retrieved through taxes, as happens now with family allowances. As a result, the costs of the proposal would come from individuals who do not earn much additional income. This society already spends considerable sums on social services for such individuals. In 1987, for example, the combined social services budget in Canada was almost $60 billion, an average of about $2,400 for each person in the country.[26] If this expenditure were distributed across the lowest quarter of the population, it would average $9,600 per person; for a family unit of four, this would be an income of $38,400. Although not too much can be made out of these figures,[27] they suggest that Canadians already spend substantial sums on subsistence and that a guaranteed basic income would not add appreciably to its cost. What is at issue, therefore, is not the amount spent, but the terms. Since Canadians are committed to expenditures for basic income guarantees and supplements as a matter of public policy, why not make the guarantees universal and straightforward as a principle of entitlement?

Similar considerations apply to wage rates. The objection here is that a guaranteed minimum would force wages up by withdrawing workers from the lowest-paid positions. But what is guaranteed, again, is only subsistence, and no more than what is provided now under different terms. Most people will want to earn a good deal more than this, so their wage rates will not be affected. In this approach, even the worst-paid positions would not be affected very much, because these jobs still pay more than subsistence, or they *should* do so. If they do not, especially if they combine very low wages with oppressive working conditions, then few people will want to have them. No one should be required to do so, at least in an affluent society. Hence, the effects of a guaranteed minimum wage rate would be confined to the worst-paid positions, and such effects would not be undesirable.

Equality
As the previous discussion indicates, a complex relationship exists between the principles discussed in this essay and the ideals of the

egalitarian tradition. This relationship should be considered more closely.

Earlier, in discussing the benefits to be insured by the welfare state, two "packages" were distinguished. The "happiness package" focuses on getting people what they want; from this perspective, one might advocate greater equalization in power and wealth. The "autonomy package" stresses self-respect and control over the terms of one's life; here, material resources are relevant not as the means of happiness, but of effective self-direction. The aim is not to give people what they want (still less to do so equally); rather, it is to enable them to get what they want for themselves, by removing obstacles from their ability to do so. No special value is assigned here to equality as an ideal in its own right. The ideal is autonomy, or effective control over the terms of one's own life.

This approach does not oppose equalitarian measures. In practice, the autonomy package is more egalitarian than it may seem, for the following reasons. Autonomy is sometimes presented simply as legal liberty, or the absence of interference in one's affairs; but the ideal here is *effective* control over one's life. This involves more than legal liberty; at the very least, it requires entitlement to the means of meeting basic and special needs. To declare autonomy as an ideal, then, is not to agree with neoconservative criticisms of the welfare state. It is precisely the ideal of effective autonomy that underwrites the defence of the equal right of all citizens as community members to the means of a decent life.

The case for equalization is made somewhat stronger by the connection between income and status. Individual self-respect is conditioned to some extent by how one is seen (or thinks one is seen) by others, and human worth is frequently measured by income. This is both an improper way to treat people and an impoverished view of human value. So long as it predominates in this society, the level of income guaranteed by the welfare state must be correspondingly higher (to protect self-respect) than otherwise it would be.[28]

Finally, in considering questions of equalization it should be determined whether wealth is used as income or as power. There is nothing wrong with one person having more money than another, so there is no reason to redistribute it more equally. It may be redistributed to meet basic needs, but this is not because equality itself is desirable. Consequently, if some people want to work overtime in order to own three VCRs or drive Jaguars, they should be free to do so. But wealth is not used in our society merely as a means of consumption; it is also a form of power. It gives some people the ability to control others. Thus, insofar as one's ideal is effective autonomy, there is no reason to limit wealth as a means of consumption but there is every reason to restrict it as a form of power.[29]

Autonomy

A great deal of this essay's argument is supported by the idea of autonomy. This idea needs clarification. Many liberals treat autonomy as an accomplished fact. All adults are presumed autonomous, that is, individually responsible for their actions, unless they are declared mentally incapable by the courts. Autonomy, however, means more than this. While it is true that individuals are self-directing in the legal sense, the "self" is the product of a long period of socialization that has shaped it in many ways beyond its control. Thus, taking charge of one's life requires also a process of taking charge of oneself, of understanding one's identity, coming to terms with it, and ideally accepting oneself as a worthy being. For most people, therefore, autonomy is not so much an accomplished fact as an ideal to be developed. This, generally speaking, can only be done by individuals for themselves. Individuals can be provided with money and the means of satisfying various desires, but they cannot be given autonomy, because the tasks of developing autonomy are independent of material resources. This is another reason for not overemphasizing the equalization of material resources.

Autonomy is not completely independent of social structure or social resources. It can be encouraged by quality education and by counselling and support for those in crisis. Above all, autonomy is enhanced among those who grow up with a sense of solid self-respect and independence. Individuals are less likely to see themselves as worthy beings if they are brutalized, or taught to feel systematically incapable, or see people like themselves being treated in such ways. If autonomy is seriously considered in this way, society will be more concerned with the psychological tasks of developing it and relatively less with the politics of material equalization.

Neoconservative versus Social Democratic Views

So far, the social democratic view that the benefits of the welfare state should be understood as the rights of all citizens has been argued on the basis of neoconservative premises. The welfare state has not been supported on grounds of public policy, or morality, or human rights, but as a comprehensive form of insurance, in terms that imply that its protections should include the means of autonomy and self-respect. This approach shows what is attractive and supportable in each position while distinguishing these attractive features from the limitations and one-sidedness with which they are often presented.

Neoconservatives are correct to insist upon the importance of liberty and individual autonomy, but they are wrong to construe these values only in legal terms, as freedom from direct interference. Individuals can lack effective autonomy, or control over their lives, in many other ways. People with disabilities are unable to move around; the ill are unable to lead an active life; the unemployed are unable to provide for their families. In this sense, neoconservatism is a half-truth; it advocates the right ideal (autonomy), but in mistaken terms. As a result, it construes this ideal in a way that makes it impossible for all but a fortunate few.

Social democrats risk making the opposite mistake. In their haste to ensure that their fellow citizens have what they "need," they may pay too little attention to individual rights, particularly to the rights of citizens to determine what they need for themselves. Thus, wheelchairs are provided as benefits rather than entitlements, as the gifts of a public policy that state officials may revise, question, alter, or cancel as they judge best. There is no excuse for this, and there is no reason why the values rightly stressed by neoconservatives—individual autonomy, liberty, and entitlement—cannot be inscribed in the heart of more generous and humane social policies.

Society should focus less upon providing for others, and more on enabling them to provide for themselves. Individuals owe this to one another, not as a duty of charity or public benevolence, but simply to establish each person's basic right as a member of the society.

Notes

The author is indebted to Jim (Hutch) Hutchinson, who introduced him to the main ideas in this essay many years ago, and to Alain Noel and Alan Shandro for their comments on earlier drafts.

1. Although public opinion surveys indicate solid but complex support for the welfare state, it depends upon how the question is put. In general terms, Canadians are apparently unwilling to pay more taxes to support the welfare state and are even willing to cut back on services to balance the budget. On the other hand, surveys also indicate strong support for particular programs, including the most expensive services. Support for the welfare state seems to be based on a sense of fairness. See Richard Johnston, *Public Opinion and Public Policy in Canada* (Toronto: University of Toronto Press, 1986), pp. 205–216. Brian Mulroney's Conservative government discovered this the hard way early in its first term, when the minister of finance proposed to "de-index" pensions, that is, to remove the provision by which pensions are automatically adjusted to changes in the cost of living. A storm of protest ensued, and the government was forced to back down. This ended any further plans to cut back on social welfare spending.
2. Laissez faire liberalism sought to maximize individual liberty by minimizing the state (laissez faire means "leave alone"). See Chapter 3, "Political Values and Ideologies," in *Liberal Democracy in Canada and the United States*, ed. T.C. Pocklington (Toronto: Holt, Rinehart and Winston, 1985).

3. Neoconservatism adopts the same view as laissez faire liberalism, although neoconservatives are usually more concerned about protecting property than individual autonomy. Technically, one might distinguish between neoconservatism and neoliberalism in this respect. But neoconservatives typically use the reasons of laissez faire liberals to defend their position, and this is the focus of this essay.
4. This position could be held by, for example, left-wing (or "human rights") liberals and socialists. Technically, social democracy combines a welfare state or strong redistributive measures with a capitalist economy.
5. The fact that someone is human is a reason why they ought to be treated in a certain way, for example, by providing the means of life if necessary. But this duty arises from what one ought to do, not from the prior right of the other.
6. This is not hypothetical. The following experience was narrated by a Canadian who had grown up with the welfare state and first experienced the alternative while attending university in the United States. A close friend was injured in a cycling collision: "Katrina was rushed to the hospital in an ambulance; I went with her. She was unconscious the whole time, with blood gushing from a deep gash in her forehead. When we got to the hospital they refused to admit her, saying that because she was at the university she should be taken to a different hospital. When we got there, they held up her admission while they tried to check with the university that she was covered by their health plan."
7. See G. Dworkin, "Paternalism," in *Morality and the Law*, ed. R.A. Wasserstrom (Belmont, Calif.: Wadsworth, 1971).
8. This condition is essential. Mandatory participation could not be justified if the service were substandard.
9. This is especially true if contributions are collected through the tax system; in that case, no one who could afford the care could avoid paying for it, and so society could cover those in the lowest income category without encouraging anyone else to be a "free-rider."
10. The proportion of noncontributors does not matter and can be varied (within reasonable limits) without affecting the argument.
11. This argument is indebted to the work of John Rawls; see especially his "Justice as Fairness," *Philosophical Review* 67 (1958), pp. 164–94, and *A Theory of Justice* (Cambridge, Mass.: Harvard University Press, 1971).
12. This objection is considered only because it is likely to be raised by readers familiar with Rawls's work. For the reasons indicated, it does not have much force here; even in Rawls's work, the "gambling" issue has a somewhat arid character. The issue is typically posed as whether to adopt a maximum rule or some alternative, such as average utility. But the case for any alternative becomes stronger, and therefore the case for Rawls's difference principle becomes weaker, if the alternative has a "safety net" guaranteeing basic needs.
13. The objector may reply that there would be no need to insure against being in this position: one's parents would not be poor because their character would not be defective. This rests on the double inference that poverty is the product of poor character and "I know my parents couldn't have had a poor character because I don't." But the inference to the character of one's parents is only probabilistic. Would it be sensible

to gamble on this? In other words, this objection is now a version of the "gambling" objection dismissed above.

14. It might be objected here that the force of the argument is that everyone should have to pay car insurance even if they don't have cars themselves, but this confuses two questions. If one lives in a car-oriented society, then it is in one's general interest that there be car insurance whether one owns a car or not, because it is a real possibility that one might buy a car, in which case one would need the insurance. But how the insurance is funded is a separate matter; each person's general interest that there be car insurance does not dictate (as it does in the case of the welfare state) that all social positions be insured, irrespective of their specific needs, because there is no reason to suppose that the inability to pay for such insurance would be a severe disability.

15. The relationship between self-respect and autonomy on the one hand, and happiness or well-being on the other, is complex. Presumably, a happy life would include considerable measures of autonomy and self-respect; but those who see the good life as the happy life often forget this, or put a rather low priority on autonomy goods in relation to material benefits. At any rate, this is suggested in the remainder of this section. Conversely, an autonomous life would hopefully be happy, but that is not its point or its aim; and those who seek to live autonomously generally have learned the hard way that it requires the sacrifice of many elements of happiness.

16. The issue of happiness or well-being and autonomy as conceptions of the good life is also raised in this book in the critique in Chapter 7.

17. For a different view and a rejection of the claim that benefits should be established as entitlements, see Robert E. Goodin, *Reasons for Welfare: The Political Theory of the Welfare State* (Princeton: Princeton University Press, 1988), Chapter 7.

18. *The Observer*, February 17, 1980; quoted by Jon Elster in "Is There a Right to Work?" in *Democracy and the Welfare State*, ed. Amy Gutmann (Princeton: Princeton University Press, 1988), p. 60.

19. There is no question that individuals are entitled to be treated in this way. If any firm treated its clients in this way, they would take their business elsewhere. Abuses of this nature do occur in the private sector as well, but they seem to occur far more frequently in cases involving clients who have nowhere else to go.

20. An issue of power lies beneath this question of rights. Either the insurance company can dictate to the individual (by refusing a claim) or the individual can dictate to it (by requiring payment). Thus, any right is a form of power. To have a right is to be able to require conduct from others, as specified by the right. Conversely, to lack a right in this society is to be powerless, dependent, and eventually at the mercy of others. This is not true necessarily or universally, but it is true generally, if somewhat variably, in Canadian society for the reasons indicated earlier.

21. Another consideration frequently used to support supervision is the need to minimize "scrounging" by individuals claiming benefits on false grounds. Similar considerations apply here as in the foregoing argument. On the one hand, it is perfectly legitimate to limit benefits to those who qualify for them, and this entails the need to monitor qualifications. But this could easily be done, as it is now with most

insurance claims, in terms (i) that recognize that a legitimate claim constitutes an entitlement and (ii) that show some respect for the applicant in the process of adjudicating the claim.

22. This view is mistaken and shallow.

23. See C.B. Macpherson, *Democratic Theory: Essays in Retrieval* (Oxford: Clarendon Press, 1973), especially Essay 3, "Problems of a Non-Market Theory of Democracy."

24. In other words, the inequality is not problematic in itself as a simple difference in wealth. It can be problematic in other ways, particularly when it describes a relation of constraint, that is, one in which those with less are dependent upon those with more. The strategy of the guaranteed income is to counter this, not by reducing the inequality (by taking away from those with more, or giving to those with less), but rather by freeing those with less from dependence and constraint.

25. This is in addition to the internal rewards of the job. The objection here seems to assume the point challenged earlier, that work is in principle objectionable.

26. This is just for federal and provincial social services. It does not include expenditures on, for example, health and education. These would raise the total to over $122 billion, an average of over $5,000 per person. Source: *The National Finances, 1987–88* (Toronto: Canadian Tax Foundation, 1988), 4:10.

27. For example, the social services budget includes items such as family allowances and pensions, which are not restricted to those with low incomes. The point is only to illustrate that society already guarantees subsistence; the issue is how to do so.

28. It might be objected that if individuals were autonomous, they would not see themselves as seen by others. This is not only implausible as a generalization, it is irrelevant. The insurance principle argued earlier makes it plain that one would want to protect self-respect as part of the insured package.

29. See the above discussion and note 24 on equality and the guaranteed minimum.

CRITIQUE

In his essay, Don Carmichael attempts to provide a justification of the welfare state that will persuade both neoconservatives and social democrats. Specifically, he attempts to justify a welfare state robust enough to satisfy social democrats on the basis of principles that are congenial to neoconservatives. For social democrats, the benefits of the welfare state are shown to be extensive and guaranteed as a matter of right rather than charity. For neoconservatives, the improved welfare state is shown to be based on the sound, business-like principles of insurance rather than on moral considerations, and it is designed to promote personal freedom and self-reliance—watchwords of the traditional liberalism that is the conservatism of our time.

Although an expanded and strengthened welfare state is a laudable goal, it is not possible to defend such a state on nonmoral grounds, and Carmichael fails to do so. But neither is it desirable to defend such a state on the extravagantly individualistic grounds invoked by Carmichael.

This difference of opinion is not simply a disagreement about the kind of reasoning appropriate to support shared political conclusions. In my view, Carmichael's extreme individualism has important and undesirable political implications. It misrepresents human nature and thereby yields prescriptions that undermine rather than promote a healthy political community.

Insurance and Morality

Carmichael purports to justify the welfare state, not on moral grounds, but by construing it as a grand, compulsory, abstract insurance scheme, which is both rational and fair. The insurance scheme is grand in that it incorporates all citizens, not just (as in commercial insurance) those who choose to subscribe to it, and because it covers a very wide range of benefits. It is compulsory, in that all who can afford to pay for its benefits must do so, whether or not they wish to do so. It is abstract, in requiring people to ignore their actual positions and prospects and imagine that they might be anyone, including above all someone who desperately needs certain benefits but cannot afford to pay for them and has not been able to afford the insurance premiums that would pay for them.

The scheme is rational because it requires people to want and do only what it would make sense for them to want and do. People are not required to be compassionate or beneficent; no more is demanded than that they avoid the irrationality of failing to employ effective means to their own ends. Finally, the scheme is fair because it is impartial. It would be adopted by people who did not know their actual positions. Without undue stretching, this requirement of fairness could be construed as merely an elaboration of the requirement of rationality.

Carmichael purports to avoid any attempt at moral justification of the welfare state because, he maintains, a moral justification would stigmatize beneficiaries of the welfare state as recipients of charity rather than claimants of rights. Indeed, the essay maintains that "with this justification, right lies with those who give, not with those who receive." This is a remarkably thin conception of morality. Most conceptions of morality see it as having a great deal to do with what we *owe* others, not merely with what it would be *generous* to do for others.

But this emaciated view of morality is not maintained consistently by Carmichael himself. Early in his essay, he asserts that "justice is a matter of giving individuals their 'due.' " The central thrust of his critique of my discussion of Native self-government is that I underestimate the importance and power of *moral rights*. Evidently his understanding of morality is more capacious than some passages in his essay might lead us to believe. It would be odd, to say the least, if he abandoned his moral outlook simply for the duration of his discussion of the welfare state, especially in view of his insistence that welfare benefits should be guaranteed as the *entitlements* of their recipients.

Suspicion that moral considerations play an unacknowledged role in Carmichael's reasoning are confirmed by the heavy burden he places on the notion of fairness. Although Carmichael maintains that he will not attempt a moral justification of the welfare state, he argues that such a state should be implemented because it is *fair*: "the reason for supporting the welfare state even if one does not need its protections as much as others do is because doing so is fair. It is the policy all people would accept if they did not know their actual social positions." One could argue that this requirement of fairness is simply a matter of rationality; no sane person with a standard measure of self-interest would subscribe to an insurance scheme that was unfair.

Nevertheless, the fact is that fairness is usually taken to be a requirement of morality. Far more important, however, is that Carmichael's fairness requires readers to imagine that they do not know their actual social positions. But why shouldn't an uneducated, unemployed, single mother of three children keep very much in mind her own social position and use every realistic tactic to maximize her benefits? Similarly, why shouldn't the multimillionaire who doesn't need any benefits act in her own self-interest and press for shrinkage of the welfare state to a size barely necessary to prevent intolerable social disorder? The only response available to Carmichael is that it would be morally wrong to refuse to adopt the impartial perspective he recommends. Thus, he has smuggled a moral precept into a crucial place in an argument that was advertised as nonmoral.

But the most striking and most important intrusion of moral considerations into Carmichael's allegedly nonmoral, insurance-based justification of the welfare state is the insistence on the pre-eminence of personal autonomy. Throughout his essay, but especially in the final third of it, the welfare state is justified, either primarily or exclusively, as being necessary to "protect each individual's 'autonomy package,' not by guaranteeing the ingredients of happiness but rather by protecting the abilities of individuals to decide the terms of their own lives."

Carmichael is by no means shy about this point. The next-to-last section of his essay begins with the observation that "a great deal of this essay's argument is supported by the idea of autonomy." But what is the status of this "idea"? On this point Carmichael is less forthcoming, but moderately careful reading reveals the answer:

> No special value is assigned here to equality as an ideal in its own right. The *ideal* is autonomy, or effective control over the terms of one's own life. It is precisely the *ideal* of effective autonomy that underwrites our defence of the equal right of all citizens as community members to the means of a decent life. [N]eo-conservatism is a half-truth: it advocates the right *ideal* (autonomy), but in mistaken terms.

The "idea" of autonomy, then, is for Carmichael an *ideal*. It is the principal mark of an admirable person to possess it and of a worthy society to protect and promote it. His own protestations and the extraordinary allurement and subtlety of his arguments to the contrary notwithstanding, Carmichael's justification of the welfare state is a *moral* argument.

In my judgement, it could not be otherwise. Carmichael's thinly disguised moralism illustrates the adage that one can't pull a rabbit out of the hat unless one puts it in. To maintain that a good society is a society of autonomous persons and a good policy is one that protects and promotes personal autonomy, one needs more than an insurance scheme. Otherwise one is left with a hat and no rabbit.

Individuality and Sociality

The beginning of this critique supported Carmichael's advocacy of an expanded and strengthened welfare state, but it also said that his extreme individualism misrepresents human nature and thereby yields prescriptions that would undermine rather than promote a healthy political community. Before I defend this charge, I want to avoid misunderstanding by making two points about what I am *not* saying.

First, I am *not* maintaining that Carmichael is ignorant of well-established propositions about the social context of human maturation. Nothing in his essay suggests that it subscribes to the preposterous view that people acquire the wherewithal to "live on their own terms" independently of social interaction.

Second, I do *not* deny either that personal autonomy is a good or that it should be protected and promoted by the welfare state. There is extravagant communitarianism as well as extravagant individualism. The dangers of the former are almost certainly greater than the dangers of the latter, since the former can lead to fantastic visions of society as one big happy family or to the horrors of totalitarianism.

The starting point here is that the good life for the individual is a life of well-being, that the good society is one that fosters well-being, and that good public policies are those that protect and promote well-being. But this stance has no critical bite. Carmichael could easily accept it, adding simply that the main, if not the sole, ingredient of well-being is personal autonomy. But it is precisely here that Carmichael and I part ways.

Human beings have manifold needs, dispositions, capacities, and potentialities—physical, emotional, intellectual, and spiritual. Well-being is increased whenever a need is satisfied or satisfied more fully, and whenever a desirable disposition, capacity, or potentiality is allowed to flourish or flourish more fully. Any enhancement of well-being is desirable. Thus, for example, the reduction or elimination of physical pain does not need to be justified on the ground that it contributes to personal autonomy though it often does, and that is certainly a reason for commending it. It is justification enough that physical pain is almost always antithetical to well-being. Similarly, a good society or a good public policy is one that protects and enhances well-being. Personal autonomy is an element of well-being, so that a policy that increases it is commendable. But a policy that increases well-being without increasing autonomy is also commendable.

So far, my position is different from Carmichael's, but it is not a whit less individualistic. Broadly speaking, we both favour the well-being of individuals and commend societies and policies that enhance the well-being of the aggregate of individuals. We just differ about the nature of well-being. How, then, can the essay's position be condemned as extravagantly individualistic?

The essay is so captivated by, even obsessed with, the vision of autonomous individuals, living their lives on their own terms, that it neglects other, profoundly sociable, human needs and dispositions. Occupying a central place among these needs and dispositions is the aspiration to be recognized as a valued member of an ongoing community.[1] The satisfaction of this yearning to belong is therefore an element of well-being, and an important mark of a good society— and a good welfare state—is its satisfaction of this yearning. But individualism carried too far, as it is carried too far by Carmichael, undermines this dimension of well-being.

Constant emphasis on the ideal of the truly worthy person as one who lives life on his or her own terms isolates individuals and *undermines* self-respect, especially the self-respect of those who rely most heavily on the welfare state; those who, because of poverty, disability, or lack of education tend to be unassertive; and those who place a high premium on social solidarity and adherence to tradition, such as Native people. What is needed, then, is a justification of the welfare state, and more generally a social and political outlook, that is far less attentive to the autonomy of individuals and far more sensitive to their sociability.

Morality, Community, and the Welfare State

If these criticisms of Carmichael are well founded, a sound justification of the welfare state would have to be a moral justification, and it would have to incorporate a political outlook that emphasizes the values of community as well as personal autonomy. If this approach to well-being is accepted, there seems to be no difficulty in meeting these requirements.

If personal well-being is good, public policies that protect and enhance well-being are also good, and it is a responsibility of governments to enact such policies. Thus, the range of welfare-state benefits endorsed by the "well-being approach" would be at least as extensive, and almost certainly more extensive, than those covered by any insurance scheme. Moreover, if satisfaction of the yearning to be regarded as a valued member of a community is recognized as a crucial element of well-being, not only the welfare state but also other political institutions, practices, and policies would recognize and affirm the values of community.

But what has been said so far ignores a matter that Carmichael rightly emphasizes. He correctly insists that the benefits of a welfare state worthy of the name must be established as the entitlements of their recipients, not as charitable donations that may be altered or even eliminated by the priorities of the government of the day. Can the well-being approach establish welfare-state benefits as entitlements?

On the face of it, the answer to this question seems to be no.[2] If the proper end of public policy is well-being, and if there is good reason to believe that aggregate well-being would be increased by a modification of the terms of the welfare state (such as a reduction in old-age pensions to defray the costs of a major job-creation program in Newfoundland), then it would seem to be not merely permissible but obligatory for the government to make the change. Welfare benefits would not be firm entitlements but merely legal rights properly subject to regular adjustment.

This objection, however, rests on constricted and myopic understanding of the importance of fundamental rights to human well-being.[3] The long-term costs of undermining such rights far exceed the short-term benefits of curtailing them. The fact is that firm entrenchment and protection of fundamental rights—both rights that promote autonomy and rights that promote community—are crucial requisites of well-being.

In his admirable endeavour to justify an expanded and strengthened welfare state, Carmichael eschews morality and embraces an extravagant individualism. He has got it exactly wrong.

Notes

1. See David Braybrooke, *Meeting Needs* (Princeton, N.J.: Princeton University Press, 1987), p. 36.
2. The most renowned current exponent of the view that perspectives that assign priority to the good over the right are unable to give a firm grounding to rights is John Rawls, to whom the essayist expresses indebtedness. See Rawls, *A Theory of Justice* (Cambridge, Mass.: Harvard University Press, 1971), especially sections 6 and 29.
3. An illuminating discussion of the relationship between rights and well-being is David Lyons, "Human Rights and the General Welfare," in *Rights*, ed. David Lyons (Belmont, Cal.: Wadsworth, 1979), pp. 174–86, originally published in *Philosophy and Public Affairs* (Winter 1977), pp. 113–29.

Discussion Questions

1. Is Carmichael's basic argument correct? If you were designing a society without knowing your place in it, would you guarantee all the means of a decent life as entitlements? Would you worry about having to pay for them if you didn't need them?

2. Pocklington thinks that Carmichael's account is too individualistic and that the welfare state should be established instead on moral grounds. Which view is correct?

3. Carmichael argues that all the means of a decent life should be guaranteed as entitlements. Is he right? Isn't there a danger that individuals would abuse the system?

4. Is the guaranteed minimum income as good an idea as Carmichael thinks it is?

5. Neoconservatives argue that individual freedom and efficiency would be maximized by organizing medical care and higher education on market (payment-for-service) principles, with a safety net of minimal health care for those who cannot afford it. Do you agree?

6. One solution to spiralling health-care costs is a two-tiered system. This guarantees basic care for all but allows individuals to purchase nonessential and more expensive health care if they want. Do you support this?

Further Readings

There are two good introductory accounts of distributive justice and rights: N.E. Bowie and R.L. Simon, *The Individual and the Political Order*, 2nd ed. (Englewood Cliffs, N.J.: Prentice-Hall, 1986), especially Chapters 3 and 4; and S.I. Benn and R.S. Peters, *Social Principles and the Democratic State* (London: Allen and Unwin, 1959), especially Chapters 4–6. The latter work is over thirty years old but still remarkably current. The former is more recent but heavily American.

The "abstract insurance" argument can be developed through John Rawls's "Justice as Fairness," *Philosophical Review*, 67 (1958). Rawls is the most influential moral–political philosopher of our time. Robert Nozick stresses the idea of entitlement from the perspective of natural rights in Chapter 7 (section 1) of *Anarchy, State and Utopia* (New York: Basic Books, 1974). This is a readable account. The importance of work and more generally of developing human powers is stressed by C.B. Macpherson in *Democratic Theory: Essays in Retrieval* (Oxford: Clarendon Press, 1973), Essays 1–3. This work is difficult but worth the effort.

A general account of issues raised by the welfare state can be found in Robert E. Goodin's *Reasons for Welfare: The Political Theory of the Welfare State* (Princeton, N.J.: Princeton University Press, 1988). Goodin rejects the idea that benefits should be established as entitlements. A collection of articles (although few of them deal directly with the issues covered in this chapter) has been edited by Amy Gutmann in *Democracy and The Welfare State* (Princeton, N.J.: Princeton University Press, 1988).

CHAPTER 5

Gender, Justice, and Democracy

For some time now, women's rights have been central to Canadian democracy. Women have worked long, hard, and effectively to have entrenched, in the Canadian Charter of Rights and Freedoms, a guarantee of legal equality with men. This is a significant achievement, especially when contrasted with the unsuccessful attempts in the United States to have a similar provision written into the terms of its constitution.

Despite the comparative magnitude of this achievement, it constitutes only a small step in the direction that most feminists, women and men alike, would like Canada to take. Instead, the lion's share of what feminism seeks is just beginning to become plain to the broader society. Feminists in Canada and elsewhere have articulated a broad and scathing critique of women's "place" in modern society, a critique that challenges much of what has been taken for granted in our society. The central charge of contemporary feminists is that a profound and historic injustice has been done to women and that it must be redressed if Canadian democracy is to become legitimate.

This chapter assumes that this charge must be taken seriously. It assumes that the debate over women's rights has proceeded well beyond the question of equal rights to a crisis in social relations. One need only point to the horror and tragedy of the shooting deaths of women engineering students in Canada to confirm this conclusion.

What are the feminist grievances that define the increasing disquiet in Canadian social and political life? What principles could serve as principles of redress, that is, as a theory of justice regarding women and men? Under what conditions, if any, ought women continue to co-operate with men in their societies?

Pyrcz canvasses a range of views that represent the scope of the current crisis in relations between and among women and men. He considers but rejects the contention that what we must do to restore "civic friendship," is settle on one theory of justice regarding women and men on the strength of the theory itself. Instead, he argues for a strong democratic resolution to the crisis in relations between and among women and men which in this context requires near-unanimity in agreement on the basic terms of social co-operation. Such a resolution, Pyrcz contends, would auger for a distinct form of political pluralism, a regime in which no view rules society but in which all but those based on power are tolerated. The political work that such a resolution requires in the present context, he contends, involves the further eradication of patriarchy as the traditional and often implicit dominant view of Canadian society.

Carmichael argues that this proposal would not work and that, in issues of justice, any procedure, including Pyrcz's strong democracy, must be guided by principles. Carmichael also notes that, in issues of justice concerning women today, "liberal" principles must be supplemented by radical and psychological perspectives.

ESSAY

Securing justice between the sexes may appear to be a relatively straightforward philosophical task. The more challenging goal appears to be a political one, namely, the attainment and exercise of power by and in the interests of women. This appearance of the matter as a philosophically straightforward yet politically daunting issue may stem from a confidence in a longstanding notion that equals be treated equally and that distinctions in the treatment of persons respect only those aspects of persons that significantly distinguish them. That is, where unequal treatment is tolerated by justice, it must respect and extend only to *relevant* differences between persons. For example, justice requires that students be given grades that reflect their academic accomplishment. But differences in scholastic accomplishments do not justify granting the more accomplished students a greater voice in student councils or greater respect as persons. The scholastic achievement of students is, as a matter of justice, simply irrelevant to their political and human rights.

The philosophical difficulty of justice is in discerning which characteristics of persons deserve distinctive treatment, if any do, and which do not. In matters of justice between men and women, for egalitarians, this difficulty is resolved easily. It seems that there are very few, if any, differences in the qualities of men and women that justify treating them differently socially, politically, or personally. To egalitarians, differences between men and women are simply irrelevant to the rights all people possess, to the opportunities and shares of social goods that they may rightfully claim, and to the equal respect they all deserve as persons.

When behavioural differences may appear to signify relevant differences between the sexes, for example, when women display a willingness to be treated as "sex objects" or when men display greater aggression, egalitarians hold these differences to be largely artificial and due to socialization. Such differences cannot serve as bases for future justice because they are the consequences of prior injustice.

This is how the matter of justice regarding women and men has appeared to egalitarians. It is from their confidence with this point of view that the work of justice has appeared to be political. What is required is the restructuring of society and its power relations in order to develop and then secure a practice of equality.[1] Those who oppose or frustrate this work are held to be politically tyrannical and philosophically inept.

Competing Conceptions of Relations Between the Sexes

As is the case with other considerations of democracy and rights in this book, what appears straightforward and conventional proves, in the light of critical analysis, to be neither. In this instance, the egalitarian assessment of justice regarding women and men offered above is compelling primarily for its simplicity, not for its insight. But as this essay will show, this fundamental dimension of justice is neither politically nor philosophically straightforward.

The issue of gender equality is really two interwoven issues, one of justice and one of freedom. If, in the terms of the egalitarian "solution" to the issue of justice between and among women and men, justice requires the discerning of differences relevant to the treatment of persons, then who is to do the discerning? Do men and women value the world in the same ways? Do they even experience it in the same ways? Under what political and personal conditions ought those who attempt to discern relevant differences to proceed? Should women and men determine the terms of justice now, or only after society has altered the balance of powers now enjoyed and suffered by them.

Most contemporary feminists claim not only that modern society has got the differences between men and women tragically wrong, but that getting them right requires a genuine freedom for the expression of justice *by women*.[2] Resolving the crisis of our times requires, accordingly, the *simultaneous* redress of injustice toward, and the full emancipation of, women. Men and women must be free *and* equal, if they are to be genuinely either.[3]

This essay considers six competing conceptions of what justice and freedom between and among women and men require. Four articulate but don't exhaust contemporary feminism, and two challenge it. Then the essay considers a means of resolving the current crisis in the light of this divergence of conceptions: the proposition that a demanding form of democracy can achieve justice more completely than can the egalitarian principle or any of the alternatives to it that will have been canvassed.

To begin, there are the views of those who oppose feminism by defending patriarchy. Patriarchy is, in part, a system of powers and orchestrated opportunities that effectively confines women to lives defined by assumptions that underlie the traditional, hierarchically structured household. In a patriarchy, women traditionally have their work, sexuality, unique reproductive capacity, and willingness to nurture children exploited in relationships with men, over which they have little control.

Whether women spend their lives inside or outside the household, patriarchy defines their roles in terms of their function in the home. This means that generally women are permitted few leadership roles in society. They are generally expected to perform in the workplace in domestic jobs, nurturing the young and nursing the ill, and in the "service industries." It also means that issues like the right to abortion are settled broadly in society, where men play powerful roles, and not by women themselves. As well, in a patriarchy, the freedom of women outside of the household is conditional upon the continued maintenance of household values, generally by women.

Two views have traditionally supported patriarchy. The first, referred to as Patriarchy I, is the simplest (some would say most simple-minded) of the views considered.[4] Patriarchy II is more subtle.

Patriarchy I

Patriarchy I is not much of a view of justice between and among women and men at all. Those who subscribe to it believe that men who exercise power, having "won" struggles to attain it, deserve it. They contend that power, as a means to one's private ends, should always be defended, and that more power is almost always preferable to less. Crude as this may appear as a view about justice, it has a long ancestry. The view that justice is merely the advantage of the stronger, though denounced in Plato's *Republic* 2,400 years ago,[5] has enjoyed constant (though often underground) currency.[6]

This assertion about justice between the sexes is noteworthy because it aptly describes the political postures implicitly taken by some men in the debate over justice and freedom for women in Canadian society. These men maintain what is essentially a right of conquest over women.[7] Moreover, this assertion sometimes serves as the darker political undercurrent to the more philosophically respectable defence of Patriarchy II.

Patriarchy II

Patriarchy II, a view deeply embedded in both Western and non-Western cultures, defines justice for women by employing the assumptions of the hierarchically constructed household. Its basic contention is that significant and unalterable differences exist between the natures of men and women. These *natural differences* are indicated partly in sexual and reproductive relations but extend well beyond this in their relevance. Those who hold this view maintain that sexual differences, as they have been historically displayed in most Western cultures, are a reflection of essentially biochemical differences between the sexes. Moreover, they contend, attempts to ignore these differences frustrate and repress women by denying them the satisfaction of their distinctive qualities. That is, they harm women, persons who by nature are created to beget, nurture, and replenish the world morally and materially. Women, they contend, are uniquely suited to the functions of the household. Their well-being, and that of society as a whole, requires that they not be encouraged to block the expression and satisfaction of these distinctive female qualities.[8]

Those who oppose feminism by defending Patriarchy II may differ with some points of this view. They may maintain that there are women in every society whose *individual* natures predispose them to the kind of lives to which men by nature are suited. This again is an ancient view. But those who recognize such exceptions are quick to caution that the pursuit of such lives by those women must not undermine the integrity of other women, whose "female" natures do not so dispose them. For these defenders of patriarchy, society ought to provide the opportunity for some women to live "male-like" lives, but on the condition that most women do not choose them. Others in the patriarchal camp argue the proper "constraints" that define women's prospects are better understood to stem from the God-given natural duty of women and men to pursue lives governed by their natures than they are by reference to the "well-being" of women or society. On the other side of patriarchy's camp are those prepared to concede to all women the right to participate fully in society, but on condition that their exercise of this right does not undermine their "natural" roles in the family.

Notwithstanding these finer distinctions, there is a common core to these views. Patriarchy II contends that (i) the sexes' natures ought define their roles in society; (ii) the natures of women and men are significantly different and extend well beyond the sexual differences accepted by egalitarians; and (iii) these differences must be respected by protecting the historical integrity of the household, in which women are uniquely suited to nurture children, to replenish the moral and material needs of family members, and to fulfil their roles in heterosexual relations. Unlike Patriarchy I, Patriarchy II argues for what its advocates take to be the interests of women. Adherents of Patriarchy II contend that they are implicitly praising women for their moral and sexual pre-eminence in the foundations of the family and, by extension, of society.[9]

Liberal Feminism I

This essay construes patriarchy's best defence as an essentially conservative doctrine. It is conservative because it embraces the ideas that nature is fundamental to society, that there are natural duties that emanate from people's distinctive natures, that a hierarchy of natures exists, in which some are entitled to rule, and that constraining the freedom of individuals to respect their natures is a requirement of justice. It is also conservative in the sense that it seeks to recapture and protect traditional mores and lifestyles. Liberalism, in its many guises, essentially opposes this conservative worldview, and perhaps nowhere more than in the early development of feminism.[10]

Liberal Feminism I contends that the public sphere of society ought to be as open to women as it is to men.[11] Liberal feminists contend that there is nothing in the public sphere—the economy, law and politics, and culture—that women are in any relevant way less suited than men to pursue or in which to excel. Moreover, as women have the requisite intellectual, decision-making, and physical potential and skills to participate, their exclusion from the public sphere is at the unjustified price of allowing this potential to remain undeveloped and these skills to atrophy.

Liberal feminists simply do not agree that nature is fundamental to society in the way that it is held, by conservatives, to determine justice for women. Instead, they contend either that individual natures are shaped extensively by nurture, that is, by how people are raised and socialized, or that natural differences distinguish *individuals*, not the sexes. They maintain, as most liberals do, that how society nurtures its members and how individual natures are to be respected can adequately be decided only by encouraging all persons to make personal decisions for themselves and for public decisions to be made through the discussion and agreement of *all*. In short, the liberal feminist position on genderical justice is, first, that women and men all ought to be given equal and extensive opportunity to make life decisions for themselves and to pursue these decisions however they choose;[12] and second, that this preferred state of affairs can be attained by providing women with equality of opportunity to participate in the public sphere. The second contention is the focus of the feminist criticism of Liberal Feminism I. The first contention is the object of conservative derision.

Liberal Feminism II

Feminists opposed to liberal feminism express their contempt by referring to it as "liberal patriarchy." What they mean is that while it opens the sphere of public life to women, some of the deeper assumptions and constraints of patriarchy are left intact in the day-to-day lives of women, in their private relations with men, and in the private dimensions of their public lives.[13] To them, this is almost worse than some versions of patriarchy, because it gives the appearance of justice and freedom while insidiously reproducing injustice and effectively undermining the full autonomy of women.

Most relevant here, to those who stand under the umbrella of Liberal Feminism II, is the distinction between the public and private spheres of life. Feminists critical of Liberal Feminism I contend that this distinction protects the essential terms of patriarchy in the liberal regime. It allows governments to redress injustices between men and women in the workplace while treating injustices in the household as a different order of concern outside the scope of social interference.[14] There is, in Canada, a minimum hourly wage for employment outside the home that is set by provincial legislation. For employment in the private household there is none. Here, work is deemed to be in the "private sphere," and payment for it is left completely to the terms of the householders.

This point about language and politics is a subtle one. It requires a person to understand that defining the world through language can be a political exercise and that it can carry with it decisions about power. In this case, the "public/private" distinction is necessary to contend that the regulation by government of the private sphere is unacceptable while regulation of the public sphere may be required by the terms of justice. It is, thus, a distinction essential to liberalism.

But many radical feminists argue that the distinction between private and public is merely a human invention. It could just as easily, as it is in some other cultures, be drawn differently; or it could be altogether absent from our language and in the way those who employ it think and act. The distinction between the public and private spheres of society permits liberal feminism to argue for equality of opportunity outside the household, while leaving the roles of the household largely unattended as a realm of privacy beyond the considerations of social justice. It is exactly this "error" that radical feminists accuse Liberal Feminists I of committing.

Liberal feminism seems stuck with the private/public distinction as the very term of its liberalism, not its feminism. That is, liberalism has steadfastly and by definition protected a private realm free from social or state interference. This private realm is necessary *in liberalism* to guarantee the citizen the opportunity to exercise personal autonomy and to make decisions for oneself.[15] The reader may recall the discussion of the censorship of pornography, in Chapter 2, where the essayist defends what is essentially a liberal feminist position by distinguishing between areas of individuals' lives where society has a right to judge behaviour and areas that are exclusively, and by right, matters of private judgment. A women's right to abort a fetus is as well based on a distinction between what is private and what is public business.

Radical feminists reply that while all improvements in the lives of women are welcome, this distinction permits the suppression of women to continue in their private lives even while it is being eradicated in the public realm. An example is prostitution, which liberal jurisprudence considers as being outside the legitimate purview of society when parties consent to its terms. Such relations, in liberal theory, are matters to be determined by the private judgment of individuals.[16] If men and women consent to trade the use of their bodies for financial purposes, this decision is theirs alone to make; it is a private decision. Others in society may not approve on grounds of morality or justice, but it is a decision in which they have no right to intervene.

Radical feminists, for whom "the personal is political," are quick to criticize this understanding of these sorts of relationships, even when women appear to have consented to them. They simply do not accept the notion that considerations of social justice do not extend to what is understood by liberals to be the separate realm of "private lives." Moreover, they contend, prostitution illustrates dramatically the victimizing logic of the lives of many women in other "private" relations, especially those in the household. Here, as has already been noted, feminists contend that both the work and the sexuality of women is exploited in putatively "consensual" relations.

Radical feminist concerns are briefly considered here to illustrate the essential thrust of Liberal Feminism II. Liberal Feminists II accept the difficulties that exploitive relations, *"freely" consented to*, pose for an adequate theory and practice of feminism, as these difficulties are identified by radical feminists. Yet they remain deeply committed to the liberal notion of individual autonomy. They seek to define their theory and practice somewhere between the doctrines of liberal feminism and those of more radical programs. They do so in two ways.

First, they contend that only those decisions taken by persons who have the resources effectively to have chosen otherwise ought be subjects whose "judgment" is respected as private.[17] This includes the availability, for all persons, of the widest range of genuine choices. The female prostitute who consents to sexual relations because her current "station in life" presents her with neither a genuine alternative to this "consent" nor the inner resources to choose otherwise is not autonomous. She cannot be considered to be exercising private judgment. Her decisions cannot be understood to lie outside of and free from the purview of social justice. What may appear as an autonomous decision to her, or more likely to those liberals who so characterize it, is not really autonomous at all. This is also true, contend Liberal Feminists II, of the "happy housewife" who "consents" to continued household inequality and dependence because she has no discernible alternatives to such a life.[18] Neither of these decisions, according to Liberal Feminists II, can fairly be considered consensual, because the actors cannot be fairly characterized as enjoying real autonomy.

Second, Liberal Feminists II contend that it is the traditional distinction between public and private, *as it rests on the institution of the household*, that is philosophically flawed and politically tyrannical, not the distinction itself. Here Liberal Feminists II contend that just as there is no reason why men and women should not have equal opportunities in the traditionally defined public sphere, there is nothing, except childbearing, to distinguish men and women in their potential and skills in the household. Liberal Feminists II favour equality between men and women in the opportunities and burdens they share not only in the public sphere but also in the household. While maintaining a *modified* public/private distinction focusing on *empowered* decision-makers, Liberal Feminists II deny that household life is in any way relevant to drawing this distinction. They contend instead that justice and freedom are as much about the household and private sexual relations as they are about equal pay for work of equal value. Here the slogan of Liberal Feminists II might simply be "equal work."[19]

Androgyny, or Liberal Feminism III

Just as patriarchy is considered an essentially conservative doctrine, androgyny can be considered in its existentialist and essentially liberal expression. Androgyny, as a doctrine, is concerned with how people are socialized to act as either men or women. Androgynists see current forms of sex-role socialization as both harmful and unnecessary.

The common notion that androgynists and other liberal feminists share is that men and women are not at all different in their natures, except for their sexual and reproductive "particularities." All other apparent differences between the sexes are products of how individuals are conditioned to act. These differences are consistently displayed and reproduced in society to the detriment both of individuals' well-being and of the development of their widely diverse potentials as human individuals. To the extent that the sexes act differently—when men act aggressively and women submissively, or when men appear more detached and women are emotional—they are mimics.[20] The androgynist contends that genuine human life is creative; that it need not be, though it too often is, imitative.

Androgynists wish to exploit their belief that human beings, current mimicry notwithstanding, can create better social norms. As the creative sources of culture, individuals can "write" whatever "scripts" they like for the conduct of their lives. Androgynists wish to encourage and create ways of being in the world that do not mimic current male and female stereotypes. What is necessary for the full emancipation of women, they contend, is a strategy in which the life roles of men and women can be radically rewritten.[21] Women and men can and should live lives that are neither "female" nor "male." What is required, they contend, is a creative melding of the various properties of human life that are found in all individuals of both sexes, but developed now only partly in each.[22] This means that both men and women could be nurtured, especially as children, to encourage the full and complex expression of their equal potential for "assertiveness" and "submissiveness," action and passivity, analytic detachment and intense caring, and the like. These creative transformations in cultural roles and individual lifestyles are proposed for all aspects of human life "from the boardroom to the bedroom."[23]

This form of feminism, more than others, is concerned with the problem of sexist socialization and stereotypes and with the connection between complete human emancipation and feminist justice. Androgynists contend that justice between the sexes requires first a radical emancipation of both sexes, a freedom from the currently limiting lifestyles that are the products of, and "enforced" by, current social conventions. What they propose, unlike other feminists, is a radical transformation of what "gender," in the lives of men and women, means in social life and in culture. Without this transformation, they imply, all changes in the political terms of relations between and among the sexes, such as those proposed by Liberal Feminism I and II, will collapse under the weight of traditional but unnecessary social conventions.

Radical Feminism I and II

There is little doubt that the philosophy and politics of androgynist feminism are radical; androgyny calls for a major transformation in social life. But this is not what radical feminism means in the contemporary debate. Instead, it consists of a set of views that are almost diametrically opposed to androgyny.[24]

Radical feminists are critical of the liberal feminists' terms of gender and justice. They disagree with these terms in a number of ways. One of their most politically important criticisms is that they reject the individualism inherent in liberal feminisms. They believe the struggle for feminist justice requires women to understand themselves first as a *gender-defined community*, and only then as "individuals." In much the same way, some aboriginal groups, Quebec separatists, and unions insist upon a communitarian definition of emancipation and justice.

The content of this communitarianism deserves scrutiny. Radical feminists conclude that liberal feminists have mistakenly ignored or trivialized the real differences between male and female values and experience. These differences, radical feminists contend, have been exploited, and the values and experience of women have been denied by the patriarchal hierarchy. There is nothing more valuable in assertiveness, emotional detachment, or "rationality" than there is in passivity, compassion, or artistic creativity. The only reason the former "male" values have come to dominate the latter "female" values as the ruling values in this society is because men have exercised their greater aggressivity. This has been detrimental both to women, who are made to suffer male rule, and to society generally, because "female" values are insufficiently respected.

The means of redressing injustice done to women, of revaluing the experience of women, are twofold. The first is to recapture and build upon the distinct qualities of women. The second is for women to break down both the current hierarchy in society and the socialization processes that preserve it. These tasks require the separation of women from male-defined relationships.[25]

The extent of the separation from male political culture measures the philosophical distance between Radical Feminisms I and II. Radical Feminists I contend that the differences between the experience and values of men and women are partly the product of the marginalization of women by male rule in this society. Only when female values come to have the same or greater momentum in the determination of social relations than those of men can discourse between men and women justly resume. Only when the nurturing of the young is as important to society as is the making either of money or war, and only when women are given complete control over their bodies and the terms of reproduction, can social relations be reconstructed. Justice between men and women is possible, from essentially different value systems and bases of experience, but only when new ways of valuing women and men, by both men and women, are achieved.[26]

Radical Feminism II, a still more provocative view, is an *essentialist* doctrine. Its advocates contend that men and women are different at the level of experience itself, that women and men are *by nature* different.[27] This contention stems from the view that people's connection to the world is through their bodies, and that the physical and biochemical difference in the bodies of men and women presents a gap between the worlds of men and women, a gap that can't be bridged fully by any discourse, just or otherwise.[28]

The terms of these last two philosophically complex varieties of feminism are articulated only briefly here. However, for the arguments that follow, a sense of the direction of these arguments is sufficient. The rest of this essay will argue that only a strong form of democracy can adequately redress the claims of injustice and "unfreedom" that constitute contemporary feminism.[29] This argument requires agreement that while in some respects these various views are complementary, they are nonetheless politically and philosophically divergent. They are philosophically distinct because they differ on the question of whether the differences displayed by men and women are products of "nature or nurture." They are different to the extent to which they consider apparent or natural differences relevant to justice, in the degree and quality of transformation in men and women they take to be necessary to the task of justice, and in the extent to which they contend there is any real basis for meaningful political discourse between men and women.[30] Most importantly, they differ in the strategies they contend are required to achieve emancipation and justice for women and men. These differences constitute a *crisis* with respect to the relations between and among women and men. There is no commonly accepted understanding of the terms of injustice or of the possible terms of justice and freedom that could serve as the means of redress.[31]

This crisis in contemporary Canadian society cannot be resolved by society simply choosing one of the preceding views. An alternative strategy is available. It consists of a demanding form of democratic politics, defined as "strong democracy" below. Democracy can serve as an effective means of securing justice between and among women and men, but only when it is defined by demanding criteria that are well beyond those ordinarily thought to be sufficient.[32]

Why Not Entrench a Prevailing View?

It would be a mistake for Canada now to entrench, *on the strength of the view itself*, any of the views discussed above. This is not because they are unworthy of respect and political support; rather, the reasons for not proceeding with them have to do with the terms of debate between them. One reason for not accepting any one of these views as the *ruling view* of this society is that each of them relies upon assertions of fact, which have not been and may never be established with certainty.[33] The malleability of humans assumed by androgynists, the view that individuals can shape human lifestyles quite profoundly, assumes that individuals in a society are free to determine their cultural roles creatively, because human beings can adapt to a wide variety of "ways of being" and have natures bursting with diverse potential. Contrast this with the nature-based arguments of advocates of patriarchy and Radical Feminism II, who assume that the natures of men and women place strict limits on how they can define their social roles; limits that, if surpassed, damage them as human beings.

The nature versus nurture argument, which has been at the heart of most political philosophy for thousands of years and is now at the heart of the debate over feminism, is not even close to being settled.[34] How can individuals ever know, for certain, how much of their lives is governed by "given" natures? Even if they could settle this question for themselves, how could they ever know whether their conclusions were true for others? But while people have to "take a stand" on this question if they are to raise children, they needn't do so as a society. Raising children requires people to make *assumptions* about how extensively children can be "shaped" before attempts to do so damage their "given" natures. It requires this because there are no other means of approaching child-rearing except by making some such assumptions.

But need people do so for all society? Should public conceptions of justice and emancipation rest on such a decision? The contention that people ought simply to "go for it" on this issue places their sense of justice and freedom, as members of a society, on distressingly uncertain footings, as matters of mere belief and good luck. But this sort of broad social assumption is unnecessary. Society simply doesn't need to settle this issue in the absence of certain facts, because another effective way of proceeding is available, one that will be discussed later.

There is a second reason for not proceeding in this manner: the character of the competition between these views, and the political results of a decision simply to entrench any one view in lieu of certain evidence. Suppose, for example, that a new social regime of androgyny is entrenched. To achieve this, in Canada, the authorities alter school texts and nursery school pedagogy, regulate the images of the mass media, socially praise and otherwise reward androgynist lifestyles, create and highlight androgynist symbols, provide incentives for men to develop their caring, passive sides, and offer tax breaks for more women to enter small business and blue-collar jobs. Suppose further that a number of persons do not support this decision, their "genderical politics" work in a different direction. They don't feel comfortable with what their lifestyle in the new society must be if they are to succeed socially, or they think that true justice and freedom for the sexes requires quite another direction for social policy. What are they to do?

They might continue to work for their preferred view and urge others to keep the faith, to continue the struggle for true justice and freedom. Or they could retrench; they could move to ground upon which their opposition to the socially preferred view is sharper. Those normally committed to Patriarchy II could fall back to the less philosophically satisfying but sharper political position of Patriarchy I.

Those committed to Radical Feminism I could move to the ground of Radical Feminism II, a less compromising position in its opposition to androgyny. Liberal Feminists I and II could move in either direction to protect what they take to be important differences in sexual identity, even when they do not consider these to be matters of justice. They might all take more adversarial postures, not because they prefer their new positions, but because these positions are easier to defend politically.

The effect of entrenching one of the existing views, without certain evidence in support of its working assumptions, may be to drive people from their more genuine philosophical support for other positions, essentially for political reasons. This is not a point of logic; the entrenchment of one such view does not logically entail political realignment. It is a political insight. Until recently the view that "ruled" Canada was Patriarchy II, and today it is increasingly Liberal Feminism I. It seems safe to conclude that the recent success of Liberal Feminism I has induced many of those who have historically favoured Patriarchy II to the ground of Patriarchy I, and may even have driven some feminists, who would be otherwise engaged,[38] to Radical Feminism II. It also seems likely that the early entrenchment of Patriarchy II has driven many feminists to more adversarial views than those to which they would otherwise be committed.

A final reason for not choosing any of the previously discussed views is related to both of the previous points and is, regrettably, a point of political conjecture. Some believe that a society that entrenches one ruling theory of justice is essentially more stable than a society that refrains from doing so. It is more stable not only because its law is made with confidence by governments and its citizens love or come to love their constitution and their country. It is also more stable because people in this society can predict the behaviour of others and because individuals can form trusting relationships, as citizens and as friends.[36]

This connection between justice and stability is an interesting and important one. It appears at least logically correct to deduce these qualities of citizenship from the assumption of a ruling theory.[37] But would these benefits be enjoyed in contemporary Canada if Canadians adopted any of the views so far considered? Would citizens come to form trusting and co-operative relationships and moderate their claims against one another in the interest of all? Probably not.

The reasons are as follows. First, a sense of justice needs to be widespread in a society for it to provide for civic friendship. It seems unlikely that citizens who hold a sense of justice at odds with the ruling theory would have enhanced civic or personal friendships with other citizens whose views have been socially entrenched. Rather, such entrenchment would work in exactly the opposite way. It would erode currently existing patterns of friendship. Friends don't

need to hold the same views, but they do need to be equal in the social
and political advantage they enjoy by virtue of their beliefs. To the
extent that a friend is privileged by the entrenchment of a principle,
the friendship is vulnerable.

This unequal civic friendship would be worsened if it were known
that the socially entrenched view rested on "mere" belief rather
than on certain evidence about the character of human beings and
society. Is it possible to befriend people who profit from the success
of a ruling theory that one abhors and that is known to rest on mere
belief? Is civic friendship possible between people who socially
profit from the political rule of a religious view and those who abhor
such a view? It is difficult to see how this could happen.

The unlikelihood of civic friendship stemming from the mere
adoption of one of the previously discussed views would be heightened if a preference for one view were to drive individuals to more
politically effective ground. Here, not only would an individual be
faced with the prospect of befriending those who profited from an
abhorrent ruling theory, but he or she would not really know what they
in fact favoured. It would be more difficult to trust them, and thus to
form either civic friendships or effective political alliances with
them.

The entrenchment of *any* one of these views requires nearly all
citizens to share the same assumptions about human life and to
embrace politics in matters of gender, if the entrenchment is to have
stabilizing or crisis-resolving effects. This is not now the case in Canada,
nor is it likely to be in the foreseeable future. Notwithstanding this
conclusion, doesn't the requirement for a ruling theory persist, in
much the same way that parents must embrace some ruling theory
to raise their children? Couldn't one contend that no other option
for society exists, that it is as impossible to govern society as it is to
raise children without a ruling theory of genderical justice? Such
an option is, however, available to society in a way that it isn't to
parents.

An Alternative Approach

The contention that another strategy can resolve the crisis between
and among women and men requires two tasks to be completed.
First, it must be shown that there is indeed such an alternative
procedure,
which neither sidesteps nor trivializes the crisis. Assuming a "strong"
version of democracy as an alternative strategy for resolving the
genderical crisis could avoid a ruling-theory decision. Canadians
could thus protect and build upon the sense of civic friendship avail-

able to Canadian women and men. This decision would neither damage the integrity of nor undermine the prospects of any of the views advanced for and against feminist politics, except Patriarchy I. Second, it must be shown that governing society without a ruling theory of justice between and among women and men is a real, not just a theoretical, option. In this respect, governing a society is unlike raising children. These are ambitious tasks, which will be completed only partially, in skeleton form. The reader can flesh this skeleton out, if it seems worthwhile.

The term "strong democracy" is used gingerly in fulfilling these tasks. It was initially coined, but poorly developed, I contend, to defend participatory democracy.[38] Here, the concept will be altered in a number of ways. It signifies a way of defining democracy in terms much more demanding than those normally captured by the concepts of "representative" or "liberal" democracy.

What is at stake in the issue of justice regarding women and men are the very terms of liberal democracy. Patriarchy I and II implicitly contend that liberal democracy is flawed to the extent that it considers the views of women to count on issues of public policy. Liberal Feminist II contends that liberal democracy underestimates the conditions necessary to a citizen's autonomy. Accordingly, it considers all liberal–democratic consensus (consensus that does not require the satisfaction of stronger criteria of autonomy) illegitimate. What does it mean, Liberal Feminists II ask, to secure the consent of women if they are fearful of male power or can't imagine any alternative to their lives except that of the "happy housewife?" Of what moral significance is the consent of men who are now mesmerized by "men's clubs" and "girlie magazines?"

Androgynists contend that taking such a vote today, given the underdevelopment of virtually all human beings, would merely cement what is already bad work, work that could be otherwise. Radical Feminists I and II contend that liberal democracy, based as it is on competition and adversarial politics, on the notion of "the rational voter" and the like, is hopelessly "male-centric." In short, a liberal democratic resolution of the crisis will not work because most of those at odds in the crisis consider liberal democracy to be biased in favour of one of the views, liberal feminism, and antithetical to the very terms of their preferred outcome.

Democracy does not usually require that everyone's point of view be reflected in social decisions. Liberal democracy typically tolerates minority views, by providing minority rights, while ensuring that the majority rules. However, what is being considered here is not merely which policy, if any, will reign; it concerns a prior question. What are the acceptable terms of social co-operation between the citizens of a democracy?[39] The proposition of an original contract or agreement provides the first point of definition of "strong democracy." Strong democracy requires, in part, that agreement to the terms of discourse and social co-operation be understood as fundamental to, and established prior to, the processes and institutions of democracy itself.[40]

What must be decided by strong democracy, in the matter of genderical justice, are the conditions of relations between and among the sexes under which all participants would be prepared to conduct their lives. There must be agreement on the language of political discourse, between the participants of democratic society, before any real discourse can begin. But what might these conditions of original discourse be?

Consider the somewhat parallel complexity of married life, a pattern of social life to which genderical politics is no stranger. All "couples" have ways to resolve differences between them. Some rely upon affection and desire, qualities arguably absent in civic relations. But patterns of conflict resolution, of compromise, and especially of mutual respect and integrity are often secured in marital relationships by essentially political processes. They are often attained through democratic processes, by agreeing to the right to speak, the equal right to determine outcomes affecting both people, the right more or less freely to associate with others, respect for a realm of privacy, and tolerance of unresolved differences. These devices work in personal political relations, to resolve crises, only when they are already agreed upon as the accepted conditions of discourse in the relationship. If one of the couple believes in the divine right of men to rule households and the other believes in liberal–democratic principles, no amount of working within one or other of these ways of settling issues can achieve peace in the household. Nor can it achieve a shared sense of justice, even when one side appears to have won a political battle.

Such resolutions can rely upon affection to succeed, to patch up differences, but this doesn't resolve the fundamental question of social co-operation. Only strong democracy can provide the means of a lasting peace and justice between such women and men. Both must agree on a procedure, on the terms of discourse, before making any other particular decisions.[41]

The Criteria for Resolution

Three criteria for strong democracy will be employed to resolve the genderical crisis. They are more demanding than those that define liberal democracy, and they may well not be exhaustive.[42] What is being considered is whether there is any democratic means, in principle at least, to fully and fairly resolve the political crisis of gender. This essay contends that there is, but only at the level of the "original contract" and under conditions of strong democracy. The three criteria are: (i) that claims based on power not be admitted; (ii) that near-unanimity of agreement be required; and (iii) that provision for future renegotiation be a condition of any such agreement.

The first criterion seems to be the easiest to defend. It is widely held that the right of conquest is no moral right at all. Power, in and of itself, justifies nothing. All but irrepressible bullies learn early on in their lives that while supremacy of strength is not without practical consequence, it is no basis upon which to establish agreement. Men might win "the battle of the sexes" if aggressivity is the only measure, but they could not obtain the real agreement of women by such a hollow victory. Thus power is irrelevant to, and excluded by, strong democracy, because in principle it could not secure an agreement that could finally settle the issue. At best, it could push the crisis underground, as it does in some personal relationships.

Liberal democracy doesn't, however, tolerate pure power politics any more than strong democracy does. What the exclusion of power as an aspect of legitimate political discourse means is that the agreement of some participants in the debate over feminist justice is unnecessary. Their voices need not, indeed ought not, to be heard in the debate. Those who subscribe to Patriarchy I need not be considered in any original contract, that is, in any fundamental agreement about the terms of social co-operation between the sexes.[43]

The second criterion also seems obvious. If the goal is to establish the terms of social co-operation between persons, then the agreement of all of those affected by such a decision is necessary. Consider what it would mean if the terms of co-operation between an employer and employee were solely a function of the employer's determination. The relationship would be one not of social co-operation but of slavery.

This point has interesting ramifications. One feminist view considers full autonomy to be a necessary condition of binding agreement. Recall what Liberal Feminists II think of the "agreement" to household patriarchy by women who can't imagine themselves living otherwise, or who are fearful of threats made by their companions. Or note that the agreement to "marry," where one party is driven by nothing but a desperate desire to be clothed and fed, is no agreement at all. These decisions would simply be ruled out by Liberal Feminists II, as unacceptable terms for the strong democratic resolution of the genderical crisis. Liberal feminists would be loathe to agree to any "new deal" that failed to reflect the real autonomy of *all persons* affected by the agreement. Requiring near-unanimity guarantees something close to the full autonomy of persons as a condition of the agreement of Liberal Feminists II. This would, of course, be the case for all the participants to a new social contract.

All would add conditions to the process of strong democracy, conditions beyond those here considered, as extensions of the unanimity rule or, in other words, by threat of veto.

The third criterion is related to the other two and especially to their underlying notion of consent. Strong democracy requires the terms of initial agreement, whatever the parties subsequently agree to, to be renegotiable. It must always be possible for individuals who have agreed to revoke their agreement, to start fresh once again. One reason for this is that not all possible views could be represented in any one set of negotiations. No voices ought to be ruled out of court when settling issues of fundamental social co-operation. Another reason is that people do change their minds about justice and about the relevance of gender to justice. There is no good reason for holding people to an understanding as basic and important to their identity as these views. To do so would be to deny who they have become.

At stake here is the moral status of agreements that no longer enjoy the favour of those who have made them. In business it is important to respect agreements, and in friendships it is important to keep promises. But does this mean that people who no longer wish to live according to prior terms of social co-operation or previous terms of discourse, or that those who come to hold profoundly different understandings of justice and indeed of themselves, ought never to be relieved of their prior agreements? Plainly not. To hold someone to such an agreement is not significantly different, in the quality of relationship it creates, from the unacceptable agreements noted earlier, the slavery of the one-sided employer–employee relationship or the agreement of the "happy housewife."[44] This way of thinking about the matter is at the heart of Canadian's current thinking about the right to divorce.

It doesn't really matter whether the reader is persuaded by the brief justifications favouring these three criteria or not. The claim is not that these criteria *ought* to be accepted by the parties to an "original contract;" it is that at least some of the parties to any such contract *would* be so committed, because for some of those in the debate over feminism, to fail to be so committed, to accept these three criteria, would be to misrepresent the very terms of their own understanding of justice for women and men. Liberal Feminists II would insist upon all three criteria, and this would be enough to undermine any agreement that failed to satisfy them.

Strong Democracy and Political Pluralism

The previous section has shown that there is an alternative to a ruling theory of justice between and among women and men which can be accepted on the strength of the theory itself.[45] This alternative is to settle the issue politically, but through a particular form of democratic politics. The democratic procedure defended above is different from what is now understood as liberal democracy, especially strong democracy's requirement of near-unanimity on the fundamental issues of the terms of political discourse and social co-operation. What remains to be shown is that such a "resolution" of the issue would resolve anything, that strong democracy would at least provide a workable alternative to the "ruling" theory.

It might be predicted that the conditions of strong democracy would lead to a new, fundamental, and lasting "original contract" between men and women. That is, in such circumstances persons might see the basic virtue of one theory and accordingly give up their previous view. Or the desire of participants to secure "civic friendship" and social co-operation between men and women might be strong enough to cause them to accept a view other than their own.

Although this scenario is plausible for intimate relationships, it is a highly improbable outcome for society. This is partly because the existing intensity of civic friendship in Canada is not sufficient to produce such an outcome. Canadians just don't care enough for one another as fellow or sister citizens ever to give up their essential views about justice regarding women and men; enough of them simply hold their views on such matters too dearly for this to be possible. It is implausible also because the differences between views on such questions of justice are too great. Finally, it is an implausible outcome because a fundamental compromise can be avoided by another arrangement.

This alternative arrangement is for all the parties in a strong democracy to embrace *political pluralism* as a condition of continued social co-operation between the sexes.[46] Pluralism here means that individuals form political subgroups and conduct their lives with those who have achieved essential agreement about social co-operation, justice, and freedom. Such a pluralism, in its own way, is conducive to a type of civic friendship based on mutual respect and a tolerance of differences. If there are any ruling theories in a pluralist society, they must operate only within subgroups, the members of which are always and completely free to leave. There is no positive role, in such an arrangement, for the state to govern the relations between members within these groups or between these groups, except to guarantee that no members are within subgroups against their autonomous will.[47] The only role for government would be to enhance, as best it could, the continued respect of all members of society for the terms of pluralism and especially to ensure that no view came surreptitiously to rule all.[48] This role for the state would require quite extensive government action.

Before turning to this point, however, it should be noted that nothing in such an arrangement precludes individuals in one subgroup from forming civic or co-operative relations with individuals in other subgroups. Such relations would be necessary if the society were to thrive. However, such cross-cutting alignments could not be constrained or even coloured in any way by a ruling theory. They would have to be conditional arrangements freely and fully consented to by the parties; Liberal Feminists II would insist on this before they would agree to a pluralist arrangement. Here, it would be government's job to see that as full an autonomy as was possible, for all citizens, was ensured by legislative means, if necessary. The legislation might include emancipating divorce laws, sexual-harassment legislation, a guaranteed income, and so on.

Agreement to these terms of pluralism would provide, by analogy and for greater clarity, that members of a political science department, for example, could work as colleagues even while they profoundly disagreed about justice between and among women and men, to the extent that no one of them achieved advantage or suffered in any way from a ruling theory, explicit or implicit. Students in this department could neither be rewarded nor suffer from any differences in politics regarding gender except Patriarchy I advocates who would be silenced. This would be guaranteed by university rules and by effective appeal procedures.

What would this form of political pluralism mean to the distinction between the private and public spheres of society? It would plainly be a nonstarter as an alternative to a ruling theory, if it could be argued to reproduce, say, patriarchy under the guise of pluralism. Pluralism provides a sphere of private, subgroup relations between citizens, just as it allows individuals to form intimate relations on the terms of their mutual autonomous commitments. But in doing this, the pluralist state is not passive. Even though it cannot impose any ruling theory of this dimension of justice, it must see that the conditions of the agreement struck in strong democracy are assured, even in personal relations. This, again, is why Liberal Feminism II is so important in strong democracy. Its advocates would require the terms of personal relationships not to be respected unless reasonable conditions of autonomy of the parties to them were met.

What this would mean is that women could not be led to form or continue relationships because of a financial dependency upon men or because of an absence of any real alternatives to such a lifestyle. It would mean that the courts, systems of taxation, school pedagogy, and the mass media would not be permitted to undermine the autonomy of women. These pluralist guarantees may not be sufficient to satisfy radical feminists or androgynists, but they go much further than liberal feminism, which seems to tolerate patriarchy in the name of "private relations" enough to persuade other feminists to choose pluralism over a competing ruling theory. Such a pluralist compromise is especially likely for all parties to this original contract when the door is left open to an eventual resolution of the matter in favour of their preferred view and when nothing prevents the continued practice of a preferred view within a subgroup. These conditions are provided for under the umbrella of a pluralist accord.

Consider how one issue at the heart of the crisis in Canadian justice between and among women and men might be understood in a regime of political pluralism. The political crisis over abortion legislation is the focal point and testing ground of an underlying crisis over this question of justice. There have been two ways in which women's claim to make this decision themselves has been defended by feminists. The first has been to assert a right of women to control their own bodies, and by extension the terms of sexuality and reproduction, a right that has conflicted with the competing rights of fetuses, and fathers and with a religious duty to protect human life.

A second way this claim has been supported has been to assert that the state has no right to decide between competing visions of justice in such issues. The state's role, instead is simply to ensure that no theory of justice wins, even by majority rule. That is, its role is to protect a sphere of action for all who have a view in the matter to govern themselves accordingly, within groups and as individuals. This protection is held to apply, however, only to citizens. Feminists who support this political argument for a freer abortion policy contend not that fetuses have no moral right to life, but that because they are not yet citizens, their right to state protection has not yet begun. Another way of putting this is to say that the state need not guarantee all moral rights and that the right to life of fetuses is one such right that simply can't be protected, because of the essential contest over this aspect of justice.

This second way of proceeding is essentially pluralist, and it displays both the prospects for a pluralist resolution of the crisis between the sexes and the impediments blocking such a resolution. The greatest difficulty would be to secure the support of Patriarchy II advocates to such a pluralist resolution if it was seen to mean their loss on the abortion question. What, if anything, might persuade them to agree, albeit unhappily, to such an accord? First, acceptance of this resolution would not constitute acceptance of the liberalism of women's rights as the ruling theory of society. While it would not be a victory for conservatives, accepting political pluralism is not the surrender to liberalism that it would be if the *moral right* of women to abortion was guaranteed by the state.

Second, for all parties to the strong democratic resolution of genderical justice, the very possibility of civic friendship, stability, and social co-operation may encourage the resolution of the crisis in matters of justice regarding women and men. If society is to persevere, then some resolution is better than none, and the "best" is that which least threatens one's preferred view. Community is among the most important of conservative values. Advocates of Patriarchy II could, under pluralism, continue to govern their own subcommunity, albeit under the conditions of freedom or autonomy insisted on by Liberal Feminists II, by *their* ruling theory. Moreover, they could continue to appeal to others who did not share their views, so long as they tolerated and respected others' decisions to do otherwise. As well, they could develop very compelling support systems for protecting fetuses, which, if the autonomy of citizens was respected, the state could support. Financial and moral support for prospective mothers to develop fetuses to term are within the opportunities of conservatives, in pluralist societies to provide. It may even be argued to be the responsibility of the state to provide this, as the terms of respecting the integrity of this subgroup.

This reasoning has not yet persuaded advocates of Patriarchy II to give up their cause. This is partly because the question of justice regarding women and men has not yet been put to conservatives as a crisis that has the potential of ending the patterns of social co-operation upon which most citizens seem to depend.[49] But it is also because Patriarchy II continues to enjoy a certain privilege in Canadian society. The most important result of a move to pluralism from the current status quo is that the traditional privilege accorded the values of Patriarchy II, and to a lesser extent of Liberal Feminism I, would need to be dismantled in Canada.

Some judges who now hold the values of Patriarchy II would need to be retired or "retooled," as would some teachers. This would undoubtedly give both conservatives and liberal feminists reason to proceed slowly on the matter. Whether they will ever think of the issue in the way outlined in this essay depends on the extent to which politics between and among the genders continues on its "crisis" path. Whether they ought to be so influenced to reconsider is, finally, the reader's decision. Plainly, a great deal is at stake.

Notes

1. Canada's Charter of Rights and Freedoms has accomplished this, in sections 15 and 28, at least within the scope of the law, by guaranteeing women legal equality.
2. For some advocates of feminist justice, the discernment of justice would require, as well, a more genuine freedom for men.
3. While it is ordinarily useful to distinguish these values, in this issue they are inseparable. The rallying cry of the French Revolution, "liberty, equality, and fraternity," despite its undeniable insensitivity to women's freedom and equality, can also be understood as a call for the pursuit of *inseparable* values. The view of most feminists is that feminist justice

and freedom for women requires, as well, the *solidarity* of women, again, as a further inseparable term of freedom and justice. While these are crucial to the politics of feminism, this essay tries to avoid the question of whether feminism must assume a communitarian or individualist vision of social relations, except to note that some forms of individualism seem unlikely bases for an effective challenge to patriarchy.

4. The intention here, in characterizing the views by the labels used, is merely to find a means of distinguishing a variety of conceptions. There is a danger, though, in proceeding in this way. It may permit some to trivialize these views. As well, it is difficult to canvas any set of views in this way without leaving those who have developed views on the question at hand, to contend, often rightly, that they have been inadequately represented. Recommended is the more complete treatment Rosemary Tong gives in *Feminist Thought: A Comprehensive Introduction* (Boulder and San Francisco: Westview Press, 1989). See also a collection of essays that effectively illustrates the terms of the current debate within feminism: *Feminism and Equality*, ed. Anne Phillips (Washington Square, N.Y.: New York University Press, 1987). An valuable discussion of the terms of the debate, in the framework of literary theory, appears in Toril Moi's *Sexual/Textual Politics: Feminist Literary Theory* (London: Metheun, 1985).

5. Plato's *Republic* may appear to be a curious work to cite in capturing the feminist problematic because it is held, not without cause, to be a misogynist political tract. It has, however, also been heralded as one of the first statements in favour of feminist justice made by men. See Wendy Brown's "Supposing Truth Were a Woman . . . Plato's Subversion of Masculine Discourse," in *Political Theory*, Vol. 16, no. 4, (November 1988), and Steven Burns's "Women in Bloom", *Dialogue*, XXIII (1984), pp. 135–40.

6. Another variety of this is men's propriety interest in "their women," their wives, lovers, daughters, and fetuses to which they lay claim.

7. Patriarchy I also expresses a psychopathology, that of misogyny or women hating.

8. The most commonly accepted source for these differences is that of hormonal balances, but other differences in the bodies of men and women serve the argument as well.

9. On the strength of such characterizations of the view, some women in Canada (for example, some who belong to R.E.A.L. Women) have organized to oppose feminist politics and abortion and more generally to protect the traditional role of women in the family. Some men, however, champion feminist conceptions of society, and some women champion Patriarchy II. Patriarchy II satisfies the formal conditions of justice considered in the early part of the essay, but draws hierarchical rather than egalitarian conclusions in its discernment of differences.

10. While feminist politics has a long and vital history in the relations between the sexes and while the writings of women have a long tradition (only recently being recovered by feminist scholarship), the intellectual turning point in the development of feminist political philosophy was the publication by Mary Wollstonecraft of *The Vindication of Women's Rights* (1792), an essentially liberal argument for feminism.

11. This is parallel to the egalitarian view of genderical justice presented early in this essay.

12. Often this claim is made by virtue of an essentially property-based right women are held to have to their own bodies to an equal right to liberty. The claim that liberal feminists make to their own bodies seems to be of a different order from that advanced by radical feminists, though investigating this difference is well beyond this essay.

13. For example, this is where the appearance of sexual submissiveness of women or sexual play by women is a condition of advancement in the public sphere, more so than are the "complimentary" attitudes of men.

14. Except where harm, such as that resulting from physical assault, can be shown.

15. For an assessment of the importance of this realm free from interference, see Judith Sklar, "The Liberalism of Fear," in Nancy L. Rosenblum, *Liberalism and the Moral Life* (Cambridge, Mass.: Harvard University Press, 1989).

16. The distinction between the private and public realms of society is not, even in liberal legal and moral theory, as crisp as it is represented in this example. But the example still effectively displays the distinction between private and public decisions entailed by liberalism.

17. This type of argument is employed by this author in his critique in Chapter 2.

18. Lives like these are *not prohibited* by Liberal Feminism II, but are allowed only when quite demanding conditions of autonomy known as "real consent" are first fulfilled.

19. There is an important connection here between Liberal Feminism II and democratic socialism. The concept "liberal feminism" is preferable because of the centrality, in this view, of autonomy. However, it is a radical form of liberalism.

20. The relationship between "toadyism" and freedom is unsatisfactorily discussed in Richard Flathman's *The Philosophy and Politics of Freedom* (Chicago: University of Chicago Press, 1987). Those who wish to contemplate further how liberal theories can serve to tolerate inner impediments to the freedom of women might consult this work.

21. Androgyny, as a doctrine of feminism is both liberal and radical. It is liberal because it is centred on the concept of autonomy, of people making their own lives.

22. A literary treatment of this proposal is found in Marge Piercy's *Women on the Edge of Time* (New York: Knoppf, 1976). Other articulations can be found in the works of Virginia Woolf and the philosophy of Simone de Beauvoir.

23. This is the focus of much of the criticism of androgynist feminism both by conservatives and, interestingly, by radical feminists: such a program would undermine the achievement of sexual identity among the young. See Jean Elshtain, "Against Androgyny," *Feminism and Equality*, ed. Anne Phillips (Washington Square, N.Y.: New York University Press, 1987).

24. Radical feminism is here characterized as an *essentialist* doctrine. There is a second way of characterizing these views, though, and that is to contend that the difference between women's and men's experiences, is a function of what it is to be a woman or man in contemporary society; that is, these differences are products of the suppression and

marginalization of women in their experience of the world, and they are products of socialization. This way of proceeding has been chosen because most of the second distinction is captured in the radical doctrine of Liberal Feminism II.

25. Julia Kristeva contends that what needs to be deconstructed is the binary (oppositional) relations entailed in the man/woman distinction. See Julia Kristeva, *Desire in Language: A Semiotic Approach to Literature and Art* (New York: Columbia University Press, 1980).

26. See Angela Miles and Geraldine Finn, eds., *Feminism*, 2nd ed. (Montreal: Black Rose Books, 1989); and Alison Jaggar *Feminist Politics and Human Nature*, Totowa, N.J., Rowma R. Allanheld. A brief and compelling discussion of Jaggar's work can be found in Virginia Held's "Feminism and Epistemology: Recent Work on the Connection Between Gender and Knowledge," *Philosophy and Public Affairs*, Vol. 14, No. 3 (Summer 1985).

27. It is in the articulation of this view, more than any others, that it may be unacceptable for a man to speak because if radical feminists are right, men have no real means to understand the experience of women, as male and female experience is fundamentally divergent.

28. A statement of this view can be found in Carol Gilligan, *In a Different Voice*, (Cambridge, Mass.: Harvard University Press, 1982); Luce Irigary, *This Sex Which Is Not One*, trans. Catherine Porter with Carolyn Burke (New York: Cornell University Press, 1977); or Adrienne Rich, *Of Women Born: Motherhood As an Experience and Institution* (New York: W.W. Norton, 1976) and is discussed in Jaggar, above.

29. Ben Barber's concept of strong democracy is used here, even though in a number of respects this argument is different from, and in some respects at odds, with his, a view articulated in *Strong Democracy: Participatory Politics for a New Age* (Berkeley: University of California Press, 1984): Richard Flathman employs the concept of "unfreedom."

30. A splendid discussion of the language of political discourse in genderical politics can be found in Mary Hawkesworth's "Feminist Rhetoric: Discourses on the Male Monopoly of Thought," *Philosophy and Public Affairs*, Vol. 16 (August 1988).

31. This way of understanding the problem is drawn from the work of Jurgen Habermas's *Legitimation Crisis* (Boston: Beacon Press, 1975). This essay is also indebted to a striking critique of Habermas by Seyla Benhabib, "Liberal Theory versus a Critical Theory of Discursive Legitimation," in Rosenblum, pp. 143–57.

32. Readers will discover a similarity of approach in this argument and in that favouring of limiting the freedom of expression of journalists, in Chapter 8 of this book.

33. This concern, of course, parallels the one identified by the essay on the issue of the prohibition of pornography in Chapter 2.

34. Other assumptions are similarly divergent and uncertain in this debate. Some contend that a private/public division is essential to the well-being of persons conducting social life and others that is a mere social convention and is harmful; some believe that women can achieve justice only through community, while others contend that communitarianism is insidiously conservative in the social and political practice it encourages. These are not completely matters of fact but they are so in part, and are therefore not easily nor soon to be resolved.

35. The assertion, however, is not that Radical Feminism II is unworthy either as a philosophical view or as a political program. It is, instead, that it would not proceed satisfactorily, grounded in the kind of political "logic" it has just been suggested it might "enjoy." It is obvious why it would not be a good thing were those who are now devoted to Patriarchy II to be induced to the ground of "the right of conquest."

36. These considerations are central to the works of John Rawls, *A Theory of Justice* (Harvard, The Bellenays Press of Harvard University, 1971) and John Dunn, *Rethinking Modern Political Theory: Essays: 1979–83* (Cambridge, Cambridge University Press, 1985). The argument offered below can be traced to a consideration of Rawls's work as much as it can to that of Habermas and to their recent feminist critics. See, for example, Susan Moller Okin's "Justice and Gender," *Philosophy and Public Affairs*, Vol. 16, No. 1, (Winter 1987), and Seyla Benhabib, as above.

37. The connection between civic friendship and regime integrity is a long-standing one, deeply embedded in the political philosophy of antiquity. See Jane Mansbridge's *Beyond Adversarial Democracy* (New York: Basic Books, 1980).

38. Barber's book, *Strong Democracy*, has enjoyed widespread popularity despite, or perhaps because of, its somewhat reckless abandonment of any constraints upon democratic discourse. Barber's essentially Foucaultian argument is worth considering as another means of democratically resolving the genderical crisis. This essay's treatment of "strong democracy" is more Habermasian and more effectively sympathetic to feminist politics than is Barber's.

39. There are always two decisions to be made in democratic politics. The first is, under what conditions, if any, ought one to "play?" Resolution of the question of genderical politics, as a matter of the terms of social co-operation between women and men is, in this way, a matter of the fundamental conditions of democratic politics and not merely an outcome of democratic choice. This point is well secured in Rousseau's *Social Contract*. Rousseau contends that there must be some basic agreement about social co-operation that is fundamental to the life of any sort of regime. Rawls makes the same point when he insists that decisions about justice are prior to decisions about institutions. He seems to argue that such decisions require near-unanimity, even though his unanimity technique is, like Kant's, abstract. Reasoning for this distinction includes, of course, a concern about regime stability, a function of which, it is contended, is a shared sense of justice.

40. This is the notion of the "original contract" in Rousseau's *Social Contract*.

41. This is part of Rawls's point in his phrase, "justice as fairness."

42. They are, though, somewhat less demanding than those favoured by Habermass, who requires that democratic discourse be "rational," that it must reveal the essential human qualities of the species. The notion that "rationality" is central to humanity is one of the propositions challenged by radical feminists. They do not contend that it ought to be irrational, but that this way of proceeding is too reductive; it narrows human qualities unjustifiably, to the detriment of women. This essayist wishes to favour conditions that stop short of Ben Barber's. For Ben Barber, virtually anything goes, as long as it is participatory.

43. This, again, is Plato's point, in part, early in the *Republic*.
44. Neither this essayist nor Liberal Feminists II believe that all decisions of such women are illegitimate in this way. This depends solely on the conditions of autonomy for these women, not on the content of the agreements they make.
45. In doing so, this essay is indebted to others, especially the critique of Habermas by Seyla Benhabib; to an essay and discussion delivered by Jane Mansbridge to the Conference for the Study of Political Thought at Acadia University, October 22, 1989; and to a discussion offered by Angela Miles at Acadia University in February 1990.
46. Such an arrangement, though it is not presented in a context such as the one now being contemplated, is defended effectively by Nancy Rosenblum's "Pluralism and Self Defence," in Rosenblum, pp. 207–227.
47. Liberal Feminists II again would not agree to a pluralist option without a full principle of autonomy. Here, it seems that only Liberal Feminists I might disagree, but the pluralist one is so much closer to what they could live with than the adoption of any ruling theory other than their own, that they would likely be prepared to accept these conditions. That is, they would need only to consider the other real options, once theirs had been rejected, to find much to value in the pluralist option.
48. This is not a general principle. It is the particular qualities of genderical politics that require the application of such a principle.
49. Earlier legislation, that of the Trudeau administration, was pluralist in its rationale, and abortion "on demand," a state of the law for months before the current Conservative legislation, was principally liberal. The difference between the latter two is that the Trudeau legislation, at least as it was administered, seemed to assume that the full autonomy of women was better ensured if some limited impediments were placed in the way of women's decisions to abort a fetus; basically that physicians were prepared to recognize the importance of the decision to the woman's life and identity. Many feminists considered these impediments an indication of a desire to have a largely male medical profession exercise control over women's bodies and decisions.

CRITIQUE

In his essay, Greg Pyrcz proposes a unique approach to issues of justice concerning women. Since there is no agreement (he calls this a "crisis") about what justice requires in such issues today, he argues that they be settled "democratically." The issues should be left for individuals to work out for themselves by a special procedure, a form of "strong" democracy involving unanimity or near-unanimity, which operates through decentralized or "pluralist" subgroups.

This approach is distinctive. Most theorists try to handle such issues by using principles to determine what justice requires and how to realize it. Each of the perspectives surveyed in the first part of the essay attempts precisely this, but it is not Pyrcz's own approach. Instead of devising principles, which might then be imposed upon individuals, Pyrcz devises a democratic procedure whereby those involved can settle the issue for themselves. In part, this focus on democracy reflects a concern with what works politically, as opposed to what might be "true" philosophically.

But there is also a more general disposition to focus on the democratic needs of the community. Pyrcz particularly wants to avoid the "liberal" trap of focusing on individuals apart from their community, as though individual rights were a fence separating each person from the rest. For Pyrcz, individual rights are important, but they must be understood and dealt with through the politics of the community. So here again he abjures any approach to justice based on abstract principles in favour of an approach that lets individuals devise their own solutions.

There is much to be said for this approach. It is clearly desirable, *if* it is possible, that solutions to problems be devised by the parties themselves—solutions they can agree to, live with, and adapt to changing conditions. However, Pyrcz's approach makes a basic mistake: it relies on procedures *instead* of principles, whereas, in issues of justice, both are needed *together*. This can be argued by indicating three problems with Pyrcz's approach: (i) his "strong" democracy is unworkable, in a way that undermines his reliance on procedures; (ii) his "purely procedural" approach is itself undermined by the reasons he gives for adopting it; and (iii) no such procedure on its own could be adequate as an answer to questions of justice.

Does It Work?

How does the proposal work? The aim is to devise a democratic procedure that will deliver justice on issues concerning women. But there is no guarantee that justice will be delivered by normal majoritarian voting. Recognizing this, Pyrcz proposes a procedure of strong democracy, meaning that decisions must be unanimous, or very nearly so.[1] Why? No explanation is given, but the near-unanimity rule gives each individual an effective veto, and this presumably guarantees justice by enabling individuals to veto anything they regard as fundamentally unjust.

The problem with this approach is that nothing can be established on this basis. As Canadian constitutional conferences have repeatedly and boringly proven, it is almost impossible to get unanimous agreement on anything, even with only eleven participants. Imagine that everyone in Canada is involved, including the various patriarchs, liberals, and radical feminists surveyed by the essay, and that they must agree, almost unanimously, on policies regarding abortion, pornography, hiring of women in public service management positions, and running the household. Could they agree on any policies here? Clearly not; the near-unanimity rule makes agreement impossible.

Recognizing this, Pyrcz proposes a "pluralist" procedure, that policies be adopted by subgroups instead of by society at large. He seems especially to have in mind voluntary associations and intimate relationships, and it is clear that his proposal would work at this level. Individuals can and do decide how they want to be treated by others, and they choose their friends, social groups, and sexual partners on this basis.

But what about larger social groups, such as churches, political parties, trade unions, professional associations, schools, and businesses? These are some of the main arenas in which questions of genderical justice arise. It is clear that near-unanimity would be impossible in such groups for the same reasons that made it unattainable in the society at large. Imagine that quotas are proposed for hiring women in each department at Canadian universities. Would there be near-unanimity on this?

The same problem arises with more general social policies. How will policies on abortion and pornography be established on a society-wide basis? Since these problems directly raise issues of justice for women, policies governing them could only be adopted if they met the near-unanimity test. No policy at all could be adopted on this basis. The alternative is to leave the issues to various subgroups to decide, but this would result in no policy at all. Some subgroups would ban pornography, while others would promote it; individuals would decide which groups to join on the basis of whether they liked pornography or disliked it; and candy stores would be free to sell it to anyone they choose.

The same problem arises even where the proposal seems to work—in small, voluntary associations. Would there be any restrictions on the kinds of groups one could join? Suppose there were groups dedicated to the practice of patriarchy. Women would be welcome to join, but they would be expected to be subservient, docile, and adoring in relation to men. Pyrcz opposes this on the ground that subgroups must respect the autonomy of women as understood by Liberal Feminism II. His reason is that Liberal Feminists II "would insist on this before they would agree to a pluralist arrangement." He is correct in saying this but fails to note that patriarchs would oppose the principle, and their agreement is supposed to count as well. So the near-unanimity rule would not be met.

This is fatal to the proposal. If subgroups are to be restricted by rules adopted on a society-wide basis, then *no* such rules could be adopted and *no* subgroups would be established. The subgroup proposal cannot get off the ground. This is not surprising; subgroup pluralism was proposed only because Pyrcz recognized that the near-unanimity rule could not be met on a society-wide basis. But if principles of justice cannot be established on a society-wide basis, neither can principles governing social groups. The very consideration that creates the need for subgroups prevents them from being established.

It is possible that Pyrcz fails to see this problem because he takes the principle of respect for the effective autonomy of women for granted. Several passages in the essay suggest that subservience by women is contrary to their best interests, that it indicates a lack of full autonomy, and that it is the effect and evil reflection of patriarchal dominance. This may be correct, but it is a *principle*. To adopt it is to abandon the hope of a purely procedural approach. Pyrcz might have adopted the principle, but it would require justification. It cannot simply be assumed as part of a magical agreement.

Without some such principles, Pyrcz's proceduralism collapses. It does not allow restrictions on social groups; it would not work at all in large groups; and it does not permit social policies to be established. As an account of justice for issues involving women, this is not much.

Is the Procedural Approach Necessary?

Pyrcz claims that this purely procedural approach is required because there is a lack of fundamental agreement (a "crisis") on issues of justice concerning women. Why should this be a reason for not adopting a theory or principle of justice? When fundamental disagreement occurs in other areas of life, such as science, religion, or politics, no one treats the disagreement as a reason for not adopting a position, so why is it done here? Questions of justice inevitably involve disagreement because they are contentious: people raise conflicting claims about what they are "owed" as matters of justice.

So this is the one area of practical life where disagreement should be expected, and this is why principles are required. The fact of disagreement should be a reason for adopting principles, not for abjuring them.

In any event, the essay's reasoning is odd. It is said that proceduralism, involving a near-unanimity rule, is necessary because of fundamental disagreement. But the disagreement means that near-unanimous agreement is impossible. Thus Pyrcz's proceduralism is rendered impossible by the reason given for adopting it.

Does the Approach Work on Issues of Justice?

Why, then, doesn't the proposal work? It isn't just because the near-unanimity requirement is too severe. Rather, this requirement is imposed by the needs of justice. Agreement might be obtained by using a simple majority vote, but this would not guarantee justice. So the real problem with the proposal is not that it is too severe, but rather that it is inadequate as a treatment of justice.

Consider this more systematically. The pure procedural approach has important advantages, *if* it can be made to work. But it works more successfully in certain conditions than in others. For example, the idea of having people "work out" solutions for themselves presupposes—or works best in—small groups in which individuals can confront one another directly and continuously. This possibility is diluted as the group gets larger, and it disappears entirely in very large and anonymous groups such as cities, provinces, and countries. As the group gets larger, individuals get smaller, less able to influence decisions, and less able to protect themselves from adverse decisions. As the group gets larger, therefore, the case gets stronger for liberal rights to protect individuals from majoritarianism.

If this is correct, it explains why size is a problem for the essay's proposal. It is not that the near-unanimity requirement is too severe in large groups, although this is true. The basic problem is that pure proceduralism itself does not work in large groups. It can work well in small groups, but in larger groups principles of justice are needed to protect individuals against abuses of majority, or "democratic," power.

Two further conditions deserve brief mention. Problem-solving groups are more likely to be successful and are more likely to achieve unanimity when their members have a sense of compromise and fair play. Conversely, groups tend to be less successful when their members adopt entrenched positions and do not trust others to deal fairly with their concerns. By the same token, groups work better when they are organized fairly; they are less successful if some members believe that others in the group have unfair advantages over them. However, these conditions—a sense of compromise and fairness within the group—cannot be presumed in cases of *justice*.

Individuals who make claims of justice are not moved by a spirit of compromise. They are demanding what is due, or owed to them. This is perfectly reasonable, because if they are correct they are entitled to their claims and others are obliged to deliver. People who are owed money do not compromise and split the difference! Moreover, injustice implies that the individual has been denied what is owed, even the minimum. These individuals are not likely to think that their claims will be met with fairness by others. This is particularly the case if the injustice concerns the group itself, if individuals believe that they have been disadvantaged by the organization of the group.

These are the kinds of claims made today by women about justice in their relationships, social groups, and the social structure itself. The procedural approach is an inadequate response to these claims. The pure procedural approach tends to be successful when the group is small and the problems are not issues of justice, especially issues concerning the organization of the group itself. In large groups, especially where justice is an issue, this approach does not work. The result is more likely to be an entrenchment of positions than agreement.

Concluding Remarks on Justice

Pyrcz's proceduralism is inappropriate as an approach to justice. Consequently, the need for principles in determining justice cannot be bypassed. In seeking to understand issues of justice affecting women, it would be a good idea to work through the several perspectives identified in the first part of the essay; they are excellent outlines. But something must be said about these perspectives as they specifically concern justice for women.

It is a good idea to start with the principle that it should be each woman's right to live on her own terms. As a point of justice, society should be organized to facilitate this, for both women and men, by minimizing interferences in individuals' lives and by guaranteeing the security and minimal resources they need.[2] This entails respect for the choices individuals actually make, whatever one thinks about them. Pyrcz, however, is reluctant to respect relationships, such as prostitution or patriarchal marriage, that are not based on the autonomy prized by Liberal Feminism II.

But one must be careful here. Subservient relationships may not be chosen autonomously, and as a result they reflect what is truly evil about patriarchal domination. But where these relationships are chosen freely, the choice must be respected, whatever one thinks about it. Conversely, to prohibit such choices as nonautonomous is to combine a true belief about the lack of autonomy with a complete lack of respect for the person involved. Whether the woman is a prostitute or a "patriarchal" wife, it is her life; her choices must be respected.

It may seem that this focus on "choice" adopts one of the "liberal" perspectives outlined in the essay. But this is not so. Although one should "start" with respect for the right of women to live on their own terms, a great deal more is required. Major gender-related inequalities of power exist in Canadian society. There is much truth in the critique of what Pyrcz calls Radical Feminism I. Genderical injustice is not merely a question of insufficient equality of opportunity, although this is the case. Canadian social institutions also reflect the priority of men's interests and male values, with the corresponding marginalization or denigration of women's interests. For example, the raising of children, a traditionally female occupation, is rarely given the social importance it deserves. It should be on a par with such traditionally male occupations as law and medicine.

Also, women are vulnerable to violence and psychological abuse in ways that men are not. Yet very little is done about this. For this reason, one might expect that basic self-defence for women would be a central part of the school curriculum. It is not, because school boards do not see the need for it. This is bizarre. So, more generally, the question of justice in relation to women's concerns is not just an issue of equality of opportunity; the effective ability of women to live on their own terms requires some radical changes in the values and power structure of Canadian society.

There is also a psychological dimension. Liberal perspectives place great emphasis on autonomy (as in Liberal Feminism II). But two senses of "autonomy" should be distinguished: one is the *right* of individuals to live on their own terms; the other is their *ability* to do so. Liberalism generally treats autonomy in the second sense—the ability to be self-directing—as an accomplished fact, when in reality taking effective charge of oneself is an ongoing challenge realized only incompletely in anyone's life. Some people will deny this, believing themselves to be fully self-directing. But they are either pretending or mistaken; the people closest to autonomy are those who realize that their lives are not fully in their own power, who have tasted the bitterness of their own limitations, and who have worked to come to terms with them.

These remarks are dreadfully opinionated, but they have an important implication for genderical justice. For most people, gender—being male or female—is central to their identity and sense of themselves. It is precisely in this respect that we are radically incomplete. We draw our sense of gender identity from our earliest experiences with our parent figures, when we are most vulnerable. The parent figures are woven deeply into the texture of our identities, and we reproduce them in our adult relationships.

Usually there are two parent figures. This means that both gender roles typically play a role in any individual's identity. This has two implications. First, there is much to be said for complementing what Pyrcz calls radical feminism with psychological perspectives.[3] Second, the fundamental social changes required by radical feminism must to some extent be worked out within individuals and through their closest relationships.

This harks back to Pyrcz's proposal that issues of genderical justice should be left for individuals to work out among themselves, presumably in their closest relationships. Although this is inadequate as an account of what justice requires, it may be the best way to bring justice about.

Notes

1. The essay also suggests two other criteria, the denial of claims based on power and the right to renegotiate. But these are treated as byproducts of the near-unanimity rule, with the suggestion that other criteria might be implied in the same way. This critique will focus only on the near-unanimity rule.
2. This is developed further, although not with reference specific to women's issues, in Chapter 4.
3. An excellent short account can be found in Chapter 5, "Psychoanalytic Feminism," of Rosemarie Tong's *Feminist Thought: A Comprehensive Introduction* (Boulder and San Francisco: Westview Press, 1989).

Discussion Questions

1. Would all of those Pyrcz characterizes as having different views about "genderical justice" accept the "strong democratic" resolution of the problem? Would they do so to protect the integrity of their preferred view?

2. Is Pyrcz right to believe that no one ruling theory could resolve the "crisis" without undermining all prospects for "civic friendship"?

3. Is there really a crisis in genderical political relations?

4. Are stability , social co-operation, and civic friendship worth the price of pluralist compromise? Isn't pluralism just a front for the status quo?

5. Is "strong democracy" really possible as a political mechanism in large societies, or only in very small ones? Is it possible in any society?

Further Readings

Readers should consult the works cited in the notes to this chapter. They represent a wide scope of the scholarly and political work of contemporary feminism. However, because many of these works are aimed at a readership that is well acquainted with feminism, three of them are recommended to beginners: Rosemary Tong's excellent survey of feminism, *Feminist Thought: A Comprehensive Introduction* (Boulder and San Francisco: Westview Press, 1989); Angela Miles and Geraldine Finn, eds., *Feminism*, 2nd ed. (Montreal: Black Rose Books, 1989); and Anne Phillips, ed., *Feminism and Equality* (New York: New York University Press, 1987). All three works provide an introduction to contemporary feminism that is more complete and certainly more direct than that provided in this chapter.

Those who wish to explore the intellectual roots of patriarchy will find them in Book One of Aristotle's *Politics*. A powerful and well-written critique of the male-centric political philosophy in Western political thought is Diana H. Coole's *Women in Political Theory: From Ancient Misogyny to Contemporary Feminism* (Boulder, Colo.: Lynne Reiner, 1988). One of the best works of recent philosophy also sheds considerable light on the traditional debate. See Martha Nussbaum's *The Fragility of Goodness: Luck and Ethics in Greek Tragedy and Philosophy* (Cambridge University Press, 1986).

CHAPTER 6

Abortion and the Right to Life

This chapter explores the abortion issue by focusing on two major claims. Support for abortion is frequently justified on the ground that it should be each woman's right to decide what happens to, and in, her own body. Opposition to abortion is often argued on the ground that it violates the fetus's right to life.

In the essay, Don Carmichael supports a moderate position on the morality of abortion but he argues that it should be each woman's right to decide this for herself. He argues that the attempt to identify the point at which the fetus becomes "human" is irretrievably arbitrary and that the moral justification for abortion should become more stringent as the fetus develops. However, he also argues that there is no point at which abortion is blocked by a fetal right to life. There is no such right because the idea of a right to life presupposes capacities that the fetus completely lacks. Thus, to say that abortion violates the fetus's right to life is like saying that it is wrong to torture cats because this violates their rights.

A major thrust of this argument is that it separates the moral and legal–political aspects of abortion. In contrast, the standard positions tie the legality of abortion to its morality. They hold that abortion should be forbidden because it is wrong or that it should be allowed because it is a woman's right. Carmichael, however, argues that views about the morality of abortion must be supplemented by an independent respect for the right of individuals to live on their own terms, even—perhaps especially—where others disagree with them. This respect might be blocked if there were a fetal right to life. But once it is shown that a fetal right to life does not exist, it follows that the morality of abortion should be left for each woman to decide for herself. The result is a moderate view on the morality of abortion and a "pro-choice" view on its legality.

This distinction between law and morality is the focus of Tom Pocklington's critique. Pocklington does not completely reject Carmichael's view, but he is unsure whether it can be maintained consistently. For him, the question is whether a moderate view on morality may make it impossible to assert a pro-choice view of the law, and vice versa. Pocklington raises this question in three ways. First, a moderate view on morality means that human beings have some duties to fetuses; the grounds of these duties might also establish rights, including a right to life. Second, although Canadian society respects the right of persons to live on their own terms, there are limits to this right. If one individual believes that another is acting immorally in having an abortion, why should the individual respect the other's right to do so? Third, the essay seems to permit abortion in terms that would also permit infanticide, and this is objectionable.

Abortion is a complex and controversial issue. Support for abortion can be understood to deny the sacredness of life and the special love and protection that is due to the young. Opposition to abortion seems to deny the right of individuals to decide the terms of their own lives, especially the right of women to control their own bodies. Both views are morally contentious and touch people's deepest emotions in ways that are easily inflamed. For many people, the issue is haunted by memories of personal grief and tribulation, and it is not surprising that abortion is a "fighting issue" for so many.

Current views on abortion tend to polarize into two positions that may be broadly characterized as "pro-choice" and "pro-life." The "pro-choice" position is that abortion should be a right, because it should be the right of each woman to control what happens in her own body. The "pro-life" position is that abortion is wrong in a way that is akin to murder, because it violates the fetus's right to life.

This essay, however, will argue for a position that is moderate on the morality of abortion while supporting the right of women to decide the issue for themselves. The abortion issue raises two questions: the morality of abortion, and the right to decide to abort in a particular case. The moral justification for abortion changes during a pregnancy because abortion becomes more difficult to justify as the fetus develops. But at no point is it blocked by the fetus's right to life; this "right" simply does not exist. As a result, the decision to abort can properly be left to the woman bearing the fetus to decide for herself.

After a brief review of the background to the controversy, this essay's argument will be presented in three stages. First, the idea of a fetal right to life will be examined to determine why it is so central and yet so difficult to establish. Next, a now-classic argument in support of abortion, based on the right to control one's own body, will be considered. This essay will argue that, notwithstanding the importance of this right, it does not entail a right to abortion. Finally, by considering the nature of rights in general, this essay will argue that the narrow focus on rights is inappropriate and, in particular, that the idea of a fetal right to life is unintelligible.

Political–Legal Background

Until 1988, Canada's Criminal Code required that abortions could be performed (i) only in accredited hospitals and (ii) only if the hospital's therapeutic abortion committee deemed the pregnancy likely to endanger the life or health of the woman.[1] Violation of this law carried a maximum penalty of life imprisonment.[2] In 1973, Dr. Henry Morgentaler was charged with violating this law by operating an abortion clinic in Montreal. Morgentaler was a licensed physician, and his technique was medically safe; but his clinic violated the law by enabling women to obtain abortions without going through the cumbersome process stipulated by the law. At trial, Morgentaler was acquitted by the jury, but on appeal this was overturned and a conviction was substituted.[3] Eventually, Morgentaler spent ten months in jail.[4] Further charges were laid, and a jury acquitted him on these charges as well. A retrial was ordered on the first charge, and again the jury acquitted him. The government concluded that the law was unenforceable and decided not to prosecute further offences. Released from jail, Morgentaler continued to operate his Montreal clinic.

In 1983, Morgentaler opened similar clinics in Winnipeg and Toronto. In each case, he was charged immediately. After a highly publicized trial, the jury acquitted him. The result was appealed to the Supreme Court of Canada. The verdict, announced in January 1988, was a bombshell. In a five-to-two decision, the court struck down the abortion law as a violation of the "liberty and security of the person" guaranteed by section 7 of the Canadian Charter of Rights and Freedoms.[5]

The issue returned to Parliament. In the summer of 1988, Parliament debated six proposals for a new abortion law. In a free vote, all the proposals were defeated. It seemed that the politicians, like the Supreme Court, were more comfortable saying what they opposed in the abortion issue than what they supported.

At this point, there was no law on abortion. The issue might have been left in abeyance permanently, especially because of the divisions on the issue that existed in the Conservative caucus. But the following summer, it became a public issue again when women in two separate actions were prevented from having abortions by injunctions granted to their former boyfriends. In one case, the injunction was quashed on appeal. The woman in this case had an abortion and then declared that she regretted it. In the other case, the appeal court postponed its decision until after the twentieth week of the pregnancy and then quashed the injunction. By this time, the woman had obtained an abortion in the United States.

The intense feelings unleashed by these cases forced the government to bring forward new legislation. At the time of writing, Bill C-43 was before Parliament. If adopted, it would permit abortion on the broad grounds of the mother's physical, mental, and psychological health, as attested by one doctor. Few abortions, if any, will fail this test. Thus, the legislation would make abortion a criminal offence, but in terms that mean that no one would be prosecuted. But the issue is not likely to be settled in the immediate future, whatever Parliament and the courts decide. Because of the significance of abortion as a moral issue, any such decisions are bound to be rejected by those who consider them mistaken or illegitimate. Legislative and judicial decisions in this case are more likely to extend the controversy than to end it.

The Terms of the Argument

The pro-choice position is that abortion, and easy access to abortion facilities, should be a right because (i) every person should have the sole right to determine what happens in her (or his) body; (ii) pregnancy refers exclusively to a condition in a woman's body; therefore, (iii) the pregnant woman should have the sole right to decide whether to continue her pregnancy.

The pro-life position is that abortion violates the fetus's right to life. Consequently, abortion can be justified only in extreme cases, that is, when it is necessary to save the mother's life. This position does not permit abortion for any other reason, for example, physical or mental health, financial limitations, immaturity, or convenience. The argument is (i) that every human being has a right to life; (ii) that the fetus is a human being; therefore, it follows (iii) that abortion should not be allowed because it violates the fetus's right to life.[6]

These two positions are not the only ones in the dispute,[7] nor are the above arguments the only way they can be supported. They are, however, the most frequent terms of justification, and they simplify the issue considerably by stating clear-cut positions.

In each case, the core of the position is a right. The pro-choice argument is that any restrictions on abortion would violate the rights of the pregnant woman. The pro-life argument counters this by arguing that abortion would violate the right of the fetus. Thus the simplicity of the two positions derives from the rights they assert.

This simplicity, however, is achieved at a price. These positions are clear, but they are also extreme: the pro-choice position allows abortion in *all* cases, while the pro-life view allows them in almost *none*. By contrast, most Canadians hold more moderate positions. The great majority, about 63 percent, supports abortion in certain circumstances but not as a general right.[8]

The irony is that the moderate position of the majority is more difficult to justify than are the extreme positions. The problem with justifying the moderate position is to explain why one's reasons support abortion in a particular case *but not in others*. Suppose that in a particular case one thinks it should be the woman's right to control what happens in her own body. This principle, however, applies in all cases; hence, to support abortion on this basis is to endorse it universally. Conversely, if one opposes abortion in particular cases in which one believes the fetus has developed into a human being, one would have to explain why the fetus is not human in other cases. This, as will be shown in the next section, is impossible. In short, to oppose abortion on this basis in any particular situation is to oppose it in all cases. Thus, moderate positions, such as supporting abortion in some cases but not in others, may seem attractive but they can be more difficult to justify.

The more extreme pro-choice and pro-life positions do not have this difficulty, precisely because each takes the same view—support or opposition—in all cases. Although it may seem that they avoid the difficulty because of the general rights—the right to control one's body versus the right to life—that they assert, this is not so. Asserted in general terms, these rights have no particular implications for abortion. Everyone, including moderates and partisans of both extreme positions, can agree that generally individuals have rights both to life and to control their own bodies. Rather, the crucial distinction between the pro-choice and pro-life positions lies in how they see pregnancy and the fetus. This also distinguishes them from more moderate views. The pro-life position holds that abortion is always wrong because the fetus is a human being. The pro-choice position holds that abortion is always a right because pregnancy is just a bodily condition. Hence, the fetus is not an independent human being, and any claims on behalf of the fetus are subordinate to the woman's right to control her own body.

In effect, the validity of each position turns on two basic questions. First, is the fetus human? Second, if the fetus is human, does its right to life defeat the woman's right to control her own body?

Is the Fetus a Human Being?

It is clear that the fetus develops *as* a human being during pregnancy, but this does not mean that it *is* a human being, with an independent right to life, throughout this development.[9] A pro-choice advocate might argue that a zygote immediately after conception has none of the physical or psychological characteristics of human beings: it does not look human, it has no personality, and it is utterly dependent upon its mother's body for survival. On the other hand, a pro-life advocate can point to the state of the fetus just before birth: at this point it is an independent human being. Before this, the fetus is not some other kind of entity; rather, it is developing *as* a human being. Even a postconception zygote may not look human, but it has a genetic code that contains all the elements of full human development, including that of a mature personality.

There are two "pictures" here. In one picture, the fetus is a developing human being; in the other, it is just part of the tissue of its mother's body. Which picture is correct?

It is difficult to agree entirely with either picture. Each seems true at one end of the pregnancy and false at the other. Both pictures err in treating the fetus as the same thing throughout gestation—as fully human throughout, or not at all—when the central fact of gestation is that the fetus *develops* from one condition to the other. Therefore, it seems more plausible to distinguish stages within the development of the fetus. One could then say that it is "human" at some point but not earlier, for example, just after conception.

But there is a problem here. Although several stages of fetal development can be distinguished, it is not clear why any one of them should be understood as the stage at which the fetus becomes human. For example, some consider that the fetus has become human by the time that it is "viable", or capable of surviving outside the womb. It is plausible to suppose that the fetus must be human by this stage, because it is an independent being, and there may be nothing to distinguish it from a prematurely born baby. Therefore, if the premature baby is human, then the viable fetus must be human as well. But this does not mean that the fetus becomes human at viability, or that it was not human before, because there is no obvious connection between the ability to survive and being human. Ants, fish, and worms are all viable; this does not make them human. Conversely, some people with chronic illnesses or severe disabilities are not capably of surviving on their own. If viability were the criterion of humanity, it would mean, perversely, that such persons were not human and had no right to life.

In short, the fact that the fetus may be human at the point of viability does not mean that viability is the criterion of humanity or that the fetus was not human before this. There is an important difference between a fetus that is viable and one that is not. It is not that one fetus is human, in contrast to the other, but merely that it is capable of surviving outside the womb. Therefore, viability cannot be used as the criterion of fetal humanity, because there is no connection between viability and being human.

The same problem will arise if other criteria are used. One may want to regard the fetus as human by the time it indicates, say, neural activity or "quickening" (motion); but one cannot say that it *becomes* human at this stage or that it was not human earlier, because there is no connection between neural activity and being human. So the problem is that while there are many important stages in fetal development, none of them is a point at which the fetus can plausibly be said to become human or cease to be pre-human. The result is that the only point at which the fetus can be said to become human is conception.

The Problem of Arbitrary Distinction

Any criterion of fetal humanity, however reasonable it may seem, will be unavoidably arbitrary in its application. Imagine twin fetuses, A and B, conceived together, but not quite at the same time. Their development is identical, but A is just slightly ahead of B. On a continuum from conception to birth, A will always be slightly ahead of B.

Consider the point at which A becomes just barely viable. Here, B is immediately behind—almost viable, but not quite. If viability is the criterion of fetal humanity, it will follow that A is human and has a right to life, but that B is not human and may be killed without particular justification. But A and B are virtually identical, and it is a principle of justice that similar cases should be treated in similar ways. If so, what is true for A is also true for B: if A is human, then B is also. But B is not yet viable. Therefore, if B is human, viability must be abandoned as the criterion of fetal humanity.

The same problem will defeat any attempt to distinguish a stage in gestation at which the fetus becomes human. Whatever criterion is used, whether it is neural activity, quickening, or full organ development, there will be a time at which A meets the criterion (and therefore is human) but B does not; yet, because B is almost identical to A, it should be treated in the same way. This can be represented graphically by imagining a series of fetuses: C, whose development is parallel to but just behind that of B; D, who is just behind C; and so on, stretching back to Z at the point of conception.

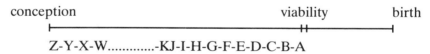

Every fetus in this series is virtually identical to those just behind and just ahead of it. This means that no point can be distinguished in this series as the stage at which the fetus becomes human. The choice of any point (for example, M) will result in some fetuses (M, L) being considered human, while other, virtually identical, fetuses (N, O) will be considered nonhuman. The distinction is arbitrary; consequently, it is impossible to identify any point of fetal humanity.

This argument may seem absurd. Even if there is no difference between A and B, there is a considerable distinction between A and Z. The problem is that one can only say that A is human and Z is not by distinguishing a point of humanity somewhere in the series, such as at M, and every such distinction is arbitrary. In respect of humanity and the right to life, therefore, all fetuses must be treated identically. Either all are human, or none are.[10]

This problem lies at the core of the abortion controversy and explains why the standard positions are pushed to extremes. The pro-life position argues that the fetus must be considered human from conception because it is human at birth and there is no point in its gestation at which humanity can be said clearly to begin. The pro-choice position counters this by denying that the fetus is human, at least up to the point of viability. As a result, the only defensible views are the extreme positions, which most people do not hold.

However, both views ignore the central fact about gestation: the fetus *develops*. It is not the same at the end as it was at the beginning. If it is human at birth, this does not mean that it has been human since conception. Although it is true (as the pro-life position insists) that the fetus is a *potential* human being throughout gestation, it follows that while it is developing it is *not* a human being and has *no* basis for any right to life. On the other hand, this is not to say that it may be aborted. To say that the fetus is not a human being while it is developing does not mean that it is just tissue in its mother's body or that its potential for human development can be ignored.

The question of abortion must be considered in terms that respect the development of the fetus. Because it is impossible to distinguish any reasonable point in this development at which the fetus becomes human, the pro-life position concludes that the fetus must therefore be regarded as human from the moment of conception. But a different conclusion might be drawn; perhaps the impossibility of establishing the point of fetal humanity comes from trying to impose an "either/or" dichotomy of human/nonhuman on a process of continuous development. If fetal development is continuous, it cannot be dichotomized; trying to locate a magic point at which the fetus becomes human or acquires the right to life simply rests upon a mistake.

Before considering the implications of this position, another view must be considered: that of women's right to control their own bodies.

The Right to Control One's Body

If women have the right to control their own bodies, it may be argued that the controversy about whether the fetus is human is irrelevant. Even if the fetus were a full human being and had a right to life, it would not follow that abortion is wrong. This is the thesis of a now-classic essay by Judith Jarvis Thomson.[11]

Her argument is based on the following analogy. She invites you to imagine that you wake up one morning in a hospital bed, connected to a famous violinist. He suffers from a potentially fatal kidney disease. During the night, a group of music lovers have kidnapped you so that your kidneys can be used to cleanse his blood. It is only for nine months: after that, he will be cured. But if you disconnect yourself sooner, the violinist will die.

Would you have the right[12] to disconnect yourself? Virtually everyone who reads this analogy answers "yes." But if you do so, the violinist will die. Wouldn't this violate the violinist's right to life? In Thomson's view,[13] the violinist has no right to use anyone else's kidneys in the first place. You might agree or refuse to let him do so, but it would be your right to decide. It is not something you owe him. If you decide to disconnect, therefore, this will not violate the violinist's right to life (even though he would die) because the right to life does not include any right to use another person's body.

Thomson intends this as an analogy to the abortion issue. She suggests that if one has the right to disconnect oneself from the violinist then one surely has the same right (that is, to abort) in the case of the fetus. She does not think that the fetus is the same as a violinist, or that it has a right to life from conception; her own view[14] is that the fetus becomes human in this sense only later in gestation. Her point is to show that even if the premise of the pro-life position were true—that the fetus has a right to life from conception—it would not follow that abortion is wrong. Is this correct?

Although virtually everyone agrees with the right to disconnect oneself in the analogy, not everyone agrees that this implies a right to abortion. One objection is that the situations are too different and that Thomson's analogy is simply too removed from the experiences of the abortion issue to be useful in illuminating it. In one way, however, this is precisely what makes the analogy useful. It focuses on a basic issue—the right to control one's own body in relation to another being's right to life—in terms that are not clouded by the grief and anger of the abortion controversy. This is why it is an example to which men and women can both relate equally. It is sometimes said that men discuss the abortion issue with less under-standing than they would have if it directly affected *them*. The specific complaint is that many men who oppose abortion would not dream of doing so if they thought that pregnancy might happen to them. Without taking sides on this issue, the advantage of Thomson's analogy is that it depicts a situation that would affect men and women equally. Although its application to the abortion issue can be contested, the analogy must be contested in a particular way. It is not enough to say that the two situations are different; it must be shown that they are different in a relevant way. Since people agree with the right to disconnect in the violinist example, those who oppose the right to abortion must show what is different between the two situations in terms that explain specifically why there is a right in one case but not in the other.

One difference that may be argued here is that the violinist example is involuntary: the reader has been kidnapped against her will, while pregnancy is the result of voluntary sexual activity. Hence, one has the right to disconnect oneself in the former case but not in the latter.

Is this true? Pregnancy is voluntary if a woman deliberately seeks to become pregnant, but it is not when she does not want to become pregnant, especially if she takes precautions against it. "Not so," the critic may reply: "Pregnancy is a foreseeable outcome of sexual intercourse, and a woman who becomes pregnant did not do the one thing guaranteed to prevent it, namely, abstain from intercourse. Instead, she took a chance by relying on a device with a known risk of failure. She took the risk willingly, so the pregnancy was voluntarily incurred." An unwanted pregnancy, however, is *not* "voluntarily incurred." The sexual activity was voluntary, but the pregnancy was not.

Consider another example: when one drives a car, one incurs a risk of accident.[15] The risk can be minimized by driving carefully and staying sober. Even so, one may be hit by a drunk driver. Is the sober driver responsible? He has done nothing to cause the accident and everything possible to avoid it. It is absurd to say that he is responsible for the accident because he could have avoided it by not using the roads.

For the same reason, it is absurd to regard an unwanted pregnancy as voluntarily incurred. In each case, there are risks of unwanted outcomes, but engaging in the activity—especially where one does everything possible to minimize the risks—does not mean that one consents to an unwanted outcome or that one is responsible for it. A woman is not any more responsible for an unwanted pregnancy than for being hit by a drunk driver.

The case is not significantly different if the pregnancy results from carelessness or ignorance, neither constitutes consent. If one goes for a walk alone at night through a tough part of town, one puts oneself in a situation where one may get mugged. This might be careless and irresponsible, but it does not mean that one consents to being mugged or that one cannot take steps to stop it.

It may be also said that Thomson's analogy fundamentally distorts the nature of pregnancy by comparing it to being kidnapped, a situation that is abnormal and a violation of a person's natural integrity. Pregnancy is not like this; it is a normal process, because it is the biological unfolding of a woman's maternal nature. Abortion interferes with this natural process; therefore it is wrong.[16]

However, even if motherhood is a natural and fulfilling condition for many women, why should every woman be bound by it? If a woman does not want to raise children at a particular time in her life, why is it not her right to make this decision? The objection that there cannot be a right to abortion because it is unnatural merely shifts the question: who should have the right to decide[17] what is "natural" and binding for any individual? Surely this right should lie with each individual. The only alternative would be for someone else, or society, to say, "*We* have decided that this is how you must live because it is your nature, whether you like it or not." This would be bizarre. One could reply, "If it is *my* nature, then *I* should have the right to determine it for myself and to change it if I choose. Indeed, if I do not have even this right, it is difficult to see what other rights I might have."

Consequently, two questions are raised by the objection: (i) what is "natural," and (ii) who should have the right to decide this for any individual? As to the first, although pregnancy is natural, this is no reason to forbid abortion. On the contrary, any legislation on this basis would imply that each person's nature is to be decided by society and that individuals do not have the right to decide this for themselves. This would assert a massive authority of society over the individual to regulate thoughts, especially the thoughts individuals develop about themselves and their identities.

This massive power is claimed by *any* attempt to regulate conduct on the basis of beliefs about what is natural for the individual; every such attempt denies to individuals the right to determine this for themselves. Therefore, abortion cannot reasonably be restricted on the grounds of its alleged unnatural character. There may be other reasons for restricting it; but if it is a question of the proper nature of women, then this is surely a matter that can rightly be decided only by each woman for herself.

This principle can be illustrated by a final reference to Thomson's analogy. The analogy requires the reader to stay connected to the violinist for nine months; otherwise, he will die. Suppose, however, that the period is only one hour. Would this make a difference?[18]

Two things might be said here. First, if one can save a life at small cost (one hour), then one ought to do so: This is a clear moral duty. Second, it should still be one's right to decide whether to do so. It is still the reader's life; she has not given away any rights over it, for example, through a contract with the violinist. The fact that it is only for one hour, and that she would have a duty to agree to it, would not justify anyone else in kidnapping her for the hour or in forcibly preventing her from disconnecting herself if she chose to do so. Thus she has a duty, but it is also her right to decide this for herself.

Suppose that someone wants to disconnect herself from the

machine (i) because her father is going to die in the next hour and she wants to be with him, or (ii) because she wants the hour free to read the newspaper. These reasons are qualitatively different: a person would be justified in disconnecting for reason (i) but it would be despicable and immoral to do so for reason (ii). However, this does not mean that there is no right to disconnect in case (ii). Since it is the right of individuals to disconnect if they choose, they must have the right to decide this for their *own* reasons. If these reasons are unjustified, then the act and the individual may be criticized as immoral. But individuals' right to act, as they choose and for their own reasons, must be respected. Otherwise, individuals are stripped of their ability to live on terms of their own choice. Here again, the right to act and the reasons for doing so must be distinguished. A right must include the right to act for one's own reasons and to decide these reasons—like the terms of one's nature and identity—for oneself.

A Critique of Thomson
The strength of Thomson's argument is that it presents the abortion issue as a special case of the more general right of individuals to decide the terms of their own lives. But what of her main claim, that a fetal right to life would not establish the impermissibility of abortion? This thesis, if correct, sidesteps the tangled controversy about when the fetus acquires the right to life. Unfortunately, this is the one part of Thomson's argument that does not work.

There is a peculiarity in the way Thomson states her thesis. She does not assert that abortion is a right, but only that it is "not impermissible." This is a weak assertion. If abortion is a right, then it must always be allowed; if it is "not impermissible," then it may be allowed only sometimes. Thomson states her thesis in the weaker form because she believes that some abortions should not be allowed. She thinks that it is a merit of her account that it permits a distinction between abortions that are permissible and those that are not.

Thomson does not go into detail, but she suggests that abortion would be permissible in the case of a fourteen-year-old rape victim but not in the case of a woman who wants an abortion in her seventh month of pregnancy to avoid having to postpone a trip. These cases are clearly different, but the question is whether Thomson's argument lets her say this. Her argument permits an abortion in the case of the young rape victim; how could it deny an abortion in the other case? The reason, presumably, is the stage of the pregnancy: by the seventh month, the fetus is fully developed. But Thomson cannot say this; she assumes (for the sake of argument) that the fetus is fully human from the point of conception. Thus, in this argument there is nothing to distinguish a fetus in the seventh month from one in the first month; the justification of an abortion in the seventh month must be the same as one in the first month.

The same problem arises with the reasons for wanting the abortion. Although the justification for having an abortion in the seventh month just to avoid postponing a trip is clearly questionable, Thomson's argument seems to permit one in the first month for this reason. At the same time, her assumption of full fetal humanity means that there is no difference between an abortion in the first month and one in the seventh month. Therefore, an abortion for any reason late in a pregnancy is the same as one earlier; there is absolutely nothing to distinguish the two. This is an absurd conclusion that Thomson herself rejects, but it is entailed by her argument. Contrary to Thomson's claim, then, her argument does not permit us to distinguish permissible from impermissible abortions.

This is not an incidental problem. Thomson wants to show that abortion would not be blocked by a fetal right to life *because* a sensible approach to abortion would distinguish permissible from impermissible cases, and it would do so by taking into consideration precisely such factors as the stage of the pregnancy, the life circumstances of the woman, and her reasons for wanting the abortion. The problem is that Thomson's account does not let these factors be considered, because she shows that abortion is not always impermissible through an argument that entails that it always *is* permissible. This suggests that the question of fetal development cannot be sidestepped by assuming it away.

In any event, Thomson's analogy fails to prove its point. The analogy supposes that one's rights have been violated in being kidnapped. But pregnancy is not like this; even where it is unwanted, the fetus does not violate a woman's rights.[19] This difference matters because, as a rule, individuals are permitted to act in cases of self-defence, or when their rights are violated, in ways that would not be justified in normal situations. For example, one may use force or even kill in self-defence, but not in other cases. Consequently, the right to disconnect oneself in the violinist example does not mean that one could take equivalent action in the case of a pregnancy. The former is an act of self-defence in response to a violation of one's rights; the latter is not.[20] Thus Thomson's analogy has no implications for abortion.

Is There a Fetal Right to Life?

The failure of Thomson's argument means that the question of the fetus's right to life cannot be sidestepped. A sensible approach to the abortion issue must accommodate both the right of women to control their lives and the need to protect developing human life. This accommodation should be anchored in the recognition that the fetus *develops*, and therefore that the case for abortion weakens as the pregnancy continues. However, this accommodation is hindered by the idea of a fetal right to life, which denies the reality of fetal development by treating it in terms of a single and dichotomous (all-or-nothing) distinction.

This section will argue two theses. First, the idea of a fetal right to life is a mistake. It is a basic misunderstanding of what such a right requires. Second, the morality of abortion is not decided by asserting or denying a fetal right to life because the justification of an act does not depend simply upon whether it violates rights. In this sense, the focus upon fetal rights is much too narrow a perspective upon the morality of abortion.

Rights and Morality

It may seem that denying the fetal right to life opens the door to abortion, because of a general view that the morality of any act depends upon how it affects the rights of others. Thus, abortion would be wrong only if it violated the fetus's rights. This view is prevalent today and attests to the great rhetorical power of rights, but it is mistaken.

In the first place, some wrong acts do not involve rights at all. It is wrong to set cats on fire, but this does not violate any rights: cats have no rights. It might be objected that the act would violate the rights of the cat's owner, but is this why it is wrong to set cats on fire? If so, there would be nothing wrong with treating one's own cat this way: imagine buying a kitten or catching a stray in order to set it on fire. Such acts are wrong, and this means that whether something is wrong is not just a matter of whether it violates someone's rights. It might then be said that such acts are wrong because they violate the cat's rights. But to talk of a cat's rights here is just a way of saying that it is wrong to set cats on fire, without actually saying this. So there is no reason to invent the cat's rights in the first place.

It would also be wrong to buy a painting with the intention of destroying it, or to strip the bark off a tree and expose it to disease, or to despoil a beautiful beach. These acts are wrong, but they do not violate rights. Consequently, those who believe that acts are only wrong if they violate rights must suppose that paintings, trees, and beaches have rights that are violated by such acts. These are like "cats' rights": just a way of saying that certain acts are wrong. Here again, however, it might be said that the rights of other persons are violated by these acts; but others have no rights to these objects. The claim that "the rights of others are violated" in such cases is fictitious: the so-called rights are simply invented, like those of the cat.

In short, "wrong" cannot be equated with the violation of rights, because some wrong acts do not involve rights at all. The converse is also true: sometimes it is not wrong to violate a person's rights. Suppose a woman sees a man drowning and takes a nearby boat to go to his aid; as she does so, the owner of the boat forbids her to use it. She would still be justified in using the boat, although this would violate the owner's rights. It might be objected that the owner has no right to forbid her use of the boat, because this violates the swimmer's right to help; but this is not quite correct. The boat is the property of the owner. He has the right to forbid the woman's use of it, but he is morally wrong to do so. Similarly, anyone who knew that someone had bought a cat in order to torture it would be justified in stealing it, even though this would violate the owner's rights. Thus, not all exercises of a right are justified, and not all violations of rights are wrong.

Consequently, if "wrong" cannot be identified with the violation of rights, there is no reason to suppose that the denial of a fetal right to life is approval of abortion. Nor is there any reason to invoke such a right in order to oppose abortion. The morality of abortion in various circumstances must be judged on its own account.

Strong and Weak Rights
Two questions now emerge. First, an act may be wrong if it violates rights, but this is not the only way an act can be wrong; sometimes it is not decisive, and sometimes it is not even relevant. Why is this? Second, it does not make sense to ascribe rights to animals and inanimate objects such as trees, beaches, and paintings. Again, why is this?

These questions can be answered by considering some of the rights Canadian citizens have and how they use them. First, the right of property or ownership: this is the legal right to use a designated good in the way one chooses, to dispose of it, and to prevent others from using it. Second, the right of contract and voluntary agreement, in which one creates rights in another by committing himself or herself to specific undertakings. This right means that the other individual is entitled to require performance of the undertaking under stipulated conditions. If A promises to pay B $50 at noon tomorrow, then B has the right to require payment as stipulated.

The rights of property and contract are a valuable means of control over one's life. They permit individuals both to act in specified ways and to require specific performances by others. Rights which limit the freedom of others by requiring stipulated performances from them may be called "strong" rights.

Strong rights, however, are not the only kinds of rights.[21] The term "rights" is also used in making claims about how persons ought to be treated. For example, it may be said that a drowning swimmer has a right to assistance, which means that those on shore have a duty to help the swimmer. But this is a much weaker kind of right;

it states only how the swimmer ought to be treated. It does not stipulate an area of free choice for the swimmer. Neither does it designate any capacity that enables the swimmer to limit the freedom of others or require specific performances from them. Thus, rights of this type are much weaker than the strong rights of property and contract.

There is, however, one similarity between strong and weak rights. Both rights entail correlative duties, that is, they stipulate how an individual ought to be treated. This similarity makes it easy to confuse the two, but the differences between them are important.

(i) The relation between rights and duties is fundamentally different in strong rights and weak rights. In a strong right, duties are imposed and controlled by the right. If one person owns a boat, then other persons have a duty not to use it; they have this duty *because* of the owner's right. With a weak right, it is exactly the reverse: a drowning swimmer's "right" to help is merely a way of saying that others have a duty to help the swimmer.

(ii) As a result, the form of the argument is different. In the case of a strong right, the inference is that "A has a right; therefore B ought (or has a duty) to do what this requires." The right provides a reason for ascribing the duty. With a weak right, it is the reverse: the argument is "A ought to be given something; therefore A has a right to it." Here the "right" does not provide any reason for the duty; it merely asserts that there is one.

(iii) A strong right includes the right to *require* the performance of the duty. The owner of a boat is entitled to require that others stop using it; if A has promised B $50, B can demand payment. This is not true of a weak right. The swimmer's right to receive help does not mean that this help is required from anyone in particular. Similarly, if C is poor and D is wealthy, D might have a duty in charity to give C $50, but C would not be entitled to require it from D. This is a distinctive feature of a strong right: it establishes a right to the performance of a specific duty in terms that include the right to limit the freedom of specific persons in stipulating how that duty will be executed.

(iv) A strong right designates an area of free choice for the individual: the owner of a car may use it, sell it, or destroy it at will. In contrast, the drowning swimmer's right to help does not involve any freedom of choice; it only means that other persons have a duty.

(v) Strong rights usually include the freedom to waive or transfer them. If A has promised B $50, B can forgive payment or transfer the right to C. The idea of a promise itself presupposes this freedom; by promising, A gives B the right to require specific conduct from A. In other words, A transfers the right over some part of their life to B. But it would make no sense to speak of a drowning swimmer waiving or transferring the right to help.

(vi) Finally, the duties are different in the two cases. In general, there is a duty to respect individuals in the exercise of their strong rights. But these rights can be exercised in ways that are morally wrong, and in these cases the duty to respect the right may be offset by other moral duties. For example, if A accepts $50 from B to torture a cat, A has a duty to do so; but it would be wrong. By contrast, a weak right cannot be exercised in a way that is morally wrong because the right itself is just a way of saying what, in that situation, ought to be done; hence the duty is morally decisive.

To summarize, a "strong" right is a capacity that is basic and controlling in relation to any duties; it defines an area in which individuals are free to live on their own terms; it protects this freedom by enabling individuals to require specific performances from others; and it usually allows individuals to extend their control over their lives by transferring the right itself if they choose. Weak rights have none of these features. They simply assert that there are certain moral duties. It is important, therefore, not to confuse this weak sense of right with its stronger cousin.

This is not a complete analysis, but it helps to answer the two questions at the beginning of this section. In answer to the first question, rights in the strong sense are sometimes not compelling or even relevant in deciding moral issues because the right may be exercised in ways that are morally wrong or because the duty to respect it may be offset by some other moral duty in that situation. An agreement to torture a cat establishes a right, but it would be wrong to respect it. Consequently, in the attempt to show that an act is wrong—whether it is torturing cats or aborting a fetus—nothing is accomplished by invoking rights.

In answer to the second question, why it does not make sense to ascribe rights to animals and inanimate objects, the reason is that rights presuppose capacities that these things lack. The idea of a right in the strong sense entails the ability (i) to decide the terms of one's life for oneself, (ii) to limit the freedom of others by requiring specific performances from them, and (iii) to place oneself under a similar obligation by transferring some of one's rights to others. When these capacities are absent, the idea of a right does not make sense. While it may be true that people should not treat cats, trees, and beaches in certain ways, there is no way to consider these things as being able to decide the terms of their own lives, or being able to limit the freedom of others, or being able to obligate themselves. So duties exist in relation to cats, trees, and beaches, but these duties do not exist because of any rights.

The same reasoning applies to the rights of the fetus. At no point in its gestation does it have the ability to judge the terms of its life for itself, to limit the freedom of others, or to obligate itself. Therefore, it is impossible for the fetus to have a right to life. The assertion of such a right implies that the fetus has capacities which it clearly lacks. Consequently, since the fetus develops as a human being throughout pregnancy, people have genuine duties to respect it, but these duties do not imply a right to life. Here, one might refer to fetal rights in the weak sense, but this would be misleading, like asserting the rights of cats or trees as a way of saying that people have duties in relation to them. In this case, the duties would be weak; the claim would say only that abortion is sometimes wrong. In reality, those who assert a fetal right to life mean that abortion is always wrong because it violates a strong right. This is impossible; it is a kind of nonsense. The idea of fetal rights, like that of cats' rights, misunderstands the nature of rights and their value.

Who Determines the Morality of Abortion?

Three conclusions flow from this analysis. First, the conclusion that the fetus is a developing human being does not mean that it has a right to life in any significant sense. The existence of such a right presupposes capacities that the fetus lacks.

Second, the absence of a fetal right to life does not settle the morality of abortion. It does not mean that people have no moral duties in relation to it. The life and potential of the fetus as a developing human being impose duties upon people to provide it with love, care, and protection. The absence of a fetal right to life means, however, that these duties can be determined more appropriately—not in an all-or-nothing fashion that applies equally throughout a pregnancy, but rather in terms that take into account both the development of the fetus during the pregnancy and a range of other factors such as a woman's right to control her own body. The conclusion is that abortion can never be stopped by another person, but it requires more stringent justification with the passage of time.

But this conclusion concerns the morality of abortion. When and by what considerations may it be justified? An entirely separate concern is, who should have the right to determine this morality? The earlier discussion of the Thomson analogy indicated that it is sometimes important to let individuals determine moral questions for themselves—even in ways that seem mistaken or improper—in order to respect their right to live on their own terms. The importance of this right, and the absence of a fetal right to life, dictate that the morality of an abortion is best determined by the woman bearing the fetus and that the right to decide this should be vested in her alone.

Notes

The author is grateful to Linda Trimble, Holly Turner, Tom Pocklington, and Alan Shandro for their comments on an earlier draft of this essay.
1. A detailed account of the political–legal controversy in Canada up to the fall of 1988 appears in Robert M. Campbell and Leslie A. Pal. *The Real Worlds of Canadian Politics* (Peterborough: Broadview Press, 1989), pp. 165–226.
2. The maximum penalty for a pregnant women was two years.
3. Following this reversal, and largely as a result of it, the law was changed. Now, if an appeal court overturns a jury acquittal, a new trial must be ordered; a conviction cannot be substituted.
4. Campbell and Pal, pp. 185–86.
5. The Supreme Court of Canada also rules that, in the future, counsel may *not* invite jurors to consider whether the law is wrong. This was important because there was never any doubt in the several Morgentaler trials that, technically, he was guilty; This was why the jury acquittals were always overturned on appeal. But Morgentaler was always acquitted because his lawyers persuaded the jurors that the law should not be enforced. In forbidding such arguments, the court sustained Morgentaler in a way that would have made his jury acquittals almost impossible to obtain in the first place.
6. For simplicity, it is assumed throughout this essay that this position would permit an abortion when it was necessary to save the mother's life.
7. For example, there has been a major change in the way the pro-life position is generally stated. Today, the objection is that abortion violates the fetal right to life. A generation ago, it was that abortion was wrong. The criticisms of this essay are directed primarily against the contemporary version.
8. Lorne Bozinoff and Peter MacIntosh, "Majority Believe Woman's Request Is Paramount in Abortion Decision," Gallup Canada, Inc., August 24, 1989: 26 percent of the respondents indicated that abortion should always be legal, 10 percent said it should never be legal, and 63 percent said it should be legal only under "certain circumstances." The certain circumstances included dangers to health (84 percent), conception due to rape or incest (78 percent), a strong chance of a serious defect in the baby (75 percent), agreed upon by the woman and her doctor (55 percent), within three months of conception (49 percent), very low family income (39 percent), and within five months of conception (31 percent). The same poll found that a majority of both men (58 percent) and women (55 percent) supported an abortion in cases where the woman requests one but the man disagrees.
9. For more elaborate arguments along the lines indicated in this section, see Roger Wertheimer, "Understanding the Abortion Argument," *Philosophy and Public Affairs*, Vol. 1, No. 1 (Fall 1971), pp. 67–95, and Michael Tooley, "Abortion and Infanticide," *Philosophy and Public Affairs*, Vol. 2, No. 1 (Fall 1972), pp. 37–65.
10. It may be objected that society can draw the distinction anywhere it chooses. This is true, but irrelevant. The fact that society has the legal power to decide at what point the fetus becomes human for the purposes of legal protection does not mean that any such decision would be

reasonable or just. With the same legal power, it might declare that people with a particular skin colour are not human.

11. Judith Jarvis Thomson, "A Defence of Abortion," *Philosophy and Public Affairs*, Vol. 1, No. 1 (Fall 1971), pp. 47–66.

12. The following discussion takes some liberty with Thomson's argument by treating it in terms of whether one would have "a right" to disconnect, whereas she states it as whether doing so would be "morally permissible." This is done because Thomson expressly argues from "the mother's right to decide what happens in and to her body" (48) and because it seems that the force of her analogy is that it treats the abortion issue as a special case of being free to determine the terms of one's own life. The issue is better stated in these terms: it allows for a distinction, which Thomson does not make, between the morality of an act and the right to decide this for oneself.

13. Thomson, pp. 55–56.

14. Thomson, pp. 47–48.

15. See Thomson's own discussion of this issue at pp. 57–59.

16. In one of her examples, Thomson compares a woman's body to a house (52–53). The body, however, is natural, whereas a house is artificial, and this difference affects the kinds of rights one can have in each. One has the right to sell one's own house, to own several, and to live in someone else's. It is silly to talk of a right to one's body in any of these ways. Because the body is natural, it is presupposed by, and limits, one's rights; or so it is objected.

17. It may seem odd to refer here to "deciding," rather than discerning or discovering, what is natural. The issue, however, is not just the claim that "x is natural," but the authority to decide that one must do x because x is natural.

18. Thomson considers a somewhat similar distinction between a Good Samaritan and a Minimally Decent Samaritan (62–65). However, she does not distinguish the question of whether an act is justified from that of whether the individual should have the right to decide this.

19. See Baruch Brody, "Thomson on Abortion," *Philosophy and Public Affairs*, Vol. 1, No. 3 (Spring 1971), pp. 335–37; John Finnis, "The Rights and Wrongs of Abortion: A Reply to Judith Thomson," *Philosophy and Public Affairs*, Vol. 2, No. 2 (Winter 1973), especially pp. 141–44; and Thomson's reply to Finnis, "Rights and Deaths," at pp. 146–59 of the same issue.

20. Technically, the fetus has no right to the use of its mother's body, but this does not mean—as the analogy suggests—that it violates the mother's right in doing so.

21. Another category includes rights as entitlements, that is, the rights that arise when individuals are entitled under a system of rules to be treated in specific ways. These are intermediate between strong and weak rights.

CRITIQUE

The most challenging feature of Don Carmichael's thought-provoking essay is his thesis that one can—and indeed, should—hold contrary positions on the morality and legality of abortion. The commonly accepted position is that one's views on the legality of abortion must follow one's views of its morality.

It is usually held that there are three views about the morality of abortion, each with its corresponding position on abortion law. Those who believe that abortion is usually akin to murder are in the pro-life camp, in which case they must favour a law that makes abortion a criminal act, except in extraordinary circumstances. At the other extreme, those who believe that abortion is not morally wrong are pro-choice, in which case they must oppose any law forbidding it. Finally, those who believe (like most Canadians) that abortion is sometimes morally right and sometimes wrong are moderate, in which case they must favour a law that makes some abortions permissible and others criminal.[1] Carmichael challenges this neat scheme. He argues for a moderate position regarding the morality of abortion and an extreme, pro-choice, position regarding its legality.

I do not argue that Carmichael's position is mistaken; indeed, I attempt to strengthen one of his arguments. The reason for my comparatively gentle treatment of the essay's thesis is quite simple: I do not know whether he is right or wrong. It seems clear, however, that he ignores some implications of his arguments—especially implications relating to the idea of the fetus as a developing human being—that are inhospitable to his own position. The object, then, is to show that Carmichael's view should not be accepted without further reflection.

The essay makes seven major claims: (i) woman have a right to control their own bodies; (ii) there is no nonarbitrary point in the gestation of fetuses at which they can be said to be human; (iii) fetuses do not have a right to life (or, for that matter, any other right) at any point in their gestation; (iv) acts can be wrong without being violations of rights; (v) although fetuses do not have rights, they are developing *as* human beings, so that "the case for abortion weakens as the pregnancy continues;" indeed, "the life and potential of the fetus as a developing human being impose duties upon people to provide it with love, care, and protection;" (vi) it is important for individuals to have the right to decide some moral questions for themselves, even when others think their decisions are wrong; (vii) because the right to decide moral questions for oneself is so important, and in the light of the fact that fetuses have no rights, it should be the right solely of the woman bearing a fetus to decide whether to abort it.

Carmichael bases his moderate position on the *morality* of abortion on the claim that fetuses, though they are not human beings, are developing *as* human beings. He maintains that people have duties to fetuses that become more stringent as they mature. Abortions late in pregnancy are likely to be immoral.[2] His extreme pro-choice position on the *legality* of abortion, in contrast, is based on two considerations: (i) that it is important for people to have an extensive right to decide moral questions for themselves, and (ii) that fetuses have no rights. It follows from these propositions (although Carmichael does not say so) that there should be no law limiting the conditions under which women may procure abortions.

Something must first be said about Carmichael's denial of fetal rights. Carmichael makes an error here. Readers who notice this error may underestimate the strength of his argument. He maintains that, for any being to have a right, it must have three abilities: to decide the terms of its life for itself, to limit the freedom of others by requiring specific performances from them, and to take on obligations by transferring some of its rights to others. These requirements are far too demanding. Three-year-olds can't meet them; neither can the senile or those with severe mental illnesses. But all these people have rights, so Carmichael must be wrong.

In some contexts, it would be right to focus on this mistake, but in regard to the issue of fetal rights it is far more important to defend the general thrust of Carmichael's line of argument than to attack it. Although its criteria for possessing rights are too demanding, no *plausible* less-demanding criterion or criteria yield the conclusion that fetuses have rights. It is sometimes maintained that fetuses have rights, specifically a right to life, simply because they are members of the species *homo sapiens*. But this is untenable; mere membership in a biological species cannot be the basis of rights. The claim that a fetus has a right to life simply because it is generically human carries as little weight as the claim that a mosquito has a right to life simply because it is generically an insect. Thus, in spite of the inadequacy of its premises, the conclusion that fetuses have no rights is surely correct.

This means that the dominant pro-life argument is refuted. Only the moderate and pro-choice positions remain to be taken seriously, and Carmichael takes both positions very seriously. He supports a moderate position with regard to the morality of abortion and a pro-choice position with regard to its legality. It is this combination that raises doubts. Three of these doubts will be explored, mainly by making use of a line of reasoning employed by Carmichael himself, namely, that it is arbitrary to make distinctions between stages in the continuous process of human development.

In the first place, Carmichael maintains that people have duties to fetuses that become more powerful as the fetuses mature. This can be inferred from Carmichael's contention that "the case for abortion weakens as the pregnancy continues." But why do people have duties to fetuses at all, let alone more demanding duties to more mature ones? Carmichael insists that beings can have rights only if they have characteristics that generate rights. The same surely holds true of duties; if people have duties toward beings, this must surely be because those beings have characteristics that constitute the grounds of the duties.[3] Unfortunately, Carmichael does not provide a basis for people's duties to fetuses.

Suppose that this oversight could be remedied without difficulty. Assume that some characteristic, C, is the basis of people's duty to provide relatively mature fetuses with love, care, and protection. Assume further that a particular fetus possesses C at time z, so that people then have duties to it. Now bring in Carmichael's postulate that it is arbitrary to make distinctions in the continuous process of human development. Does it not follow that the fetus possesses C at time y (a second, a minute, or an hour before time z), and also at times w, v, u, and so on, right back to the moment of conception? If so (and it is difficult to see how Carmichael can avoid this line of reasoning), people have duties to fetuses at all stages of their maturation. Moreover, they have no reason to believe that these duties become more stringent as the fetus matures. They must give it love, care, and protection from beginning to end.

Surprisingly, Carmichael's view of the duties owed to fetuses seems to support a pro-life stance. It is superior to other defences of that position in not invoking the preposterous idea that fetuses have rights. This reasoning cannot give much comfort to pro-lifers unless they can find a basis for duties to fetuses. But it is even less congenial to Carmichael's effort to defend a position that is morally moderate but legally pro-choice. It looks as if Carmichael can maintain a position that is pro-choice in law only by rejecting duties to fetuses and thereby adopting a position that is pro-choice also in morality.

A second, similar, problem arises in connection with Carmichael's view that it is very important that people should have the right to decide some moral questions for themselves, even when others regard their decisions as mistaken or perverse. Few people in this dominantly liberal culture reject this generalization. Many who regard as wrong such practices as homosexual acts, suicide, and interracial marriage believe that those who choose such conduct have a right to do so. But there are also definite limits to this tolerance. Except in rare circumstances, violence against persons or property are not regarded as acceptable ways of living life on one's own terms. Broadly speaking, people are content to let other people live as they choose only when they do not regard the conduct as very harmful to themselves or others.

This observation affects Carmichael's argument. He maintains that the case for abortion weakens as pregnancy continues and, by implication, that people have duties to care for and protect at least relatively mature fetuses. This suggests that, in his view, abortion in the later stages of pregnancy inflicts serious harm on another. But if this is so, abortion late in pregnancy must be (except in unusual circumstances) quite wrong, wrong enough that it should be impermissible even though fetuses have no rights and women have the right to control their own bodies. If abortion is very wrong in the later stages of pregnancy and if it is arbitrary to make distinctions between stages in a continuous process of fetal development, then abortion must be wrong also in the earliest stages of pregnancy. Once again it appears that, if Carmichael wants to maintain a pro-choice perspective on the legality of abortion, he must recant his moderate perspective on its morality.

Finally, the essay runs into problems with regard to infanticide. It maintains that fetuses have no rights but does not apply a similar yardstick to children. The precept that it is arbitrary to make distinctions between stages in the continuous process of fetal development has not only backward-looking implications (from an advanced stage of fetal development back to conception) but also forward-looking ones (from any stage of fetal development forward to the stages beyond viability or birth). If fetuses, lacking the characteristics requisite for any being to have rights, do not have rights, neither do infants or young children. Therefore, unless people do have, as Carmichael maintains, a duty to provide love, care, and protection to newborns, infanticide is no less defensible than abortion.

All that can be said here is that infanticide is almost always repugnant. I lack any principle with which to support this sentiment; it is for this reason that I do not know whether Carmichael is right or wrong. He *should* be right, but it cannot be said that he is right until defensible grounds—something stronger than my sentiments— are provided for saying that there is a point at which people acquire a duty to give rightless fetuses care and protection.

Notes

1. I hasten to emphasize that I do not subscribe to the view that whatever is deemed immoral should be illegal. Like Carmichael, I believe that there are wide realms in which people should have the right to decide for themselves how to live their lives.
2. As the "likely" in this sentence suggests, Carmichael's argument is oversimplified here. He does not maintain that stage of gestation is the only consideration relevant to the morality of abortion. However, this space-saving oversimplification is not used to do injustice to his position.

3. This does not imply that all duties must be based on the same characteristics. It seems more than likely that one's duty to one's wife, one's
employer, and a drowning swimmer are based on different
characteristics.

Discussion Questions

1. What are the clearest circumstances in which abortion should be permitted, and the clearest circumstances in which it should be forbidden?
Is it possible to allow and forbid abortion in these cases consistently,
or do the reasons for allowing abortion in one case make it impossible
to forbid it in the other?

2. Neither Carmichael nor Pocklington take very seriously the claim that
people have rights and duties because they are members of the same
biological species. Could the fetal right to life be based on this view?

3. If, as Carmichael argues, people acquire duties to the fetus as it develops, why doesn't the fetus acquire rights at the same time?

4. Pocklington suggests that there may be limits on people's duties to
respect the rights of others to live on their own terms. Carmichael
provides an example from Thomson: a woman who wants an abortion
in the seventh month of pregnancy to avoid the inconvenience of having
to postpone a trip abroad. This would be wrong. But should the woman
have the right, as Carmichael argues, to decide this? If not, how could
women have the right in any other case?

5. Suppose you were kidnapped, as in Thomson's analogy, but the other
person on the machine is your parent. Would you have the right to
disconnect yourself?

6. Carmichael's view means that infants do not have the right to life. Does
this justify infanticide?

Further Readings

The legal and political background of the abortion controversy in Canada
up to 1988 is outlined in Chapter Four of Robert M. Campbell and Leslie
A. Pal, *The Real Worlds of Canadian Politics* (Peterborough: Broadview
Press, 1989). The majority opinion by Justice Blackmun in the leading
American case, *Roe v. Wade*, also provides useful background.

   Judith Jarvis Thomson's article, "A Defence of Abortion," is lively and very readable. It was published originally in *Philosophy and Public Affairs*, Vol. 1 (Fall 1971), pp. 47–66, and has been widely reproduced since.

John Noonan argues that abortion is almost always morally wrong, not because it violates a fetal right to life, but because the fetus is human, in "An Almost Absolute Value in History," in *The Morality of Abortion: Legal and Historical Perspectives*, ed. John T. Noonan (Cambridge, Mass.: Harvard University Press, 1970), pp. 1–59.

Roger Wertheimer's "Understanding the Abortion Argument" outlines the logic of the argument, distinguishing liberal and conservative positions, and arguing that each is the other, "turned inside out," in *Philosophy and Public Affairs*, Vol. 1 (1971), pp. 67–95. Jane English argues that the abortion issue cannot be resolved by deciding whether the fetus is a person. She also argues that the liberal and conservative positions are both too extreme in "Abortion and The Concept of A Person," *Canadian Journal of Philosophy*, Vol. 5 (1975), pp. 233–43. L.W. Sumner argues a similar view in Abortion and Moral Theory (Princeton, N.J.: Princeton University Press, 1981). His view is criticized by Lorenne Clark, "Reply to Professor Sumner," in *Canadian Journal of Philosophy*, Vol. 4 (1974), pp. 183–90.

Many of these articles (and others) can be found in Joel Feinberg, (ed.), *The Problem of Abortion*, 2nd ed. (Belmont, Cal.: Wadsworth, 1984).

CHAPTER 7

Native Canadians and the Right to Self-Government

Both Tom Pocklington, the author of the main essay in this chapter, and Don Carmichael, the critic, are proponents of Native self-government. This chapter, however, is not mainly a defence of that position; it is about *how* to argue for (or, for that matter, against) Native self-government.

Pocklington's main claim is that both supporters and opponents of Native self-government have placed far too much emphasis on moral rights and far too little on considerations of well-being. He maintains that greater emphasis on well-being would yield arguments that are more cogent both philosophically and politically. In particular, he holds that arguments based on moral rights do not carry as much philosophical weight as is commonly believed, because sometimes they should be qualified, overridden, or waived by those who possess them. He also holds that, politically, such arguments are insensitive to people's concrete needs, interests, and aspirations.

Carmichael holds that moral rights are far more powerful, both philosophically and politically, than Pocklington allows. He maintains that the authority of any social group must be based on the fundamental moral right of individuals to decide how to live. In his view, Pocklington's emphasis on the well-being of both Native people and non-Natives fails to establish a strong case for Native self-government. It fails because it allows non-Natives to dismiss Native claims simply by stating that the satisfaction of those claims would diminish their well-being. Carmichael also argues that Pocklington's failure to recognize the force of moral rights leads inescapably to embarrassing positions on related issues, such as abortion and the censorship of pornography.

E S S A Y

Canadian Native leaders are increasingly, and vociferously, demanding the recognition of a right of Native self-determination and thereby,
for the Native collectivities that choose it, a right of self-government.
These demands are being made not only by Indian leaders, but also
by leaders of the other constitutionally recognized aboriginal peoples,
the Inuit and the Métis. Should such rights be embodied in law, perhaps
by constitutional entrenchment, and in political practice? This essay's
answer is yes; but its purpose is not the defend that opinion. It does
not deal with *what* the answer to the question should be, but with
how the question should be answered.

Considerations of Native self-government usually employ one
or more of three approaches: the legal approach, the political–
institutional approach, and the rights-based approach. This essay
will discuss a fourth approach, the well-being approach, and argue that
it is morally and politically more cogent than the others. This
approach brings the disagreements between those who favour and
those who oppose increased Native political self-determination[1]
down to earth, but not so far down that the issue becomes mired
in a swamp of pragmatism and divorced from considerations of
principle.

Preliminary Considerations

Before this discussion goes any further, a straightforward question
needs to be answered: Why should Canadians care about Native
self-government? To answer that question, it is unnecessary to enter
into complex questions about the historical injustices endured by
the first permanent human residents of the country now known as
Canada. It is ample reason for concern that the conditions of life
of the Native peoples, who together are the fourth-largest ethnic
group in Canada[2] are abysmal. Consider the following comparisons
between status Indians (who are not worse off than other Native
people) and the Canadian population as a whole.[3] The average life
expectancy of Indians is forty-three years, compared with sixty-seven
years for the population as a whole. The Indian infant mortality rate
is double that of the entire population. Accidents, violence, and
poisoning
account for one-third of all Indian deaths, as compared with 9 percent for the population as a whole. The Indian suicide rate is about
three times the national average, and suicide accounts for over one-
fourth of the "accidental" deaths of Indians between the ages of

fifteen and thirty-four. It is estimated that 50 to 60 percent of Indian illnesses and deaths are alcohol-related.

The annual per capita income of status Indians is about one-third of the national average. Their unemployment rate is about five times the national average, and, of employed Indians the percentage who work less than half a year is three times the national percentage. Over half the Indian reserve population receives social assistance or welfare payments, compared with 6 percent of the national population. Well under half of reserve houses have running water, and only about one-fourth have indoor toilets, indoor baths, or telephones. As to formal education, about 80 percent of working-age Indians have completed grade eight or less, compared with about 37 percent nationally. At the other extreme, only 5 percent of Indians, as compared with 27 percent of the population as a whole, have completed some postsecondary education. Native people (not just Indians) constitute less than 4 percent of the Canadian population but almost 9 percent of the inmate population of federal penitentiaries. In Saskatchewan and Manitoba, more than half the people incarcerated in provincial correctional institutions are Native.

The picture of Native life that emerges from these statistics is grim. It becomes even uglier when one reads the vivid portrayals of the suffering and despair of particular Native individuals and communities in such works as Maria Campbell's *Halfbreed*, Heather Robertson's *Reservations are for Indians*, and Anastasia Shkilnyk's *A Poison Stronger than Love: The Destruction of an Ojibwa Community*,[4] even though these writers reveal the vibrant as well as the terrible aspects of Native life.

A number of thoughtful Native leaders, as well as Native and non-Native observers, have argued that the picture would be brighter if Native people acquired more control over their own destiny. At the same time, no one sees Native self-government as a panacea. They may be right or they may be wrong, but there is no denying that it *matters* whether they are right or wrong. Those who care about anything at all in their role as citizens should care about the desirability and practicability of proposals that might significantly improve the lot of some of the worst-off of their fellow citizens. That is why Canadians should care about the issue of Native self-government.

This essay will not attack or defend increased Native political self-determination. It will propose an approach that is superior to the three now commonly employed. It will first compare the well-being approach with the other three approaches. The rights-based approach is the only serious competitor to the well-being approach, because basic rights cannot be ignored in any treatment of Native self-government. Accordingly, the main argument of the rest of the essay, its central thesis, is that too much attention has been given to moral rights and too little to considerations of well-being.

The essay then discusses the limitations of rights-based arguments that favour increased Native political self-determination. This is followed by a consideration of the limitations of rights-based arguments opposed to Native self-government. Then it is argued that a perspective that places much greater emphasis on the well-being of both Native and non-Native people provides a far sounder basis, both politically and philosophically, for assessing Native claims to greater political self-determination than do perspectives that focus exclusively on moral rights. Finally, instead of summarizing the earlier arguments, this essay attempts to clarify and defend its central thesis by rebutting two important objections to it.

Approaches: Rights and Well-Being

Three main approaches are taken to the issue of native self-government: the legal, the political–institutional, and the rights-based. Sometimes these approaches are combined; nevertheless, they are all seriously flawed.

Those who employ the legal approach attempt to develop or undermine arguments for Native self-government by appealing to and interpreting practices, documents, and rules that have, or can be argued to have, legal standing. Until recently, most lawyers whose field is Native law have been preoccupied with other matters, especially land claims. But issues relating to self-government are now coming to occupy the foreground, as a result of the shift of attention of Native leaders in that direction. Lawyers have already produced some imaginative and well-considered pieces on the subject,[5] and they will undoubtedly produce some worthwhile insights concerning Native self-government. Nevertheless, the legal approach has inherent moral and political limitations. The most that lawyers can do is explain what can and cannot be done legally in regard to Native self-government. They cannot say (*qua* lawyers) whether Native people have a *moral* right to govern themselves and whether it is *desirable* for Native people to have greater political autonomy.

The legal approach has political as well as moral limitations. It is a safe bet that no Canadian court will find that any group of aboriginal people has a surviving right to govern itself.[6] Even in the unlikely event that the Supreme Court of Canada did issue such a ruling, it is inconceivable that the court system would become involved in designing and endorsing systems of government adapted to the needs and aspirations of the extraordinarily diverse Native collectivities in Canada. The decision whether to endorse some type of Native self-government is inescapably a political question. Although lawyers can be very perceptive and sensitive in developing moral and political arguments, when they do so they are not employing the legal approach.

Those who employ the political–institutional approach concern themselves both with the practicability of Native self-government in general and with the workability of various ways in which self-government might be embodied in particular. One of the best books on Native self-government, Michael Asch's *Home and Native Land*, generally takes this approach. Asch assumes that increased Native political self-determination is desirable and gives reasons for believing that one way of implementing it is especially promising in the light of Canadian political realities. Similarly, in a recent book, Donald V. Smiley, one of Canada's ablest political scientists, disposes of the question of the desirability of Native self-government with the observation that "some considerable progress towards an enhanced range of aboriginal self-government is likely in the foreseeable future."[7] His discussion of Native self-government concentrates on institutional forms that could be adopted by Native governments; obstacles to self-government deriving from the Constitution Act, 1982; the difficulties involved in fitting such governments into the fabric of Canadian federalism; and the conflicts between some of the basic values of aboriginal people and those of other Canadians.[8]

There is no denying the relevance of political–institutional inquiries to the issue of Native self-government. Any consideration of enhanced Native self-determination involves the application of principles to a set of particular cases; otherwise, they wouldn't be *principles* at all! It follows that a defensible case, either for or against, depends not only on the invocation of the right principles but also on a clear understanding of the particular cases to which the principles are to be applied. Thus, even the most enthusiastic proponent of Native self-government should be grateful to be reminded, for example, that the term "Native people" refers to a wide range of individuals and collectivities, which are unlikely to be served well by a single form of government; that there are reasons why invoking the notion of "sovereignty" may be inimical to the interests of native and non-Native people alike; and that there will be difficulties in accommodating self-governing Native communities within the well-established Canadian institution of "executive federalism."[9] It is certainly a merit of the political–institutional approach that it recognizes the inescapably political character of self-government. However, it suffers from a serious limitation: it simply does not address the question of whether increased Native self-government is desirable.

The rights-based approach, whether it is used for or against Native self-government, invokes fundamental moral rights. Proponents of Native self-government commonly appeal to a God-given, or human, or natural right either of aboriginal peoples to control their own destiny, or of distinct peoples to national self-determination, or both. Opponents commonly appeal to fundamental rights, which, though embodied in law, are thought to be moral as well as legal rights. Pre-eminent among the moral rights invoked by opponents of Native self-government is the right of equality before the law.

The rights-based approach is not unique in its concern with rights. The concern of anyone who favours, opposes, or hasn't made up his or her mind about Native self-government can be expressed in the question: Should such a right be embodied in law? That question is as central to the well-being approach as it is to the rights-based approach. What is distinctive about the rights-based approach is that it takes moral rights as *fundamental* to political argument. The most common pattern of reasoning employed in rights-based arguments is as follows: X (an individual or a group) has a moral right to A. Those who have a moral obligation to respect X's moral right to A are not doing so. Therefore, X's moral right should be made more secure by enacting it as a legal right.

Since rights play a prominent role in the well-being approach as well as in the rights-based approach, it is important to clarify the difference between the two approaches. For purposes of illustration, it is useful to deal with a subject other than Native self-government. Suppose that Alice (a proponent of the rights-based approach) and Bob (a proponent of the well-being approach) are both distressed by discrimination against homosexuals. Basing her views on what she regards as a fundamental moral right to treatment that ignores differences in sexual orientation, Alice calls for a law prohibiting discrimination on the basis of sexual orientation. If Alice has her way, homosexuals will acquire a *legal* right to nondiscrimination based on a prior *moral* right to nondiscrimination.

Bob also seeks a legal right of nondiscrimination against homosexuals. However, instead of arguing that this legal right would simply enact a prior moral right, Bob argues not only that enacting the legal right would increase the well-being of homosexuals but also that it would increase, or at least not decrease, the well-being of heterosexuals. To do this, Bob has to advance "positive" arguments showing, for example, that homosexuals are just as likely as heterosexuals to be good mathematics teachers and "negative" arguments showing, for example, that homosexuals are less likely than heterosexuals to molest children. Despite the fundamental difference in the structure of his reasoning, Bob could be as enthusiastic as Alice in supporting the enactment of legal rights beneficial to homosexuals.

This analogy can be applied to considerations of self-government rights. With her rights-based approach, Alice might maintain that

Native people should have a legal right to increased political self-determination because they have a prior moral right to it. Or she might maintain that they should have no such right, because while there are no moral rights connected to aboriginality, there is a moral right of all people to equality before law. Likewise, Bob, with his well-being approach, might either support or oppose the enactment of a legal right of Native self-government, depending on whether or not he saw such a right as conducive to well-being. Thus, the difference between the rights-based approach and the well-being approach is indeed a difference in *approach*. Adherents of the two approaches may agree or disagree about which rights should be enacted into law.

The rights-based approach does not share the fundamental short-coming of the legal and political–institutional approaches. Unlike them, it *does* address the overriding question: Should a legal right of Native self-government be enacted? Why, then, does this essay commend yet another approach to the issue? The full answer occupies the rest of the essay, but some general comments are in order here. The rights-based approach is defective philosophically and, especially, politically. People have moral rights; even groups of people may have moral rights. And if there are collective rights, an aboriginal right of self-government may be among them. But there is no compelling *argument*, as opposed to innumerable *assertions* and implicit *assumptions*, that Native people do have a moral right of self-government. This absence provides a somewhat insubstantial foundation on which to base a position on an important political issue.

But the objections to the rights-based approach presented in this essay are not aimed primarily at the presence or absence of its basic philosophical underpinnings. Even if these moral rights exist, the rights-based approach needs to be supplemented by much fuller attention to considerations of well-being. In discussions concerning Native self-government, far too much emphasis has been placed on moral rights and far too little on considerations of well-being. This imbalance needs to be redressed.

The rights-based approach has two major limitations. One has to do with the *tone* of political discourse, the other with its *substance*. Both defects stem from the same feature of rights. Rights are "things" that one either has or lacks; they cannot be possessed in greater or smaller measure. They can differ in the degree to which they are *respected* by the public and *protected* by state officials, but not in the degree to which they are *possessed*. Rights, unlike well-being, which can increase or decrease in degrees, can only be conceded or denied.

This feature of rights has consequences for the tone of political discourse. Because rights do not exist in degrees, appeals to rights in any controversy tend to elicit outright denials or countervailing appeals to opposed rights. If one maintains that homosexuals have a moral right to be assessed by the same criteria as heterosexuals for appointment to teaching positions in the public schools, the opposition's inclination is either flatly to deny the contention or to invoke the right of school boards to decide what sorts of persons are suitable for employment, rather than to engage in an extended discussion of the advantages and disadvantages of possible policies for the employment of teachers. Appeals to rights are conducive to intransigence and uncongenial to dialogue, negotiation, and compromise.[10]

The rights-based approach, unqualified by considerations of well-being, also has deleterious consequences for the substance of political discourse. Important political innovations, such as the introduction of medicare, the enactment of a charter of rights, and the deregulation of airlines, have different effects on different people. Some of these effects occur abruptly, others gradually; some are foreseeable, others are difficult to predict. Most involve shifts of benefits and burdens from some segments of the population to others. Not surprisingly, people who are likely to be affected by major proposed innovations want to discuss the effects at some length. The rights-based approach, however, inhibits such discussion. By its very nature, it rules out attention to the concrete implications of political innovations for particular individuals and groups. Only implications for the protection of moral rights are to the point. This neglect of the concrete, which is deplorable in general, is particularly ill-suited to the issue of Native self-government.

The well-being approach considers practices, institutions, and policies as better the more they promote (or the less they inhibit) the well-being of the people affected by them. "Well-being" is not used here in the narrow, utilitarian sense to refer to a maximum balance of pleasure over pain. It is used as a "convoy concept"[11] to refer to all the qualities of life that make life better rather than worse. It is assumed here that some components of a good life, such as knowledge and loving parents, are trans-cultural, while others, such as membership in an extended family and punctuality, are culture-specific. This perspective ignores the distinction between the very general requirements of a good life, such as having close friends, and very particular ones, such as owning electrical appliances. It concentrates on the *quality* of people's lives rather than on their *entitlements*. It is goal-oriented rather than entitlement-oriented.

Much more could be said about the differences between the moral-rights and well-being approaches, but the contrast is clear enough. The issue of Native self-government can be addressed cogently only if more attention is paid to well-being and less to moral rights. The next section considers some shortcomings of rights-based arguments in favour of increased Native political self-determination.

Limitations of Rights-Based Arguments

Even if there are an aboriginal right and a right of national self-determination that favour increased political self-determination for Native collectivities, rights-based arguments for Native self-government have severe limitations.

Few, if any, rights are *absolute* in the sense that they cannot be limited or suspended under certain circumstances. This is recognized in the Canadian Charter of Rights and Freedoms, which states that the rights enumerated in it are subject to "reasonable" limitations consistent with the maintenance of a "free and democratic society." Even if there are some absolute rights, such as the right not to be subjected to cruel and unusual punishment, political rights are not among them. Even political rights regarded as especially precious in Canada, such as the right to vote, are limited: children and prison inmates, among others, are denied this right. Canadian law provides for the limitation or abrogation of political rights during periods of real or apprehended emergency. Finally, and perhaps most directly relevant here, the jurisdiction of various governments (which may be considered as rights to enact and enforce laws within a given area) are not written in stone. They may be constricted or expanded.

The Charter is not the last word on rights and wrongs, and therefore its failure to treat political rights as absolute is not a decisive consideration. But deeper reflection about the nature of political rights confirms that they are not absolute and reveals the limitations of arguments for Native self-government based upon them. It is a characteristic of most rights, and perhaps all political rights, that those who possess them are in a position to exercise them or not exercise them (or, in some cases, to exercise them to less than the full extent permissible), as they see fit. For example, anyone who has loaned money repayable on a certain date is entitled to exercise the right by "calling in" the loan, waive it by forgiving the loan, or moderate it by requiring repayment of only part of the loan. Native collectivities, even if they have a fundamental right of sovereign statehood, are in the same position. They can exercise the right by declaring their sovereignty and putting it into effect, waive it by confirming the status quo, or—assuming the compliance of other governments—moderate it by assuming exclusive jurisdiction over only some areas of governmental activity.

These are genuine alternatives facing Native decision-makers, even assuming that they have an unconstrained right of political

self-determination. The hostility of the federal and provincial governments and of many non-Natives to the idea of sovereign Native
nation-states might well lead Native decision-makers to reject sovereign statehood as impractical and leave them with the question of
how much more modest an alternative to pursue. Moreover, in view
of the great diversity of Native peoples, the various collectivities
probably aspire to different kinds of self-government.

The initial aboriginal right or right of national self-determination
provides no assistance in addressing these issues. In order to decide
whether and to what extent to exercise a right, it is necessary to
appeal to something other than the right itself. The obvious candidate for that role seems to be well-being. In any case, a rights perspective, by virtue of its inability to specify the scope of self-government
that should be sought by Native collectivities, has serious limitations
as a standpoint from which to argue for increased Native political
self-determination.

A second and closely related point is that it is sometimes not
merely the case that right-holders *may* moderate or forego their
rights, but that they *should* do so. Returning to the loan example, if
the lender were wealthy and the borrower destitute, and if they
were close friends, many would maintain that the lender would be
committing a moral wrong by failing to forgive the loan entirely or
requiring only partial, token repayment of it. This point has direct
relevance to the issue of Native self-government. To mention only
one example, the attainment of extensive jurisdiction by one class of
Native people, such as those with a well-established territorial base,
could seriously worsen the prospects of others such as urban Métis
and non-status Indians. It could be argued that this is not merely
an imprudent but a morally reprehensible exercise of a right. The
problem here is the same as in the first case: in order to decide
whether or not a right should be exercised, or exercised fully, it is
impossible to appeal to the right itself. Some other consideration or
considerations must be invoked. Considerations of well-being are the
appropriate ones for this purpose.

A third point is that a Native right of political self-determination
can be overridden, either in whole or in part. Those who take rights
seriously will infringe them only in exceptional circumstances, that
is, only when a great good is likely to be achieved or a major evil
averted. The possibility must be acknowledged, however, that a
Native right of political self-determination may be properly overridden even in circumstances in which Native collectivities do not
wish to abridge or relinquish it. This might occur if Native communities forbade other governments to run highways across their
lands. But when are the grounds weighty enough to justify the
infringement of a right? Again, appeal to the right itself provides no

solution; an independent standard, the standard of well-being, needs to be invoked.

The final limitation on rights-based arguments for increased Native political self-determination has to do with the motivation for claiming rights rather than the justification for fixing their scope. People do not usually claim rights frivolously or gratuitously; they claim them because they believe that respect for them would contribute to the well-being of those on behalf of whom they are claimed. Although advocates of Native self-government usually first appeal to notions of aboriginal rights, sovereignty, and national self-determination, they soon turn to general benefits such as enhancing self-respect and particular benefits such as more effective child-welfare services that might flow from increased autonomy. It is perfectly reasonable that they should argue in this way. Why would anyone advocate the protection of rights that hold no promise of benefits? But if the motivational point of claiming rights is the acquisition of benefits, motivational consistency requires that, whenever benefits could be increased by abridging or waiving rights, that is the appropriate course of action. For example, if an Indian band could live in greater harmony with neighboring communities by claiming less than an unqualified right of self-government and if this harmony were deemed extremely important, the band's course would be clear. But reasoning in this way attaches major importance to well-being and not only to rights.

Exclusively rights-based arguments in favour of increased Native political self-determination clearly suffer from serious limitations. Rights-based arguments against Native self-government, however, are no less frail.

Rights-Based Opposition to Native Self-Government

Opponents of increased Native political self-determination also rely on arguments based on moral rights, but to an even greater extent than its advocates do. The advocates communicate a lively sense of their grievances and present reasons to support their conviction that greater political autonomy would ameliorate them. The opponents, in contrast, have little to say about the social, economic, and political problems faced by native people. They do not condemn the goal of Native self-government as unattainable or unworthy, or the means to it as unrealistic or counterproductive. Their antagonism is, with few exceptions, based exclusively on "theoretical" considerations relating to central precepts of liberal democracy, especially individualism and equality before the law.

Although he later changed his position drastically, former Prime Minister Pierre Trudeau stated this view forcefully in 1969:

> We have set the Indians apart as a race. We've set them apart in our laws. We've set them apart in the way governments deal with them. They're not citizens of the province as the rest of us are. They are wards of the central government. . . .
>
> We must all be equal under the laws. . . . They [Indians] should become Canadians as all other Canadians. . . .[12]

Sally Weaver, a perceptive student of government policymaking with regard to Native peoples, observes that:

> One of the most pervasive forces underlying the federal government's resistance to aboriginal rights demands is its steadfast commitment to liberal–democratic ideology. Liberal–democratic ideology stresses equality, individualism, and freedom from discrimination on the basis of race, religion, nationality, and so on. For most policy makers in government, demands for aboriginal rights are problematical because they call for the administration of services, programs, and laws on the basis of special status, collective rights, and cultural uniqueness. All of these concepts are viewed by the government as contradicting liberal–democratic ideology.[13]

As a final example, Thomas Flanagan writes as follows:

> In my opinion, these proposals [for special status for Métis] represent a disturbing challenge to one of the most fundamental principles of liberal democracy—equality before the law. They would set the Métis systematically apart from other citizens of the polity, encapsulating them as a society within a society. Even if done for benevolent motives, such a division is still a racial segmentation of society. A group of people distinguished fundamentally by ancestry is marked off for far-reaching special status under the law.[14]

The most widely shared ground of opposition to Native self-government, then, is its alleged incompatibility with basic liberal–democratic norms, especially its incompatibility with equality before the law. However, the recognition of a right of increased Native political self-determination does not violate the principles of liberal democracy, especially the principle of equality before the law, *as those principles are currently understood in Canada*, and therefore it is not a decisive objection to Native self-government. The following criticism is thus a critique of rights-based arguments against Native self-government, because the relevant liberal *principles* are formulated in the vocabulary of *rights*—above all, the *right* of equality before the law.

Opponents argue, in the first place, that a right of Native self-government is inimical to liberal–democratic principles because it is a *collective right* and therefore violates the precept that *individuals* should be equal before the law. There is a wide range of respects in which individuals should be equal before the law. The idea that people's basic legal rights, privileges, and immunities should differ according to their social status, ethnicity, sex, religion, or political connections is repugnant to most Canadians, and few would argue that there should be one law for the rich and another for the poor. Nevertheless, the recognition of some collective rights is by no means foreign to Canada's legal heritage.

One of the more striking features of Canada's legal system is that it attributes rights to corporate bodies, notably business corporations. The fact that the collective rights of members of corporate bodies are thinly disguised by treating the corporations as legal persons is just that—a thin disguise. More to the point here, Canadians' right of self-government is itself a collective right. A right of self-government is not a right of each individual to govern himself or herself but a right of a collectivity to govern itself according to procedures, rules, conventions, and institutions. Collective rights in general and a collective right of self-government in particular are not incompatible with the principles of liberal democracy as they are currently understood in Canada.

It is doubtful, however, that concerns about the recognition of collective rights lie at the heart of liberal opposition to increased Native political self-determination. Of far greater importance for most opponents is a concern about the challenge that seems to be presented to the liberal conception of equality before the law by the prospect of an ethnic group acquiring a special legal status. The depth of gut-level antipathy to this prospect is revealed by the fact that it has been condemned in some quarters as a system of apartheid.[15] Michael Asch takes this charge seriously and responds to it at some length.[16] The charge, however, does not deserve such courteous treatment. No proposal for increased Native political self-determination has stated or implied that Native collectivities *must* opt for apartness, and none has stated or implied that individual adult Native people should be denied any of the rights enjoyed by Canadian citizens if they decide not to join a self-governing Native collectivity. The suggestion, therefore, that proposals for Native self-government bear even a near resemblance to the South African regime of involuntary segregation is preposterous.

But not all objections to increased Native political self-determination that are based on the ground that it violates the principles of equality before the law are crudely and intemperately misleading. Clearly, all proposals for Native self-government, because they envisage the entrenchment of a special status for collectivities whose members are defined by characteristics that *cannot* be attained by non-members, *do* infringe the principle of equality before the law as it is understood in liberal terms.

But it is important to note that many Canadian governmental practices honour this principle in a "flexible" manner. Moreover, deviations from strict application of the principle frequently correspond to the theme of this essay—they abridge the *right* of equality before the law in the interest of the *well-being* of individuals and collectivities. Consider three prominent examples.

First, constitutional entrenchment of official-language rights and the Official Languages Act grant special status to speakers of the English and French languages. Although the provisions of these laws are expressed in universalistic terms so that they can be invoked by Canadians of *any* heritage, they advance the well-being of two linguistic groups. These provisions have their opponents, but they are now firmly established as enduring features of Canadian political life.

No doubt these provisions were enacted partly in response to stark political calculations: the constitutional provisions were an essential condition of the formation of the Canadian state, and the provisions for providing federal government services in both official languages were seen as a blow against Quebec independence and probably as a means of consolidating support for the Liberal party both inside and outside Quebec. But there is no reason to believe that these moves were dictated solely by considerations of *Realpolitik*. They were surely also recognized as departures from the liberal principle of equality before the law, designed to enhance the well-being of the country's largest linguistic and cultural collectivities. If so, it is hard to see that the establishment of self-governing Native communities would be an unconscionable departure from the principle of equality before the law, as that principle has been understood in Canada.

Second, various levels of municipal government in Canada have been granted significantly different powers, for the very good reason that the requirements of their residents and the municipalities' ability to pay for them also differ significantly. Residents of Canada's diverse communities are not equal before the law. For example, residents of densely populated cities benefit from public transportation systems denied to villagers, while the telephone and electricity rates of rural citizens are typically subsidized by the city dwellers. This flexibility in the allocation of powers to municipal governments has not excited heated condemnation on the ground that it violates the principle of equality before the law. It is not obvious that the investment of special governmental powers in native communities would been seen as a more threatening departure from the principle.

Finally, there are *already* a considerable number of Native communities that exercise powers of self-government to a greater or lesser extent. This is most obviously true of Indian reserves. Although the Indian Act still speaks of "wards of the state," and although the Department of Indian Affairs and other federal departments still exercise extensive control over reserve life, reserve Indians are demanding and gaining steadily increasing control over their lives. For example, great strides have been made under the banner of "Indian control of Indian education." But Indian reserves are not the only Native collectivities that exercise some degree of self-government. There are status and non-status Indians off reserves, as well as Métis and Inuit living in homogeneous or near-homogeneous communities, who exercise great control over their affairs.

Perhaps as a portent of the future, at least on the Prairies, there are in Alberta eight legally constituted Métis Settlements. These settlements, which cover an area only slightly smaller than that of all the Alberta Indian reserves combined, though with only a fraction of the population, have evolved in a manner similar to that of reserves. They are now negotiating with the provincial government to establish new legislation, embodying broader provisions for self-government, to be entrenched in the constitution. In short, in spite of a broad commitment to equality before the law, Canadians have been living for some time with at least some rudimentary forms of Native self-government, and this has not led them so far to riot in the streets.

The conclusion indicated by these considerations is that the principle of equality before the law has not been treated in Canadian law or political practice as indefeasible, that is, as a principle so sacrosanct that there are no circumstances in which it could properly be infringed. Moreover, Canada is not unique among liberal democracies in this respect. All of the liberal–democratic countries permit deviations from this principle—apparently with the blessing of large majorities of their electorates—when the deviations yield large compensations in the form of increases in the well-being of sizable segments of the citizenry. Thus, for example, the American constitution entitles the tiny electorate of Nevada to representation by the same number of United States senators as the huge electorate of California; France provides its agricultural sector with support denied to other industries; and Switzerland and Belgium provide for representation of their official language groups in the structure of institutions and the formation of public policy. As well, it is commonplace in liberal–democratic counties for first offenders to be treated differently by the courts than those with long criminal records, for country votes to be "worth more" than city votes, and for legislators to be immune to prosecution for remarks they make inside the legislature. Establishment of a right of Native self-government seems to require an understanding of equality before the law no more flexible than these deviations.

Arguments against increased Native political self-determination that are based exclusively or almost exclusively on moral rights are no stronger than arguments in favour of self-government based on such grounds. The fundamental precepts of liberal democracy do not preclude the recognition of collective rights; on the contrary, the cherished right of self-government *is* a collective right. And the principle of equality before the law, as it has been understood in Canada and other liberal–democratic countries, does not imply an indefeasible right of legal equality: it permits exceptions deemed conducive to well-being.[17]

The Well-Being Argument

It has been shown that arguments both for and against increased Native political self-determination that are based entirely or almost entirely on moral rights are defective. It remains to be shown how arguments based on considerations of well-being can remedy the defect. This is problematic, not because one must dig hard to mine a narrow lode but because one is confronted with an embarrassment of riches.

One of the most important criteria for evaluating political arrangements is the contribution of those arrangements to well-being. It is generally agreed that the dimensions of human well-being are many, although disagreement exists as to whether these many dimensions can be grouped into a few broad categories or even inferred from a single greatest good. But in dealing here with the specific issue of increased Native political self-determination, even if the elements of well-being could be reduced to one or a few, a discussion dealing with only the broad standards of well-being could not possibly generate criteria specific enough to address an issue that is political as well as philosophical. Accordingly, this account begins with a very general statement of the bearing of the standard of well-being on the issue of Native political self-determination. It then turns to some considerations that, though far from being matters of narrow detail, give some indication of how this standard can be given practical application.

A perspective that focuses on well-being yields the following broad principle regarding Native political self-determination: Native collectivities should have a right of political self-determination to the extent that recognition of that right promises to enhance their well-being without seriously reducing the well-being either of Native people who are not members of such collectivities or of non-Natives. This general principle has hardly any practical application, because it does not identify any even modestly concrete considerations that militate for or against Native self-government. However, in discussing particular considerations, it is worth drawing attention to two interrelated features of the general principle, because they deeply colour the specific applications.

First, the principle does not force a choice between two clear-cut and mutually exclusive alternatives, so that one must either accept or reject the proposition that Native collectivities have a right to some specified scope of self-government. On the contrary, the principle of well-being, combined with the assumption that sovereignty is not a viable option for Native collectivities, means that the issue of Native political self-determination is actually one of jurisdiction; and different jurisdictions may be appropriate for different collectivities. Second, the principle specifies that a sound case for self-government requires attention to the well-being not only of those who aspire to govern themselves but also of those who would be significantly affected if those aspirations were realized.

A number of specific considerations must be taken into account when relating the principle of well-being to the issue of Native political self-determination. Because it is not an either/or issue, considerations that militate more or less decisively in favour of Native self-government are not identified separately from those that tell strongly against it. Instead, a number of propositions are proposed that take the following form: the greater the extent to which a certain condition is satisfied, the stronger is the case for Native self-government. The converse is also implied: the less the extent to which the condition is satisfied, the weaker the case. Naturally, this scheme allows for propositions to the effect that "the greater the extent to which a certain condition is satisfied, the stronger is the case *against* Native self-government."

Two prefatory comments must be made. First, the considerations identified below are not exhaustive. The purpose of this essay is to establish that the issue of Native self-government could be addressed more cogently if more attention were paid to considerations of well-being, not to produce a comprehensive ledger of all the factors that count for and against greater Native political self-determination. The considerations should be thought of as examples of this line of reasoning. Second, this account omits the most crucial determinant of the desirability of increased Native political self-determination, namely the desire of Native collectivities to exercise it. The reason for this omission is quite straightforward: even if the issue of Native self-government is resolved primarily on the ground of well-being, enabling legislation would have to be formulated in the vocabulary of legal rights. The law would have to be worded in such a way as to *permit* Native collectivities to exercise a certain scope of governmental jurisdiction; there is no question of *requiring* collectivities to exercise authority they do not want. It is therefore unnecessary to include as a distinct consideration for or against Native self-government the question of whether Native collectivities want to exercise greater political autonomy.

To begin with, the case for Native self-government is strongest where Native collectivities have a territory within which to exercise their jurisdiction. It is certainly possible to draw the boundaries of political jurisdictions, at least in part, on nonterritorial grounds. This is done when professional associations are granted limited rights to police the conduct of their members, and there may be grounds for granting urban Native collectivities the right to form governments for special purposes, such as child welfare, medical services, and care for the elderly. But considerations of cost alone prevent any extensive moves in this direction. A right of Native self-government must be confined, for the most part, to collectivities that securely occupy a territory within which that right can be exercised.[18]

Second, the case for Native self-government is strongest in respect of those areas of life in which Native people are worse off than non-Natives. There are respects in which Native people are characteristically better off than most non-Natives, for example, in their respectful treatment of the elderly and their sensitivity to the natural environment. But there are also many respects, some of which were noted at the beginning of this essay, in which they are much worse off. Many years of effort by non-Native governments have made hardly a dent in these appalling disparities. It is not argued here that the fact that Native people are worse off in a given realm provides a conclusive reason for their acquiring a right of self-government in that realm. There may be respects in which Native people are worse off than non-Natives that would not be improved, or would even be worsened, under self-government. Neither is it argued that self-government is a panacea. It is simply maintained that a presumptive case in favour of Native self-government is strongest in respect to realms in which the disparity between the well-being of Native people and non-Natives is greatest.

Third, the case for Native self-government is stronger the more substantially it promises to enhance the self-esteem of members of Native collectivities. This point is closely related to the previous one; there is considerable evidence that poor scores by Native people on the usual indicators of well-being are closely associated with low self-esteem, especially with a sense of powerlessness. Native people—perhaps especially status Indians who have experienced the dominance of the Department of Indian Affairs—are not strangers to either the sense or the reality of powerlessness. If a perception of powerlessness is a major factor in the low self-esteem of many Native people, this consideration militates in favour of increased political self-determination.

Fourth, the case for Native self-government is strongest in respect of matters in which the members of a Native collectivity are better equipped than outsiders to identify the nature and causes of their problems. For example, suppose there is an unduly high school dropout rate in a particular Indian band. It is recognized as a problem by band members, their leaders, and others such as professional educators and prospective employers of band members. It is reasonable to surmise that members of the band would have a better understanding than outsiders of the main reasons for the excessive dropout rate in their own community. This suggests that the band should have a larger voice in formulating educational policy for the community. The same is true for other areas of policy in which members of a Native collectivity have a deeper or broader insight into their problems than outsiders.

Fifth, the case for increased Native political self-determination is stronger in respect to matters in which Native collectivities are better equipped than outsiders to deal effectively with the problems that confront them. This point is closely related to, but not identical with, the preceding one. The distinction between them is that the ability of members of a Native collectivity to identify the nature and causes of a problem does not establish that they are better able to solve it. For example, it is conceivable that members of a Native collectivity, though better able than outsiders to *explain* an excessive dropout rate, might be less able than outsiders to devise effective means to *remedy* the problem. But it is also conceivable (and in many cases more likely) that the members of the collectivity would be better able both to identify the roots of the problem and to devise an effective solution. In such instances, the case for lodging authority to make policy in the community is further strengthened.

Sixth, the case for increased Native political self-determination is strongest in cases in which members of Native collectivities have distinctive outlooks and aspirations that are not easily or widely appreciated by outsiders. Some of the Native people's "problems" are discernible *as* problems only from within their cultural perspective. Anyone who listens to or reads the words of Native proponents of self-government cannot help but notice the overriding emphasis placed on the preservation of Native "culture" and "spirituality." This is a realm in which the competence of non-Native politicians and bureaucrats is incomparably lower than that of their Native counterparts, and the bearing of that fact on the issue of native self-government is obvious.

Seventh, the case for the self-government of a Native collectivity is stronger the greater the availability among its members of strong political and administrative skills. They would certainly be necessary to deal with the complex intergovernmental relations in which a self-governing Native community would inescapably become involved. For example, there is no prospect that in the foreseeable future any but a very few Native governments would be able to provide an acceptable level of services from funds generated by their own members. Heavy reliance on funding from senior governments would be unavoidable for years to come, and formidable political skills would be required to ensure that this funding was established and maintained at an appropriate level.[19] This observation leads to a final example of the bearing of the principle of well-being on the issue of increased Native political self-determination.

The case for self-government of a given Native collectivity is stronger the greater the economic independence of the collectivity. This does not mean that a case for self-government can be made only for fully self-supporting collectivities. The federal government contributes many millions of dollars to services for status Indians and Inuit in accordance with constitutional and treaty obligations, and both federal and provincial governments devote considerable resources, including some funding for political organizations, to Native citizens. If there is a persuasive case for increased Native political self-determination independent of financial considerations, the principle of well-being surely implies that Native governments should receive funds from the federal and provincial governments to implement and maintain themselves. This generalization fails, however, to address the political reality of the situation in at least two important respects. If Native collectivities are to be genuinely self-governing, rather than mere administrators of federal and provincial government policies, they must be able to exercise discretion as to the policies they choose to pursue. If they are to exercise such discretion, they must have the resources to implement to policies they adopt.

This means that a considerable portion, at least, of funds allocated to them must be unconditional grants, that is, grants that are not earmarked for specified projects. However, both the federal and the provincial governments have been loathe to make unconditional grants to Native groups. While they might become more liberal in this respect if they were party to agreements providing for increased Native political self-determination, the track record suggests that they would be reluctant to make unconditional grants sizable enough to enable Native governments to exercise much discretion. The unavoidable conclusion is that a self-governing Native collectivity stands the best chance of success where a significant portion of the government's revenue can be generated by the collectivity itself.

A second, and in the long run probably more important, consideration supporting this conclusion is that government expenditures—especially those in the form of grants—fluctuate considerably. In times of economic recession, cutbacks are customary. It is reasonable to assume that Native communities, with their comparatively small electoral strength and limited political influence, would not be first in line to be buffered from the rigours of austerity. Native governments lacking financial resources other than the federal and provincial government grants would be in serious jeopardy in such circumstances. For this reason, too, the case for a right of self-government is strongest for collectivities that have a considerable measure of economic independence.

The foregoing discussion should show that tackling the issue of Native self-government from the perspective of well-being is immeasurably more complex than addressing it exclusively from the standpoint of moral rights. Discussing only a few considerations of well-being in the sketchiest fashion has taken several pages. The broader and deeper analysis required by an orientation that focuses on well-being would be far lengthier, more detailed, and more complex. However, if the reasoning in this and previous parts of this essay has been sound, the heavier labour imposed by the well-being perspective pays ample dividends in the currency of philosophical depth and political cogency.

Objections and Conclusions

So far this essay has ignored two objections to the well-being perspective. One of them is stated often and vehemently by opponents of Native self-government; the other raises the ire of many of its proponents. The first ground is that it would be unfair, unjust, or simply inappropriate to single out Native people for the special treatment involved in granting them a right to govern themselves. From one point of view, so the argument goes, Canadian history has been a history of successive waves of immigrants whose early generations suffered from all, or almost all, of the disabilities confronted by Native people but who assimilated themselves into the mainstream of Canadian life and, by dint of very hard work, achieved a level of well-being comparable to that of Canadians whose ancestors arrived earlier. Favourite current examples are East Indians and Southeast Asians, who confronted poverty, cultural distance, and racism no less severe than that experienced by Amerindians but are "making it" by sheer effort and willingness to make sacrifices now for benefits in the future. Why, then, it is asked rhetorically, should Native people be granted a status so special as to include even the right to form their own governments? And if the right is granted to Native people, why is it not granted to others?

The standard Native response to attacks of this kind, which assign to Natives the same status as other ethnic groups, is based on aboriginal right. As the first (and unconquered) inhabitants of what is now Canada, they maintain, they retain all the rights they did not cede; and they did not cede the right to govern themselves.[20] This argument is strengthened by the observation that immigrants of Canada after 1867 *chose* to accommodate themselves to an already established political system. Therefore those immigrants, unlike Native people, have no right to demand special political status. Although this rights-based line of reasoning requires considerable elaboration before it becomes compelling, it is quite persuasive. However, considerations of well-being are sufficient to establish the unique propriety of establishing a right of self-government for Native collectivities.

The argument is straightforwardly negative: there is no evidence that the establishment of a right of self-government for non-Native collectivities would increase their well-being without significantly reducing the well-being of others. To this it may be replied that the well-being perspective establishes, theoretically at least, a precipitous slippery slope; it means that *any* collectivity whose well-being would probably be enhanced significantly without serious detriment to others if it were granted a right of self-government should be granted that right. This inference is absolutely correct—and not at all embarrassing. On the contrary, if issues relating to self-government should be decided on the basis of considerations of well-being, the claim that such considerations apply only to people with the right heritage, cultural practices, and skin colour is self-contradictory and therefore genuinely embarrassing.

Finally, there is a ground on which proponents of Native self-government might object to the well-being perspective. The federal government has offered to Indian reserves a degree of self-government beyond the very limited jurisdiction allowed for in the Indian Act. Under this scheme, the federal government would pass legislation authorizing reserve governments to exercise certain powers, probably including powers ordinarily reserved exclusively to the provinces. Indian leaders are vehemently opposed to this scheme. Concerned that legislation can be amended or repealed without their consent, they insist that a right of self-government be entrenched in the constitution. However, the constitutional provision under which such a right would seem to be appropriately installed is section 35(1) of the Constitution Act, 1982, which specifies that "the existing aboriginal and treaty rights of the aboriginal peoples of Canada are hereby recognized and affirmed." It is easy to see that this essay's thesis—that more attention should be paid to considerations of well-being and less to moral rights—might be regarded as inimical to the constitutional entrenchment of a right of Native self-government, since the relevant constitutional provision refers to "existing" rights, and moral rights presumably "exist." This impression, however, is mistaken.

Although section 35 has been given far more attention than the others, it is not the only part of the Constitution Act under which a right of Native self-government could be entrenched. Section 25, which is part of the Canadian Charter of Rights and Freedoms, states in part that "the guarantee in this Charter of certain rights and freedoms shall not be construed so as to abrogate or derogate from any aboriginal treaty *or other rights or freedoms that pertain to the aboriginal peoples of Canada*" (emphasis added). Also, section 37(2) of Part IV of the Act, which requires the convening of a first ministers' conference attended by representatives of the aboriginal peoples, states that "the conference convened under subsection (1) shall have included in its agenda an item respecting constitutional matters that directly affect the aboriginal peoples of Canada, *including the identification and definition of the rights of those peoples to be included in the Constitution of Canada*" (emphasis added).

Neither of these sections refers to *existing* rights. Both of them apparently permit Native and non-Native politicians to negotiate either on a very general principle allowing for the establishment of self-governing Native collectivities or on a more specific range of rights designed to accommodate the diversity of Native collectivities. In either case, the negotiation is to be based on the sorts of considerations of well-being discussed earlier in this essay, and thereupon to entrench the provision or provisions in the constitution.

This essay has not attempted to answer the question whether there should be enacted a legal, and perhaps also a constitutional, right of Native self-government. It has tried to show that this question could be addressed more cogently if less attention were paid to moral rights and more to considerations of well-being. It did, however, state at the beginning that a legal right of Native self-government should be enacted. A thoughtful, judicious, and generous application of the principle of well-being, combined with a decent respect for the democratic right of all citizens (particularly of Native citizens, who obviously have a special stake in the matter) to a voice in a matter that will affect the future of all Canadians, leads to the conclusion that a right of Native self-government should be entrenched in the Canadian constitution. This legal right would permit different kinds of Native collectivities to exercise different scopes of jurisdiction and in some cases to acquire powers now exercised by the federal or provincial governments. But further speculation about a matter that requires investigation rather than surmise will contribute to no one's well-being.

Notes

1. "Political self-determination" as used in this essay is synonymous with "self-government." More important than the stylistic concern to avoid monotonous repetition of a single term is the desire to provide a regular

reminder that there can be *degrees* of political autonomy, a point connoted by the term "self-determination," especially as it is employed in the phrase "increased Native political self-determination."

2. Michael Asch, *Home and Native Land: Aboriginal Rights and the Canadian Constitution* (Toronto: Methuen, 1984), p. 3.

3. The data presented below are taken from James S. Frideres, *Native People in Canada: Contemporary Conflicts* (Scarborough, Ontario: Prentice-Hall, 1983), Chapter 6.

4. Maria Campbell, *Halfbreed* (Toronto: McClelland and Stewart, 1973); Heather Robertson, *Reservations are for Indians* (Toronto: James Lewis and Samuel, 1970); Anastasia M. Shkilnyk, *A Poison Stronger than Love: The Destruction of an Ojibwa Community* (New Haven and London:-Yale University Press, 1985).

5. See, for example, Noel Lyon, "Constitutional Issues in Native Law," in *Aboriginal Peoples and the Law: Indian, Métis and Inuit Rights in Canada*, ed. Bradford W. Morse (Ottawa: Carleton University Press, 1985), Chapter 6; and Brian Slattery, "The Hidden Constitution: Aboriginal Rights in Canada," in *The Quest for Justice: Aboriginal Peoples and Aboriginal Rights*, ed. Menno Boldt and J. Anthony Long (Toronto: University of Toronto Press), pp. 114–38.

6. Asch, *Home and Native Land*, pp. 52–53.

7. Donald V. Smiley, *The Federal Condition in Canada* (Toronto: McGraw-Hill Ryerson, 1987), p. 73.

8. Smiley, *The Federal Condition*, pp. 70–75.

9. "Executive federalism" refers to the practice wherein senior federal and provincial officials determine policies in federal–provincial conferences rather than more traditional political forums. The term was coined by Donald V. Smiley, who discusses it in Chapter 3 of his *Canada in Question: Federalism in the Seventies* (Toronto: McGraw-Hill Ryerson, 1972). The problems it poses for Indian self-government are discussed by J. Rick Ponting and Roger Gibbins in "Thorns in the Bed of Roses: A Social-political View of the Problems of Indian Government," in *Pathways to Self-Determination: Canadian Indians and the Canadian State*, ed. Leroy Little Bear, Menno Boldt, and Anthony J. Long (Toronto: University of Toronto Press, 1984), p. 131.

10. This is not to say that citizens should seek peace at any price, so that there are no occasions in which it is necessary to struggle for the protection of rights. It is to say, however, that fundamental political arrangements are better arrived at through processes of accommodation.

11. The term "convoy concept" is borrowed from David Braybrooke's *Three Tests for Democracy: Personal Rights, Human Welfare, Collective Preference* (New York: Random House, 1968), p. 92.

12. P.E. Trudeau, "Excerpts from a Speech Given August 8th, 1969 in Vancouver, British Columbia," in *Native Rights in Canada*, 2nd ed., ed. Peter A. Cumming and Neil H. Mickenberg (Toronto: Indian–Eskimo Association of Canada, 1972), p. 331.

13. Sally Weaver, "Federal Difficulties with Aboriginal Rights Demands," in Boldt and Long, *The Quest for Justice*, p. 142.

14. Thomas Flanagan, "Métis Aboriginal Rights: Some Historical and Contemporary Problems," in Boldt and Long, *The Quest for Justice*, p. 244.

15. Diamond Jenness, "Canadian Indians Yesterday. What of Today?", in *As Long as the Sun Shines and Water Flows: A Reader in Canadian*

Native Studies, Ian A.L. Getty and Antoine S. Lussier (Vancouver: University of British Columbia Press, 1983), p. 163 (reprinted from *Canadian Journal of Economics and Political Science*, XX (February 1954)); Don McGillvray, column in *Edmonton Journal*, November 12, 1983, cited in Asch, *Home and Native Land*, p. 100.

16. Asch, *Home and Native Land*, pp. 100–01.
17. It might be objected that this whole section proves little, if anything, because it relies on the actual interpretation of the right of equality before the law in existing liberal democracies, rather than on the *principle* of equality before the law. It is common knowledge that political regimes are defective in implementing the principles for which they purport to stand, and the case presented here could be accused of being nothing more than a recommendation that yet another hypocrisy be added to the already sizable list. There are two responses to this objection. First, it is difficult to envisage a regime in which the principle of equality before the law was adhered to with absolute stringency, making no distinction (for example) between the blind and the sighted, children and adults, and magistrates and ordinary citizens. Equality before the law in a *human* society must make room for some of the differences among people. Second, it is manifestly unjust to apply the principle of equality before the law stringently to Native people as long as it is applied commodiously to non-Natives. Unless and until the principle is applied rigorously across the board, it should not be applied with special stringency to Native people. This line of reasoning is suggested by Michael McDonald's brilliant rights-based defence of aboriginal land claims, "Aboriginal Rights," in *Contemporary Issues in Political Philosophy*, ed. William R. Shea and John King-Farlow (New York: Science History Publications, 1976), pp. 27–48 reprinted in *Contemporary Moral Issues*, 2nd ed., ed. Wesley Cragg (Toronto: McGraw-Hill Ryerson, 1987), pp. 357–74.
18. This consideration does not preclude the granting of lands to Native collectivities that lack them. Considerations of well-being and perhaps also of moral rights may dictate that lands should be granted.
19. Allan Tupper suggested that this consideration is likely, in practice, to be at war with some of those already mentioned. For example, Native groups most afflicted by low self-esteem are least likely to have a cadre of members with well-developed political and administrative skills. The point is well taken; however, perhaps contrary to Tupper's intention, this tension strengthens rather than weakens the case for the well-being approach. It is a merit of this approach that it promotes recognition of complexity..
20. See, for example, David Ahenakew, "Aboriginal Title and Aboriginal Rights: The Impossible and Unnecessary Task of Identification and Definition," in Boldt and Lang, *The Quest for Justice*, pp. 24–30.

CRITIQUE

In his essay, Tom Pocklington argues that discussions of Native self-government suffer from an exclusive focus on moral rights and that more attention should be paid to considerations of well-being. Thus the essay's thesis is double-barreled: it combines political support for a right of Native self-government with a philosophical argument about how it should be established.

The essay raises a number of issues. Many of them concern the legitimacy of a right of Native self-government. Although this is not his main point, Pocklington supports this right and hopes to strengthen the case for it. Thus readers may want to question whether the case for this right is as strong as he suggests. Three lines of argument may be pursued here. First, one might question whether this right is truly warranted by the considerations of well-being outlined in the essay. Second, one might consider whether the collective nature of the right violates individual equality before the law. Critics argue that if it is wrong to ascribe or deny rights to women as women, it should also be wrong to ascribe or deny rights to Native people as Native people. Women, native people, and everyone else, it is argued, should hold rights as individuals. Pocklington briefly rebuts this by citing three other types of collective right in the Canadian system.[1] But possibly the rebuttal only shows that these other practices are wrong as well; the essay does not show that these practices respect individual rights. Nor does it show that Native self-government would do so. So a third question arises: whether native self-government can be established without violating the rights of others. Some residents of the territory will not be members of the Native community. As such, they would not be citizens. How would their rights be protected?

These lines of argument are left to those who want to dispute the right to Native self-government. For my part, I agree with Pocklington that this right should be established in law as soon as possible, but I question his reasons for this, that is, his claim that the right should be based largely on considerations of well-being rather than on moral rights.

This claim concerns the basis of legal rights in general. Although Pocklington's essay focuses upon one right in particular (Native self-government), his argument concerns the terms on which rights in principle should be established at law, and so it applies to issues such as abortion, pornography, and medicare as much as to Native self-government. In all such cases, there are two ways of arguing that a right should be established:

(i) Moral rights: by arguing that the right should be established at law because it is a moral right; that is, that individuals or communities are entitled to it. Therefore it ought to be guaranteed by law; failure to do so is a fundamental injustice. For example, it may be argued that the law should allow a legal right to abortion because women have a moral right to control what happens in their own bodies.

(ii) Well-being: by arguing that the right should be legally established because this would improve the well-being of individuals or communities. Pocklington has already illustrated this in the case of Native self-government; in the case of abortion, it may be argued that allowing abortions would improve well-being of women by relieving them of the responsibility of raising children where they are unable or unwilling to do so.

Both approaches are relevant. I think that well-being can be a reason for establishing legal rights, and Pocklington thinks moral rights can be a reason as well. But he believes that well-being provides a better basis for legal rights. This is mistaken; moral rights are far stronger than Pocklington allows, while well-being is much weaker than he realizes. The two categories, moral rights and well-being, deserve closer consideration.

Moral Rights

In his discussion of moral rights, Pocklington draws attention to their contentious and undesirable features. This is a plausible account, but it will not persuade many people that they would be better off without rights. This is because there is a difference between the partisan rights disparaged in the essay and the idea of rights in principle.

In any political controversy, partisans on each side will assert all kinds of rights and claims, generally of a quasi-legal or historical sort. In arguments over pornography, for example, it is seriously asserted that the freedom to watch "skin flicks" must be protected as if it were the same as the right to read the Bible or Karl Marx. This is absurd but inevitable: in the heat of controversy, rights will always be asserted that do not stand up to close scrutiny. But it is not a reason for rejecting the idea of rights in principle.

This is as true in the controversy over Native self-government as it is in any other political issue. It seems that such rights are most frequently asserted and disputed in historical or quasi-legal terms. Such claims are not very compelling. The fact that a certain community did or did not have certain rights in the past is no overwhelming reason why it should or should not have such rights today. Similarly, the fact that Canadian law does or does not recognize such rights does not mean that the law in this respect is just or correct. So the first thing that must be said about moral rights in the context of Native self-government is that most of the asserted rights are simply not very interesting. If these are the rights Pocklington wants to reject, he is correct. But this is true only of the fictitious rights that are disputed by the legal partisans; it is no reason to reject genuine moral rights.

Can there be a genuine moral right to Native self-government? Consider the following argument:[2]

(i) The first step is to say that any social group (for example, the state) exists only as a set of individuals. If the social group had no members, it might still "exist" in a technical sense, as a legal entity; but it would not exist in any real way. No social group exists in its own right, apart from the individuals who belong to it.

(ii) It follows that no state or social group holds authority over its members in its own right. Rather, the authority of any group derives, like the reality of the group itself, from the individuals who are its members. The rights of these member-individuals are therefore the basis of the authority of the group. This means that *if* any state (or other social group) has legitimate authority, it must be derived from the rights of the individuals who constitute it. This implies that individuals must have such rights apart from the social groups to which they belong.

(iii) What are these rights? There is room for argument here, but one right can be asserted without dispute: individual autonomy, or the right to decide the terms of one's own life for oneself.[3] Since the concern here is with the kinds of rights that individuals have on their own account (apart from and underlying those that might be established by law), it is clear that such rights will make sense only if individuals have the *capacity* to choose for themselves how to live.[4] The right to exercise this capacity for oneself is therefore the basis of all other moral rights.

(iv) Step (ii) was asserted that the authority of any social group must be based in the moral rights of its members, and step (iii) was concluded that these moral rights must be based in the autonomy right of each individual, the right to choose for oneself how to live. The autonomy right is therefore the basis for the authority of any social group.

(v) The autonomy right includes the right to decide the groups to which one will belong and the authority relations to which one will be subject. This follows from what has been established already, and it implies that the right of self-government of any community or group can be derived from the individual autonomy rights of the group's members.[5]

(vi) This means that all individuals have the right to form themselves into groups as they choose, and to endow such groups with whatever authority they want, including the full authority of government.[6] This right, again, is the basis of the authority of Canada's legal system; it cannot be denied without undermining the legitimacy of this system.

(vii) It follows that there is a right of self-government, which Native people may exercise if they choose. It is not peculiar to Native people; it is the right of any group of individuals to govern themselves, and it must be respected as the condition of the legitimacy of our system.

This was the point to be established. Contrary to Pocklington, there is no difficulty in establishing a moral right to Native self-government. However, the fact that Native people and others have this right does not mean that they ought to exercise it. Clearly, in deciding whether and how to exercise this right, it would be prudent for Native people to consider its effects upon their well-being. It is to be hoped that they would consider the well-being of others as well. Thus, considerations of well-being should be centrally important in any discussion of a right of Native self-government. They are, however, relevant only in considering *how* to exercise it; they are not needed to show *that* it exists.

Why does this matter? It is important to recall what is implied by the idea of a right. In general, a "right" is an entitlement: something owed to individuals, which they are justified in claiming. In this sense, any right entitles the holder to limit the freedom of others[7] by requiring conduct stipulated by the right. Therefore there is a major difference between what one "ought" to do for others and what one owes them as their rights. Morally, one ought to be generous, but no one else has the right to require this. On the contrary, it is the individual's right to decide whether and how to be generous, and others have no grounds for complaint. However, if A owes B $10, B has a right to it; in consequence of B's right, she may require the money from A. Instead of A being able to decide whether and how to pay, B has the right to decide whether and how to require this.

If there is a moral right to Native self-government, accordingly, Native communities would be entitled to decide whether and how to exercise it, and it would be the duty of everyone else to respect such decisions. Presumably, Native communities would be guided by considerations of well-being, but it would be their right to decide whether and how to do so. It would not be for others to decide for them, or to say that they should not have the right, or that it was not needed for their well-being. As their moral right, this would be no one else's business.

Well-Being

Pocklington rejects this perspective of moral rights and argues that legal rights should be founded more on grounds of well-being. But what does he mean by "well-being"? He does not spell this out, but it presumably includes anything that might be a means of attaining, or part of, a person's happiness, pleasure or "good life." This may include a great deal.[8]

Now Pocklington's well-being principle for rights is stated with some care: a right, such as Native self-determination, should be established legally if it promises to enhance well-being in some cases (Native communities) without seriously reducing the well-being of anyone else (Native people or non-Natives).[9]

As this thesis is put, no one could oppose it. Because of the very broad meaning given to well-being, the principle is merely that a right should be established if some want it badly and no one else minds too much. Thus, Pocklington's alternative to the "contentiousness" of moral rights is to give everyone a virtual veto over the establishment of legal rights. This may seem attractive, but the question is whether any interesting rights can be established on this basis. Is it true of such rights that no one would mind them very much?

In the case of Native self-government, it is not true. This proposal has been opposed by some provincial premiers, because it diminishes their jurisdiction and powers; by business enterprises; by non-band members, both Native and non-Native, who live in the band's territory; and by others who simply don't like the fact that it would change the constitutional "picture" of Canada. In other words, the proposal seems—to some—to diminish their well-being. It might be argued that some of their concerns are mistaken, illegitimate, or unreasonable; but if anyone believes that his or her well-being will be reduced significantly, this blocks the proposal. It does not matter whether that person's concern is illegitimate or unreasonable. Therefore, Pocklington's principle would prevent his own preferred example—Native self-government—from being established as a right.

The same will be true of any other rights that are sought to be established. As a rule, the reason for establishing rights is to allow individuals greater control over their own lives, by entitling them to act in ways that otherwise would be opposed by others. This is true of all the rights that are important: freedom of speech and thought, religion, political participation, property, and so on. In every case, the right is important because it protects a contestable area of life. On the other hand, there are many unestablished rights, such as the right to tie one's shoes or to breathe. They haven't been established because they are not needed; and they are not needed because no one opposes these activities. The difficulty with Pocklington's well-being principle, then, is that it would allow only rights that no one would oppose or mind very much. This would limit rights to those areas of life in which protection is not necessary and exclude them from the very activities that require them the most. As a result, Pocklington's principle would exclude all the rights that are important and allow only those that no one wants.

Any right gives an individual a certain power over others by entitling that individual to limit others' freedom and require a certain conduct from them. As a result, others are bound to question or "mind" the establishment of any right, simply because it means they can be required to act in ways they may not like. Those who favour the right might ask whether the opposition to it is reasonable or legitimate. But with Pocklington's principle, any opposition— reasonable or otherwise—would block the establishment of a right. Since the establishment of a right usually entails opposition, no rights could be established.

This applies to Native self-government as well as to any other right. On abortion, for example, is there any policy that is acceptable to everyone? In the case of pornography: some persons "mind very much" the idea of allowing pornography which degrades women; other persons "mind very much" the idea of censoring it. On these and all other pressing issues, there is simply no policy that cannot be said to reduce someone's well-being as they understand it. On Pocklington's criterion, accordingly, no important rights could ever be established.

Alternative Versions

Can the well-being principle be rescued from this problem? It might be revised by dropping the "no one minds" restriction or by allowing only "reasonable" estimates of well-being to count. These revisions might put more teeth into the well-being principle in ways that would permit significant rights to be established, but only at the price of reintroducing all the problems the principle was originally intended to avoid. For example, suppose only "reasonable" judgments are allowed to count in determining whether anyone's well-being would be reduced by a legal right. How does one judge what is "reasonable," and who decides this? This criterion is as contentious and arbitrary as any claims based on moral rights, and it virtually undermines the point of establishing legal rights in the first place.

The point of rights is to allow individuals to decide for themselves how to live. The revised well-being proposal would allow individuals to do this only in areas that some higher authorities (psychiatrists? social workers?) have judged "reasonable." What is the advantage of this? Why not let individuals decide this for themselves? The situation is no better if the "no one minds" restriction is dropped. This would allow legal rights to be established wherever doing so would promote total well-being, so long as reductions in well-being for some were compensated by gains for others.

There are two difficulties with this proposal. First, it allows rights to be established only where, and because, doing so makes enough people "happy." It does not matter whether the right in question is one that individuals need, or deserve, or to which they are entitled. What alone matters is whether the well-being of enough people is advanced by it. By the same token, the "total well-being" principle would allow rights to be taken away, and some individuals to be made worse off, merely so that others could be made better off. There are circumstances in which this would be appropriate, but the "total well-being" principle could allow it in cases in which the individuals were entitled to their goods or were already extremely poor. This would be a desecration of justice. The revised well-being proposal would allow this because, in its preoccupation with total well-being, it does not care about rights or justice for individuals.

Thus the "no one minds" criterion is important. Without it, the well-being principle is morally hideous. With it, however, the principle is politically vacuous: no rights could be established.

Moral Rights and Well-Being

It follow that moral rights are stronger than Pocklington allows, and well-being is weaker than he realizes. This may seem like a small point, but it is not. What is at issue is not only the justification for rights, but also, through this, the kinds of rights citizens want to protect and the kind of society they want to promote.

A moral-rights basis permits individuals to decide the terms of their own lives for themselves. In a system based on the well-being approach, however, any such rights depend upon others. It is one thing to say that in exercising one's rights one ought to be concerned with the well-being of others. But the well-being approach asserts that the well-being of others determines whether one has any rights at all. This subordinates individual rights to collective well-being. As a result, one cannot demand legal protection for what is legitimately a moral right. Instead, one must ask this of others and hope that they will find it in their interests or consciences to agree.

This is the basic flaw of the well-being approach: it requires that people seek their rights on their knees.

Notes

1.   Critics should note the way Pocklington poses the issue: whether "the principle of equality before the law, understood in strictly liberal

terms" is violated by "the entrenchment of a special status for collectivities whose members are defined by characteristics that *cannot* be attained by non-members." This is not a feature of the first two practices he cites (language rights and municipal powers), and it is not obvious even in the third (current powers of Native communities). In other words, none of the practices Pocklington cites may have the characteristic he claims to legitimize.

2. This is only the sketch of an argument. Space limitations preclude a more detailed development, but it shows how the case can be argued.

3. This argument probably originates with Thomas Hobbes. See "The Right of Nature in Leviathan," *The Canadian Journal of Philosophy*, Vol. 18, No. 2 (June 1988), pp. 257–70.

4. This is not to say that the right is absolute. The capacity may be relatively underdeveloped (as it is in children) or damaged. Consequently, it might be stated more precisely as the right to be treated as if one had the capacity unless proven otherwise.

5. The right of self-government can be understood only in this way, as derived from the individual rights of members of the group. Pocklington apparently disagrees; he writes: "A right of self-government is not a right of each individual to govern himself or herself but a right of a collectivity to govern itself . . .." This would be unexceptionable if it merely meant that the right of self-government is not the same as the right of individual self-determination because it is, rather, *derived* from it. But Pocklington seems to regard these rights as unrelated, as if any group might hold a right of self-government on its own account, as a group, and apart from the individual rights of its members. This is mistaken, for the reasons indicated. Interestingly enough, Pocklington himself seems to agree in Chapter 9 of this book, where he denies that there is a general moral obligation to obey the law. Since rights and obligations are correlative, a right of self-government (which is the right to declare law) implies the obligation to obey it. Conversely, if there is no obligation, there can be no right. Thus, in denying a general obligation to obey the law, he seems to deny that there could be a general right to self-government.

6. This is subject only to the restriction that the right be exercised in ways that do not violate the same right held by others. Note here the third line of challenge to the idea of Native self-government, as outlined in the introduction to this critique.

7. See H.L.A. Hart, "Are There Any Natural Rights?," *Philosophical Review* Vol. 64 (1955), pp. 175–91.

8. Presumably, well-being also includes the sense of control over one's life that was the basis of the foregoing "moral rights" account. Thus, the two approaches *can* be quite similar, depending upon how much value is assigned to this sense of control in the calculation of well-being. At best, however, it is only one ingredient among others.

9. In criticizing Pocklington's principle, this critique takes two liberties with it. He states it as a basis for the right of Native self-government; it is here generalized as a basis for other rights. Also, he states the well-being criterion as a sufficient condition; it is treated here as though it were both sufficient and necessary.

Discussion Questions

1. Is Pocklington's argument seriously weakened because it says too little about well-being? Or is it a strength of the argument that it leaves it mainly to Native people and non-Natives to decide for themselves what constitutes their well-being?

2. If you accept the well-being approach, should you support Native self-government only if it is democratic?

3. If you favour Native self-government, must you also favour sovereignty or sovereignty–association for Quebec?

4. Is there, as Carmichael believes, a basic moral right of individuals to decide for themselves how to live?

5. Carmichael maintains that "the well-being approach asserts that the well-being of others determines whether one has any rights at all." Is he right?

Further Readings

Michael Asch, in *Home and Native Land* (Toronto: Methuen, 1984), presents a very well-written, brief, but wide-ranging discussion of the social, economic, political, and legal circumstances and prospects of Canadian Native people. Asch argues that the political aspirations of Native people are compatible with the dominant Canadian liberal political ideology.

Thomas R. Berger's *Fragile Freedoms: Human Rights and Dissent in Canada* (Toronto: Clark, Irwin & Company, 1981), is simply written and highly supportive of Native aspirations. Chapter 2, which deals with the too often neglected Métis, provides a brief history of the Riel uprisings and assesses the prospects for increased Métis self-determination. Chapter 7 deals with the judicial and nonjudicial protection of aboriginal rights.

Menno Boldt and J. Anthony Long, editors of *The Quest for Justice: Aboriginal Peoples and Aboriginal RIghts* (Toronto: University of Toronto Press, 1985), have compiled a collection of essays of uneven quality. The high points are a number of short essays by Native writers and two by Sally Weaver and Thomas Flanagan that discuss difficulties in recognizing and implementing Native rights.

Harold Cardinal's *The Unjust Society: The Tragedy of Canada's Indians* (Edmonton: Hurtig, 1969), remains the most powerful statement of Indian grievances. The author was one of Canada's most prominent Indian leaders.

Donald Purich's *Our Land: Native Rights in Canada* (Toronto:

James Lorimer & Company, 1986), is an exceptionally readable discussion of the history, current status, and likely prospects of the recognition of Native rights. The final chapter contains a straightforward, balanced discussion of Native self-government.

CHAPTER 8

Democracy and the Freedom of the Press

This chapter considers a right similar to freedom of expression, that of freedom of the press. Since the publication in 1859 of John Stuart Mill's *On Liberty*, a brilliant defence of the freedoms of expression and of the press, the journalist's freedom from improper influence has served as a measure of the extent to which political liberty is respected in a society.

The freedom of the press, although it is widely championed in Canada, is still controversial. Two kinds of questions have defined this controversy. The first concerns the extent, if any, to which the freedom of the press can rightly be limited to achieve a public goal, for example, to heighten a sense of national identity, to improve the terms of democratic debate, to enhance public-spiritedness, and even in some societies to feed revolutionary vigour. The second and related question focuses on the impact of ownership and control of the press. Are any limitations on the private ownership and control of the mass media required by the democratic mandate of the press to inform citizens or by the freedom of journalists? Neither of these questions has been settled, even among those who champion the journalist's democratic mandate and the freedom from improper interference to which the journalist has a right.

In the essay, Greg Pyrcz defends the idea of a "college of journalists," which has been proposed to regulate Canadian journalism. He attempts to persuade the reader that the democratic duty of journalists to inform the public as well as possible is fundamental to their freedom and that it accordingly defeats the property right of the owners of the mass media, the right of journalists to freedom of expression, and even the right of citizens to determine for themselves the quality of the news they will consume. The core of Pyrcz's argument is that the press's freedom is better defined by the requirements of democracy than by liberal rights. He contends that the journalist's freedom of expression is largely irrelevant to his or her work and rights as a journalist.

The essay favours a college of journalists to ensure the democratic performance of Canadian journalism. It asserts that such a body is necessary because the power now exercised by both the owners and the consumers of the journalist's products is blind to the real informational interests of democratic citizens. Pyrcz contends that many Canadians choose, often unknowingly, a standard of journalism that leaves them poorly positioned to act as the true citizens of a democracy. A "college" would both highlight and correct this flaw in liberal democracy; at the same time, this proposal stops short of granting the state the authority directly to interfere with Canadian journalism.

To make his case, Pyrcz critically examines the standard argument for the freedom of the press. He entertains arguments about the impossibility of objectivity in journalism to show that although something less than complete objectivity is discernible, the identification of journalistic standards of excellence is possible. Here he challenges the contention that an inescapable subjectivity in the journalist's practice makes the governing of journalism politically tyrannical. Finally, he argues that the liberty of the press is a right better understood and defended as an entailment of the principle of democracy than it is as the right of journalists to freedom of expression.

Don Carmichael's critique favours instead one variety of the liberal rendering of the freedom of the press, that of regulatory liberalism. It argues that while some restrictions may be justified to ensure that standards of quality are achieved by the press, they can be identified and defended simply as justifiable limitations upon the freedom of expression. Carmichael finds the proposed college of journalists, if not wholly superfluous, unlikely to achieve in practice what it promises in theory. The real problem, if there is one, lies in the less than ideal, yet politically legitimate, preferences that citizens display in consuming the news of the day. Here, he hints, Pyrcz's proposal reveals an elitism that is at the heart of many attempts to limit liberal rights in the name of democracy.

Liberal democracy requires a free press, one that ideally provides information-rich news and diversity in its analysis of public affairs. "Freedom of the press" is understood to mean that journalists are constrained in their work neither by government nor by private interests. Canadians respect this freedom because they believe that democracy produces effective public policy only when the citizen's democratic decisions are well and fairly informed.

One of the more vexing problems of journalism in a liberal democracy concerns the substantial power that journalists are believed to exercise over citizens. Some citizens pride themselves on their independence from the opinions of journalists and believe that they read, watch, and listen to "the news" critically; but most seem not especially adept in detecting bias and are thus vulnerable to journalistic manipulation. Even the most knowledgeable and skeptical citizens are very dependent upon journalists. In a mass society, where policy decisions are complex and where events well outside most citizens' direct experience impinge often forcefully on them, there are few accessible sources of information and interpretation other than journalism. For this reason, citizens must depend on journalists for some of the information and news analysis in the light of which their political understanding is shaped and their democratic decisions made.[1]

Some journalists exercise this power over their readers, listeners, and viewers with ingenuity, integrity, and responsibility. They refrain from using their audience's dependence upon them as a means of manipulation; they seek, like educators do, to improve the public's understanding of complex issues. They also seek, modestly and critically, to strengthen their own grasp of political affairs and processes and are prepared to ferret out the information upon which citizens depend.

Lamentably, few contemporary journalists appear to be governed by these professional standards. Many claim that they are, typically in ads extolling the virtues of their columns or programs, but few really "deliver." As a result, many citizens suffer unnecessarily emotive or "hot" news analysis, sensationalism, boosterism, unabashed bias and manipulation of opinion, the abbreviation and trivialization of complex issues, ideological naivete, deference to politicians and elites, the competition of political symbols rather than the clash of ideas, "pretty" faces and "reassuring" voices rather than information and analysis, the medium as the message, and journalistic laziness.[2] Why is this, and what can be done about it?

Some people contend that there isn't much that can legitimately be done in liberal democracy to improve the practice of journalism.

They argue that bad journalism simply "sells better" than good journalism and that those who are unsatisfied with the quality of journalism are free to choose otherwise, that is, to choose more responsible newspapers and radio and television stations. For those opposed to intervention in the practice of journalism, the freedom of the press ensures that citizens get exactly the sort of journalism they want.[3]

This situation presents a dilemma. Citizens of a democracy require high-quality journalism to exercise their democratic rights effectively. Much journalism is of low quality, yet most citizens appear to be satisfied with it. Most of what might be done to improve this situation appears to challenge the freedom of the press and the liberal right of citizens to determine the terms of their own lives. As a result, few real changes occur, although superficial stylistic changes abound.

Much of this dilemma has to do with the ownership of the mass media. The more such control over the mass media is concentrated in a few individuals or corporations, the less competitive journalism becomes and the greater is the opportunity for manipulation. The concentration of power usually gives greater scope for its effective employment, because the owners of the mass media are often linked to other elites, many of whom have an interest in controlling the content of the news. These points are now commonplace and are well rehearsed in the literature on the mass media and in royal commission findings.[4] Although the problem of news media ownership continues to be important politically, it is no longer as theoretically interesting as it once was. Neither does it tell the whole story.

This essay considers a second aspect of journalism's dilemma in a democracy. It concerns the commercialization of the journalist's product, a problem that is related to but not fully captured by the conventional concern about ownership. At least part of the dilemma of journalism in liberal democracy stems from how citizens misunderstand the freedom of the press and how governments, news firms, and journalists react to this misunderstanding. The conventional misunderstanding is that freedom of the press is an extension of both the citizen's democratic right to information *and* the journalist's freedom of expression. Journalists, in this view, cannot legitimately be denied access to any information they think relevant to the citizen's deliberations in a democracy. Nor can they be prevented from expressing, as information or analysis, what *they* think is important in this work. This connection of freedom of the press with freedom of expression may stem from J.S. Mill's *On Liberty*, in which Mill justifies freedom of expression and freedom of the press on virtually the same grounds.

These two conventional justifications of freedom of the press are joined by a third, and increasingly important, one. It is the claim that citizens have a right to determine the style and content of news and public affairs analysis. Citizens are thought to exercise this right by choosing between a number of diverse news formats in a marketplace of offerings. This right is referred to as "consumer sovereignty."

The proposition defended in this essay is that freedom of the press need not and ought not be understood as the journalist's freedom of expression, even though the journalist is rightly protected from untoward interference. Nor need the press be understood to be subject to the exercise of consumer sovereignty. The misunderstanding that both freedom of expression and consumer sovereignty define the practice of journalism generates the dilemma in journalism and democracy, in which democratically unsatisfactory news is the apparently preferred fare of the majority of citizens.

It must be conceded that the freedom of the press is the right of journalists to some forms of noninterference. But it is not properly understood as an extension of the *liberal rights* of free expression nor the marketplace. Instead, it is a right extracted from and limited to the terms of the citizen's *democratic right* to information. This distinction—that freedom of the press is a right extracted from the terms of democracy, not liberalism—carries with it implications about how citizens can legitimately govern the press. Principally, it provides a means by which they may free themselves, as the citizens of a democracy, from an ineffective dependence upon bad and commercialized journalism.[5]

An alternative way of stating the thesis is that the citizens' right to information, as an essential term of democracy, defeats both the journalists' freedom of expression and the citizens' right to determine the scope and content of the news through consumer sovereignty. In this, the citizens' democratic right to information is not their right to determine how the news is to be rendered; it is the right to be informed. The freedom of the press simply cannot stand as a liberal right, even though it protects journalists from some interference by state and society, and even though, historically, it has enjoyed the support of liberals.

The thesis will be argued indirectly to provide a practical context for it. What is required is that journalists be governed by a body similar to those that now govern the medical practice. This "college of journalists" would be an active and powerful governing body, at a long-arm's distance from government, which would make difficult, if not impossible, the kind of commercialized journalism from which democracy now suffers. This body would impose dramatic sanctions upon journalists who served up the news only as their audience or favoured elite appeared to like it served.

There are three persuasive arguments against the existence of such a governing body: (i) it would threaten the journalist's right to freedom of expression;[6] (ii) it would be elitist in character and anti-democratic in effect by requiring journalists to disregard what the public wanted and instead to give them what they needed to know to exercise their democratic rights and fulfil their democratic responsibilities; and (iii) unlike the practice of medicine, journalism is not founded on any certain criteria of excellence; it is the incorrigibly subjective expression of the journalist's point of view. If this challenge is true, there is much to be said for protecting the integrity of a journalist's work, as is done with that of artists, namely, by invoking "freedom of expression."

Each of these arguments will have to be rebutted for the proposal for a college of journalists to win acceptance and for the case for a proper understanding of freedom of the press to succeed. But first the proposal for a college of journalists must be outlined in detail.

The Mandate of the College of Journalists

The college of journalists would identify and protect high democratic standards of journalistic excellence that were free from the influence of owners, managers and editors, *and consumers* of the mass media. It would defend these standards first by licensing and then, if necessary, by threatening journalists with the suspension of their license to practice. Journalists who failed to present the credentials that the college deemed consistent with its democratic mandate would simply be denied a licence to ply their trade. They might continue to work but would not be allowed publicly to present themselves as journalists; they might become like those who write for the tabloids sold at supermarket checkouts. Journalists who initially secured a licence and then subsequently fell below the criteria of performance established by the college would have their licences suspended and, as a final sanction, revoked. Finally, no news firm that wished publicly so to declare itself could hire a journalist without a licence. The college would prohibit its member journalists from working for a firm that employed unlicensed journalists.

The democratic mandate and the authority of the college to impose sanctions would be secured by legislation. The legislation would define the principles of democratic journalism and empower the college to apply the above-noted sanctions to defend these principles. This would guarantee an arm's-length relationship between the government and the college.

Journalists working under such a regime would need to approach their work with an understanding, much better than many now appear to possess, of journalism, democracy, ideology, pedagogy, and the legitimate scope of their power. Journalism schools too would be transformed, as more demanding and explicit criteria of democratic excellence were made the conditions of a journalist's employment and as the schools revised their pedagogy accordingly. Journalists would be required to understand that their professional conduct was to be governed only by criteria derived from their democratic responsibility to inform the citizenry. They would understand that their *sole* mandate, as journalists, was to provide the best information and analysis possible with which citizens might exercise their right to democratic choice. This understanding would be reinforced both by better training and by the threat of sanctions.

In the language of journalists, this means that there would be a strict, widely shared, and singular definition of "newsworthiness." What would be newsworthy would not be whatever captured the largest audience or pleased employers or elites. Instead, journalists would be required only to provide, as effectively as possible, what citizens needed to know to make informed democratic decisions in matters of public policy. Moreover, it would mean that all "stories" would be given a depth and scope made possible by the developing cognitive powers of citizens and the relative lack, under such a regime, of competing superficial and narrow renderings of the news.

At present, the responsibility for democratically excellent journalism rests with the intellectual and pedagogic skills, democratic insight, and willpower of *individual* journalists. They must withstand both the influences of others who seek to shape their work and their own material ambition, if they are to fulfil their democratic role.[7] Under the regime of a governing college of representative journalists, they would be responsible for nurturing and protecting the democratic integrity of their work *collectively*. This is the essential change entailed by the proposal to legislate this body into existence.

Colleges of medicine, also known as colleges of physicians and surgeons, have a parallel role. They too license, regulate, and govern the education of those to whom they grant the authority to practice. The sole criterion employed by these colleges is the quality of health of those its members are to serve. This criterion is met, in part, by counteracting the influence of others upon the physician by threatening sanctions. For example, physicians who prescribe medication solely at the behest of patients are subject to disciplinary action. The authority exercised by these colleges is given by statute, but provincial governments maintain no direct, and little indirect, control over how this authority is exercised.

A college of journalists would effectively prevent those who controlled the mass media from citing the preferences of their audience in order to influence a journalist's work. If a journalist was requested to cut a story down to a certain length to make it "hotter" or to edit out its more complex or controversial content because ratings or opinion surveys suggested that the audience preferred its news this way, the journalist would be *required* to refuse or would lose his or her licence. Should the journalist's job be threatened, the college would act to prevent all of its member journalists from working for the firm in question. Even if such influence from editors or producers was absent, journalists would not be allowed to cater to their audience's news preferences in the hope of garnering a wider following. Nor would they consider themselves free to express their own values and predispositions as elements of the news. Instead, they would be required to rely only upon their democratic obligation, defined both by their improved understanding of the rights and democratic responsibility of journalists and by their licensing association's commitment to having this understanding honoured.

The college, while intended to limit the influence of citizens in shaping the nature and defining the scope of "the news" by the expression of subjective preferences, would also constrain the power of government, advertisers, elites, and owners to manipulate or bully journalists. It would work against all such influences in the everyday life of journalists with a coercive support system.

The Subjectivity of Journalism

Some might argue that the analogy between a college of journalists and a college of medicine is misleading: Journalism, unlike medicine, has no objective criteria of performance. Journalism, it might be asserted, is essentially a subjective activity, more of an art than a science. It might be contended that, just as with the study of history, there are for journalism no objective descriptions of events and analyses of political affairs. All descriptions of events are inescapably subjective reconstructions, it might be said, at least in the sense that they aren't complete and that they reflect judgments about what is important and what is not. As such, all journalistic descriptions are the subjective and selective renderings of events.

It might also be contended that journalism is about the description of events that are themselves value-laden, that the "patient" defies objective description. The fact that journalism is largely about describing politics is telling in this regard. Or, more simply, it might be argued that it is impossible for journalists to free themselves from either their personal or professional values in the events they cover. How, it might be asked, is it possible for feminist or anti-feminist journalists to cover events without these events being described in their favoured light?

These are undeniably difficult issues, well beyond the scope of this essay. Despite this, their force, as criticisms of the proposed college of journalists, may be met without fully resolving these deeper issues. First, the practice of medicine is not the concrete, certain, and objective science that it is sometimes made out to be. Much of it is a matter of judgment, selection, interpretation, and especially, a matter of the patient's own values. Whether patients are considered ill or not is, in an important respect, dependent on how they understand themselves in particular contexts. But such a response sidesteps the challenge.

Consider instead that the proposal calls for principles of democracy to serve as the governing principles of the journalistic practice, not the criteria of truth. What this means is that for every event the journalist covers, the question is not what is true, but instead what must citizens know to exercise their democratic rights effectively? Although the issues of objectivity in journalism are not irrelevant, they are not as daunting as those confronting the historian. Journalists would need to make sure that no reconstruction of an event was biased in such a way as to lead a citizen to make a choice based on the bias. They needn't capture an ultimate truth to meet democratic standards of excellence. While this might be a difficult task, it is not an impossible one; university instructors do it when they provide students with information and analyses that are at odds with their own convictions.

Still, the rendering of events undeniably requires something less than completeness in the scope and depth of the description and analysis of an event. Some subjectivity, some limits of both the journalist's and the audience's own understanding, abilities, and commitments, will persist. These are the terms of the problem of description and explanation as its deeper level; complete, objective information is impossible to achieve. It does not, however, follow that "anything goes."

Suppose a constitutional crisis occurs in Canada. Suppose further that four "levels" of description of the event are available. The first assumes that what is important is who is drinking what brand of scotch, who is wearing what colours that day, who is romancing whom while negotiations are underway, or how the journalist feels about being in Ottawa at this time. The second maintains that what is at stake is mainly a great battle of the wills of two or three major players, that what must be described is the theatre of battle: who wins, who loses, who is defiant, who is pathetic. The third describes the essential terms of the debate, the provisions that are in contention, the reasons and considerations that underlie the contest of views, the terms that might favour one view rather than another. Here, the opinions and impressions of the players would take a back seat to an analysis of the reasons for their actions. The fourth is an advanced course in the history, economics, and political, anthropological, and psychological terms of this and previous constitutional debates. It is a course in the political philosophy of constitutions, a complete demographic and social analysis of the current context that tries to bring to light the complete terms of the debate and tell the story objectively. Few would dispute that this fourth level is unacceptable as the standard of excellence in journalism. It does not follow, however, that any of the other three is as good as the others, simply because journalism is unable to live up to the terms of the fourth.

It might also be contended that forcing journalism to maintain the standard implied by the third level would lead to homogeneity and elitism in journalism. Imagine a world, critics might challenge, in which all television news broadcasts were required to feature the democratically excellent news provided by MacNeil-Lehrer!

This concern is unwarranted. If homogeneity is the result of the pursuit of excellence, there is little to explain the remarkable diversity of intellectual approaches within any university's faculty of arts. The news need not be the same for it to reflect similar standards of excellence. It would not be at odds with democratically excellent journalism for one journalist to probe the economic terms of a constitutional debate and the other to pursue its cultural terms. Nor need such treatments be elitist or intellectually snobbish. Universities have enjoyed considerable success in layering the intellectual demands of introductory, junior, senior, and graduate courses, without leaving pedagogy to the whim of the instructor's feelings or to some students' acquired taste for spoonfed simplicity. Intellectual diversity coexists with devotion to academic excellence. Diversity does not stem simply from competition alone, if at all, but reveals the genuine diversity that evolves from the desire to supply what students need to know if they are to understand what they wish to. Just as different teaching styles are employed by different university teachers, so can the news be presented in various ways.

The problem of journalists' interests and values pervading their work is also misleading. It is made to appear to be an impediment to good journalism for reasons very similar to those offered above. Although complete distance from events is impossible, it does not follow that no distance is as good as some. Democratically excellent journalism requires only that journalists do what they can in this regard, not that they be perfect. It also requires that those unable to do this ought probably to seek another livelihood.

In short, although the problem of objectivity is a difficult one, especially for journalists, the lack of complete objectivity fails to justify the conclusion that standards of democratic excellence are indiscernible and that journalism governed by them is unattainable and undesirable. Nor does it mean that such standards would produce a boring homogeneity.

The Duty of Journalists

A defence of the authority of the college of journalists must argue that the freedom of the press is not, even in part, to be identified with the journalist's freedom of expression. One reason for this is obvious: journalists and their employers often use this contention to block attempts to regulate them.

A second reason, not quite so obvious, needs to be considered as well. One must also challenge the notion that freedom of the press is, in part, the individual journalist's freedom of expression in order to constrain consumer sovereignty in the practice of democratic journalism. Otherwise, journalists can choose simply to mimic the apparent preferences of their audiences as if these preferences were their own. Consumer sovereignty can, in this way invade the practice of journalism under the guise of the journalist's freedom of expression. It is for this reason that many owners of the mass media are so eager to champion their journalists' freedom of expression. It permits the commercialization of their product.

Journalists undeniably possess the right of freedom of expression. A college of journalists could not legitimately discipline a journalist for speaking his or her mind on a soapbox, campaigning for a preferred political candidate, participating in controversial public debates, dressing "punk," or writing provocative poetry or philosophy. Protecting the freedom of journalists to conduct such activities might instead be one of the secondary roles of the colleges. This does not mean, though, that the journalist's freedom of expression defines his or her freedom as a journalist, nor that it cannot properly be constrained in the journalist's practice. Journalists possess the right to free expression as citizens and as persons, but it does not necessarily follow that the freedom they enjoy in their work as journalists flows from this right. Nor is it true that freedom of expression is an absolute right and that no restrictions upon it are warranted. It does not, by analogy, offend a surgeon's freedom of expression to insist that, during delicate operations, the surgeon refrain from creative cutting. These mistaken ways of understanding their rights too often define and defend the work of practising journalists.

Journalists occupy a position of institutional power over citizens. This stems from the fact that citizens simply cannot experience directly all those events and activities relevant to the effective exercise of their democratic rights. As a result, journalists assume the institutional responsibility of relaying "events" to citizens. This is part of the reason for granting journalists easy, full, and often unique access to public figures and events.

The assumption that journalists have an institutional responsibility to inform citizens is essential to the logic of contemporary democracy. Without information, citizens simply cannot express their preference in public policy. Neither can they choose an agent to represent them without possessing information upon which to do so, information that is beyond their ability reasonably to acquire for themselves. Representatives such as members of Parliament can be democratically effective only when they understand their constituents' interests and preferences. However, representatives must also understand the terms of the issues relevant to their constituents. Otherwise, they would be unable to serve their constituents' interests and preferences effectively.

To select a democratically effective representative, then, citizens must be in a position to judge whether the various competitors for the job have the requisite understanding of issues in which the citizens have an interest or preference.[8] To do this, in turn, citizens must know the terms of the issues in which their representatives are to represent them. Only then can citizens effectively evaluate their suitability as representatives.

Consider the following simplified example. In federal-provincial matters, citizens would reject out of hand representatives not versed in the subtleties of Quebec politics. They might choose from a different set of contenders if the rights of the aged were at stake. Some representatives would serve better in the first case, others in the second. Normally, citizens must select representatives who understand a variety of issues. But they cannot select a representative effectively unless they understand the issues at stake in the mix of public policy decisions that define the scope of their interests and preferences. Therefore, the democratic requirement of journalism—to empower democratic citizens with information—is not easily set aside. Information beyond that practically available to the citizen is a requirement, even in the less direct business of electing political representatives.

To see that the freedom of journalists cannot be the same as their freedom of expression, consider that it is often impossible for journalists both to exercise their freedom of expression and to satisfy the informational needs of democratic citizens. Events can be reported to citizens in such a way as to permit them to affect policy decisions, directly or indirectly through her elected representative, only if these events are not altered or skewed by the creative impulse of the journalist. If it is otherwise, the citizens' preferences in public policy would wrongly be informed by the creative expression of journalists, not by the actual terms of those events and issues in which citizens have an interest or with regard to which they wish to have their preferences heard. In cases like these, there is a simple yet debilitating conflict between the journalist's freedom of expression and the citizen's right to information.

This conflict is common in the practice of journalism. In virtually every act of a journalist, a tension exists between the informational demands of the citizen and the creative or ideological impulse of the journalist. All "stories" can be "improved" by journalists indulging their freedom of expression. If the informational needs of the citizens of a democracy are to be met, however, journalists must partially or completely repress this desire. The freedom of the press cannot be understood as being derived from or an extension of the freedom of expression without creating a conflict between the journalist's freedom and the requirements of democracy.

This essay has maintained that the freedom of the press is not synonymous with the freedom of expression of journalists and that, where it is so construed, it conflicts with a citizen's right to information.[9] There is a further consideration that is relevant here. Freedom of expression is a right possessed equally by every citizen of a democracy, partly because all citizens are capable of and improved by the expression of their own personalities and opinions and by access to the personalities and commitments of others. It is also because it is through diverse expression, in which no privilege is accorded any opinion, that progressive understanding is achieved. But the opportunity must be available to all if public decisions are to reflect the consideration of all points of view.

To define a journalist's freedom as freedom of expression formally gives journalists an access to the consideration of citizens not enjoyed by other citizens. Why should journalists have more opportunity to express their preferences, tastes, ideological orientations, and creative impulses as the terms of the citizens' dependency upon them in exercising their democratic rights? Why should journalists be granted greater access to the attention of others in this regard? Clearly they should not be so privileged if the egalitarian terms of democracy are to be respected. Even if journalists are more and better informed about events and policies than citizens are, a democracy cannot afford institutionally to give some a greater say in public decisions, at least if it is possible to do otherwise.

There are real problems in the contention that freedom of the press is an extension of a broader right to freedom of expression. Most of these have to do with the implications this proposition carries for democratic practice. To so construe the right, that is, to construe it as the journalists' freedom of expression, pits their freedom from untoward influence against the citizens' democratic right to information. This contest is an unhappy and unnecessary one.

Freedom of the press is, instead, a special *democratic* right.[10] As such, it is the freedom of journalists to investigate, define, and report the news of the day free from those democratically intolerable influences that, if effective, cause them to misrepresent events. This democratic freedom includes freedom from the influence of governments of the day, from the church, from elites, from the owners of the media, from advertisers, and from the consumer.

Journalists thus enjoy both the right to free expression (as persons), and the right (as journalists) to practice their profession free from democratically untoward interference. The latter right is the content of the freedom of the press. Journalists enjoy it exclusively as the terms of their democratic role, as those whose work positions them, and them alone, to serve the legitimate interest all citizens have in knowledge of the events and issues of the day. Journalists possess a special, institutional right against intervention, just as police officers possess the right not to be hampered in fulfilling their institutional duty. Both instances involve freedom from improper intervention, and both stem from the special role they perform in the interest of citizens. Both are limited, by the terms of the role they perform, in the subjectivity their possessors are free to express. Both must constrain the exercise of some of their rights as citizens and persons when they are "on duty."

The duty of journalists to provide democratically effective news to citizens is correlative to the citizen's right to information, while the freedom of the press is an extension of this democratic right. Freedom of expression and freedom of the press are not the same right, and the democratic duty of journalists, when engaged in professional activity, ought to limit their exercise of their right to free expression. These two rights, the citizen's to information and the journalist's freedom fully to provide it (as the freedom of the press), are complementary. They cannot conflict because the second is an extension of the first.

Although this formulation does not provide the complete freedom longed for by some journalists and exercised by others as their freedom of expression, neither does it consider the freedom of the press inconsequential. Journalists are free, under this rendering of the principle, to pursue stories wherever such pursuit might lead. Moreover, as was argued in the previous section of this essay, nothing prevents journalists from presenting diverse accounts of the events they cover, because multiple renderings of single events are not at odds with objectivity. Journalists are not free, however, either to serve the news up to citizens "as they like it" or to serve it up as the expression of the journalist's subjectivity.

The Role of Consumer Sovereignty

The effect of consumer sovereignty on journalism has been noted by Robert Fulford, former editor of *Saturday Night* magazine:

> Journalism itself accommodates, and often exploits, an image entirely different [from that of the ideal product of journalism schools]—the raffish, highly independent, sometimes eccentric, not notably educated "personality" reporter. This man (sometimes now it is a woman) is an affront to all that journalism schools teach. Frequently, he is irresponsible and frequently his opinions are not closely tied to the facts. . . . But readers

tend to identify with him and love him, and editors, too—and publishers, while sometimes made uncomfortable by him, tolerate him with that special geniality we reserve for those who are helping to make us rich.[11]

Fulford's statement cites consumer preference as a damaging influence on the integrity of journalism. The issue remains a compelling one in public debate. However, it is more startling to assert the opposite point, that citizens who have a right to elect governments should also be permitted to influence the work of journalists, who, in their democratic mandate, are the citizen's servants. This is the argument that will be made here.

One view of the terms of the right to information are provided by T.C. Pocklington in a statement that summarizes a current consensus in democratic theory:

> If voters cannot have a right to comprehensive information, because such a right would be impossible to satisfy, they can at least have the right to seek out the best information available as to the probable consequences of opting for one alternative rather than others. And this right really resolves into two related rights . . . (freedom of speech), and the right of access to the opinions of others . . . consist(ing) mainly in the right of free assembly.[12]

According to this statement, citizens do not have the right to *be* informed. Instead, they enjoy a (right-secured) *opportunity* to seek out information without interference. They are also at liberty to give expression to their views and to share them with others. Together, these rights constitute the freedom of the press. In this respect, the rights and duties of journalists are the same as those of other citizens; journalists just exercise them more vigorously than other citizens typically do, because for them it provides a livelihood. In so doing, journalists may aid citizens in exercising their democratic rights and responsibilities by providing the best information possible about alternative proposals for democratic choice, but they needn't do so. Citizens have a right to information, but this right guarantees only the *opportunity* to seek out and collect the best information possible. It does not entail the correlative duty of journalists to provide it for citizens, even when citizens pay for their services. Let the buyer beware! This relationship between journalist and citizen, where both equally enjoy the opportunity to ferret out the best information possible, exists even though citizens are dependent upon journalists for some of the information necessary to exercise their democratic rights.[13]

Pocklington states that he accepts this reading of the right to information because complete information for the citizen is simply impossible to achieve. Such a requirement, he contends, ignores the complexity, extent, and uncertainty of virtually all matters of public choice. Moreover, he appears to hold the view that the right to information is a negative right, that it entails only a duty upon others not to interfere.

Contemporary democratic theorists such as Pocklington are undeniably right to insist that perfect knowledge not be taken as requirements of democratic choice, though the problem of objectivity is not as great for democratic politics as it is sometimes thought to be. Even though "perfect" information on matters of public life is impossible to achieve, this does not mean that some information is not simply better than other information. Nor are such distinctions in the quality of information irrelevant to citizens' democratic right to information. It is a mistake, for example, to think that where better information is available, the democratic citizen is not entitled to it. Pocklington concedes these points. However, does the citizen's *opportunity* to ferret out information satisfy this entitlement to better information? Here, democratic theory must go further than it does in Pocklington's treatment of the right to information. The right to information need not and should not be construed as thinly as Pocklington and others hold that it must be.

Imagine a government that insisted, in a matter of national urgency, that citizens be given only glossy and superficial summaries of the background information on the matter. Suppose that the summaries satisfied the citizens' expressed tastes and that they decided not to inquire any further. To contend that their democratic right to information had in this way been satisfied is to misconstrue the importance of information to democratic decisions. Does this example demonstrate a democracy at work?

It is, however, possible to exercise choice on the basis of "bad" information. Most people do this regularly, sometimes because they do not have the time or make the effort to seek out better information. But this is quite different from making choices based upon information that is insufficient, misleading, ideologically biased, or unnecessarily sensationalized from those upon whom citizens must depend. In such cases, when people cannot realistically do otherwise, the decisions they make are not their own decisions at all. They make choices that are not only bad, but that are not choices at all.[14] They must believe that the persons upon whom they are necessarily dependent are not manipulating or misinforming them when providing them with the information upon which they make decisions, if those decisions are to speak for them. Stating the right to information as thinly as Pocklington and other democratic theorists wish to do does not necessarily mean that democratic decisions will be compromised, but it does mean that they could be.

The above example of government-provided summaries showed

that choices based on these informational terms could not be characterized as democratic because it would be impossible to say that a majority view was discernible, even were it expressed. Indeed, no one in this case would be in a position to express a view on the issue because no one would have had access to any real information upon which to form such a view. The government in the example does have such an ability, because it alone possesses substantial information, but it does not believe itself to be under any duty to share this information unless and until it is demanded by the citizens. Citizens, believing that they already have the information, lose the desire to pursue better information. If the press had better information but decided not to offer it to the citizens, nothing relevant to the example changes. As long as the citizens don't ask for it, the provision of the best information possible from governments or journalists is not entailed by the citizens' right to information, at least in the argument Pocklington and others advance.

This is the first point against the thin reading of the right to information (the "opportunity" conception). For citizens who are dependent on journalists for information, more than the opportunity to acquire it is required by democratic principles. Instead, journalists have a duty, correlative to the citizen's right to information, to deliver the highest possible standards of information and news analysis.

A second reason supports this contention. Citizens, at least in Canada, enjoy quite different occasions to exercise the opportunities to which they are held to have a right. This is especially plain in the issue of the opportunity to pursue information. Most Canadians do not have the time to peruse all the available sources of information. They cannot read all the newspapers at the end of the work day, and the library is seldom open long enough for them to do all their civic homework. In this way, as well, a thin reading of the right to information is unsatisfactory. The largely inescapable terms of their lives make some citizens more dependent upon "bad" information than others are. In its favour, the "thicker reading" of the right to information provides a more egalitarian distribution of one of the means of exercising democratic choice, the achievement of the best information available upon which to do so.

The problem remains, however, that the right to information conflicts with consumer sovereignty, the purported right citizens possess to be served by their preferences even in journalism and even when these served preferences mean they are poorly informed. How is the conflict between the democratic right of citizens to be served with the best possible information and the liberal right of consumer sovereignty to be resolved, if at all?

It is argued, in favour of consumer sovereignty and against the duty of journalists to inform citizens, that citizens must be at liberty to develop and exercise their political preferences fully in society, not merely in the selection of representatives, for a society to be democratic. One of the ways in which citizens might exercise their political preferences is to select preferred journalists and journalistic firms, and thus to determine the nature of the journalistic enterprise. Read in this light, democracy seems to require a recognition of the sovereignty of citizens' preferences in journalism as a condition of democracy, even where they prefer the capricious, banal, hegemonic, eccentric, and mistaken in "their news." When citizens choose a "Conservative paper" over a "Liberal paper," they are exercising their political preferences, and they have a right to do just that.[15]

But there is a real difficulty in this easy conclusion. Asserting that such a choice is the expression of a political preference and thus that it ought to be protected by democratic right is quietly to undermine the notion, also crucial to democracy, that democratic choice is informed and considered choice. By choosing a newspaper of whose values one approves, one no longer fully entertains the information and analyses required for other, more substantial political choices. The newspaper one chooses, while meeting one's current political preferences, blocks information and assessments that might otherwise be made available and in the light of which one might make different decisions. In this way, choosing one's preferred newspaper could become one's first, last, and indeed *only* political choice. Such sedimentation of political preference is at odds with democratic decision-making, at least to the extent that there are new questions of public policy and ever-new information upon which to form political preferences.

Allowing political preferences to determine the information with which one makes other political decisions undermines the integrity of these other decisions. This does not mean that one ought not to make political commitments in a flourishing democracy, just that such commitments must not systematically close the door to the possibility of different or new commitments. A journalistic practice that merely plays to the preferences of its clientele, even when it intends to serve their political preferences honestly, is at odds with the drive to achieve the best in public policy through democratic choice. Moreover, although human development requires the exercise of real choice, this development is possible without someone in desperate but unsatisfiable need exercising choice in all matters. Citizens who have not suffered the horror of choosing between abandoning or not abandoning a loved one do not have underdeveloped human capacities. It may be useful to contemplate such choices in forming or understanding one's values, but being given a choice in all matters is too demanding and an unnecessary criterion for human development.

Another factor to consider is that it is not usually possible for citizens to make informed choices between good and bad journalism. One cannot know what adequate coverage of an event is unless one views and understands it first-hand. Making such a choice requires that one have, as a standard, first-hand knowledge of the event that the journalist seeks to represent. But citizens usually do not have such information upon which to choose their journalism, which is why they are dependent upon and vulnerable to the power of others. It may *seem* obvious that the *Globe and Mail* provides a higher democratic quality in its description of the day's events than, say, the *Toronto Sun* does, but this perception may be and sometimes is mistaken. Although readers occasionally "catch a paper out" on its treatment of an event, this discovery doesn't go far enough. The next day the same journalist's near-perfect account of another event may be rejected because of the previous day's mistake.

A citizen's democratic right to information requires that restrictions be placed upon journalistic practice. It is not enough simply to educate journalists more effectively (although this would help) or simply to limit the concentration of ownership. Both these solutions have missed a central term of the problem. If government interference is to be avoided, the collective power of journalists, especially to resist the pull of the marketplace, must be heightened.

But the most difficult problem remains to be resolved. It what is argued in this essay is accepted, then at least one democratic right will not be exercised by those who possess it. That is, citizens are to be given better information whether they want it or not. This is the result of the proposal to have the citizens' right to information correlative to the duty of journalists to provide the best information possible; and this is what consumer sovereignty is meant to protect against.

However, not all democratic institutions need to be governed by market liberalism; nor must all rights be exercised at the option of those who possess them. A number of similar rights are now considered to be compatible with democracy; for example, it is considered to be consistent with democracy (although not with full-blown market liberalism) that standards of excellence in university courses be identified and defended by those who have training in the relevant discipline, not by the students who seek credit for completing these courses. This is so even though the provision of a wide range of courses for students is a requirement of a democratic university education, and even though sensitivity to students' abilities and tastes and student–teacher interaction is a requirement of good teaching and effective learning. A good university education, like good journalism, is defined by relationships of dependence, which ought to be governed by mutual respect. Although no authority based on unnecessary dependency ought to be tolerated in a democracy, these are not relationships in which those who are dependent could be otherwise. They cannot determine the standards because they are simply not in a position to do so. If they were, there would be no reason for the dependency to exist.[16]

Consequently, the role of consumer sovereignty in journalism ought to be sharply constrained. Restricting the practice of journalism in Canada to heighten the collective powers of journalists to fulfil their democratic duty is both desirable and possible. If this argument is convincing, it is because democracy entails a positive right of citizens to information, a right that overrides their preferences in the news. The right to information entailed by democracy is unlike most other rights. In the case of most rights, those who possess them are free either to exercise them or not to exercise them.[17] However, the citizens' right to information upon which to render their democratic choices is like their right to an education, to high-quality medical care, and to a fair trial. The more a citizen demands an unfair trial, the more insistent the judiciary must be in granting a fair one.[18] The more journalists are pressured to listen to claims from their employers that what audiences prefer is thin news, the more diligent, in the name of the citizen's right to information, they must be in providing thick news.

Notes

The author acknowledges with thanks the generous editorial contribution that Herbert Lewis made to this essay.

1. For example, 70 percent of Canadians report that they receive their public affairs information from television. See "Politicians Must Bow to T.V.'s Role as a Prime Conveyor of Information." *The Globe and Mail*, April 2, 1988, pp. 1 and 5.

2. Barry Zwicker and Dick Macdonald, in *The News: Inside the Canadian Media* (Ottawa: Deneau, n.d.), have collected essays by Canadian journalists that support this assessment. There is an abundant literature on the abuses of journalism, the most compelling of which is Dan Nimmo and James Coombs, *Mediated Political Reality*, 2nd ed. (New York: Longman, 1990).

3. This assertion, referred to in this essay as "consumer sovereignty," is the pivotal idea in the development of Canadian communications policy.

4. See the background papers presented to the Kent commission, *Report of the Royal Commission on Newspapers* (Hull: Government of Canada, Ministry of Supply and Services, 1981).

5. This way of understanding freedom is defended in Charles Taylor's "What's Wrong With Negative Liberty," in *Readings in Social and Political Philosophy*, ed. Robert M. Stewart (New York: Oxford University Press, 1986), pp. 100–113.

6. The proposal for a governing body like the one contemplated in this essay is not unique. Its defence elsewhere was met with journalistic panic; an article in the *Montreal Gazette*, March 3, 1989 (CP Wire Service), noted: "Journalists should be licensed by their own profes-

sional society like doctors and lawyers so they could be punished for irresponsible stories. Julius Grey told a group of about 40 journalists Saturday that reporters . . . must be policed by a professional society. . . . The journalists at the panel discussion reacted frostily to Grey's licensing suggestion, saying it could lead to limits on freedom of expression. . . ."

7. Lucrative careers are available to otherwise poorly paid journalists who are willing to cater to the biases of majorities or to surrender to the opinions of powerful elites.

8. In Canada, this involves determining which political party seems most receptive to the electorate's interests and preferences and which seems to have the appropriate mix of understanding of the issues of the day.

9. This way of construing the right, as the citizen's right to be informed, rather than a right to access to information, is defended in the next section of this essay, in the discussion of consumer sovereignty.

10. It is special in the sense that it is of the few rights possessors do not exercise for themselves.

11. Robert Fulford, "A Sort of Reckless Courage," in *Research Studies in the Newspaper Industry: The Journalists* (Ottawa: Government of Canada, Department of Supplies and Services 1981), p. 9.

12. T.C. Pocklington, "Democracy," in *Liberal Democracy in Canada and the United States*, ed. T.C. Pocklington (Toronto: Holt, Rinehart and Winston, 1985), pp. 7–8.

13. It exists even when the opportunity for garnering information is greater for the journalist than it is for the ordinary citizen.

14. Autonomous choices are not simply those made for the public by those who control the means to information. One need only recall the "decisions" occasionally made in one's youth that were based on a parental source of (mis)information.

15. Fewer and fewer newspapers and television stations *explicitly* have an "editorial" orientation. Therefore, fewer opportunities exist to express these kinds of political preferences.

16. This is also why, as much as is practically possible, citizens should try to understand the "news of the day" free from their otherwise necessary dependency upon journalists.

17. For example, one's right as a Canadian citizen to state-financed medical care is a right one may choose never to exercise.

18. This idea is T.C. Pocklington's.

CRITIQUE

Greg Pyrcz's essay is motivated by the belief that democracy requires informed citizens and that, judged by this standard, the performance of the media[1] in Canada today is less than perfect. It realizes that any attempt to regulate the media will be said to violate the freedom of the press and consumer sovereignty. The essay aims to answer this objection by proposing a licensing agency for journalists and by considering whether restrictions on the media can be justified from a democratic perspective.

The crux of the problem, according to Pyrcz is that arguments on each side of the issue, by "market" and "regulatory" liberals, have confused the question. They have misconstrued the democratic principles of freedom of the press and of the citizen's right to be informed in "liberal" terms as principles of freedom of expression and consumer sovereignty. Pyrcz argues that, properly understood, the democratic principles allow, and may even require, restrictions upon the liberal principles.

This applies particularly to consumer sovereignty, the right of consumers to choose for themselves. This is the real villain of the essay and the focus of its last section. Pyrcz's view is that consumer sovereignty as a liberal principle may be overruled by restrictions on the media that are designed to protect each citizen's democratic right to information. As a result, Pyrcz maintains, freedom of the press means that journalists must be protected from the preferences of the citizen.

Three of the essay's points must be discussed. First, its goal: to improve the performance of the media from a democratic perspective. Would Pyrcz's proposal be effective? Second, its diagnosis: the media requires regulation. Is commercialization the problem that Pyrcz supposes it is? Third, its justification: is the democratic right to information more important than the liberal right of consumer choice?

The Proposal

Democracy requires informed citizens, and the performance of the media in Canada in this respect is less than perfect. What can be done about this? Pyrcz spends little time proposing solutions, but this is a major question that should be pursued. There are many possible solutions, for example, (i) a ban on the publication of polling results during election campaigns, and (ii) restrictions on the kinds of visuals used in brief news clips. Any proposal to improve the media's performance should be considered in terms of two constraints: whether it improves the *democratic* performance of the media, and whether the regulations it imposes upon the media can be justified.

How effective would Pyrcz's proposal for a licensing agency be? It must be assessed in the light of the problem it is intended to solve. According to Pyrcz, the problem is that journalism is commercialized. If so, requiring a licence would do little to solve the problem. Prospective journalists can be made to write exams, or go to graduate school, or swear allegiance to democratic standards; but once they are licensed, they will continue to produce for a market. The force of Pyrcz's proposal lies in its threat to revoke the licence, and thus the livelihood, of offending journalists. This would force journalists to maintain democratic standards, *if* they were frightened by the threat. But this would be an obnoxious way to defend a democratic press: we could also threaten to shoot offending journalists, or to close down their newspapers—would this be any better?

In any case, Pyrcz's proposal could not work because no one would take the threat seriously. The problem is that commercialization is popular; it seems to give people what they want. This is why, according to Pyrcz—journalists must be protected from the preferences of the people. But who is going to impose this regime? Imagine what would happen if a popular journalist were fired for "giving the people what they want." The idea smacks of victimization and censorship; no elected politician would dream of implementing it, and no nonelected body would have the power to do it. Pyrcz's "solution" is a paper tiger. It cannot work in a democracy. The licensing agency would be effective only if it were invested with autocratic powers. Is this the way to enforce democratic standards?

An important conclusion follows. It is easy to blame "the market," as though it were an alien force that has nothing to do with real people. But if the objection is to commercial, or popular, journalism, then the problem isn't really with journalism. It is with the public, and with what the public in its ignorance and prejudices makes popular. To fault the market here is to blame the people. Indeed, journalists are to be forbidden from doing what might be popular only to stop the public from having what it might want.

In this sense, the problem of the media as it is raised in the essay reflects a more general problem that has been debated at least since Plato. It can be raised not only about the media but also about politicians, teachers, doctors, and perhaps any "service" profession. As Plato asked,[2] what is the proper duty of the politician: to give citizens what they *want* or what they *need*? In a perfect world, there would be no problem. People would always want what they need, and vice versa. This is the assumption of consumer sovereignty. In reality, however, this is not always true. To give people what they want sometimes violates their interests by ignoring their needs. But every step in the direction of providing for their needs by ignoring what they want is a step away from democratic principles. Thus it can be argued that Pyrcz's proposal rejects democracy in the name of protecting it. The problem is that this proposal might be necessary. Is it?

Is Commercialization a Problem?

Is there anything wrong, in principle, with the commercialization of the news? At first glance, it seems that the mass-market media, especially print journalism, is a sea of competing sensationalism and oversimplification in the pursuit of sales and ratings. But there is something to be said on the other side.

Any judgment of imperfection assumes a standard of comparison with what is considered better or best. In journalism, imperfections are usually judged by comparisons with "quality" journalism. Even when these judgments are accurate, this way of judging means that there will always be imperfections. If one compares something with what is best, then the rest will necessarily be imperfect. However, this does not mean that the rest is inadequate or that it should be forbidden.

Further, people differ in their education, background, intelligence, and interest in political affairs. It follows that they will differ as well in the quality of journalism they prefer. Some will want depth and detail that are beyond the interest or capacity of others. As a result, the market for mass consumption will always be pitched below the level of the most demanding readers; what is commercially successful will necessarily be of comparatively lower quality. This does not mean that it is inadequate. It may simply mean that the news is being presented as adequately as possible for people at a certain level.[3] Although the commercialized version will be oversimplified and distorted in comparison with more demanding presentations, this is no reason for sneering at the inadequacies of commercialized news or of those who consume it.

Admittedly, some newspapers cannot be defended in this way. A tabloid is not making the news more accessible for its readers by running headlines such as "Doctors Prove That Ice Cream Is the Best Way to Lose Weight" or "Elvis Reincarnated in Mother Teresa's Body." But does anyone read these stories as "news"? If they do, making them read *The Globe and Mail* instead is hardly the solution!

On the other hand, much of the "quality" journalism in this country, such as *The Globe and Mail* and the CBC's *Journal*, is boring, pompous, and pretentious. It is remarkable that so many people take it seriously. Canadians should certainly be slow to legislate these examples as a standard. Few people will read the *Globe* under any conditions; if they cannot read the *Sun*, they will read nothing at all. Would this make democracy any better?

Differences in the quality of news presentations are inevitable. This does not mean that the lower-quality presentations are inadequate or that they should be forbidden. Nor does it mean that there is any problem in principle with commercialization.

The Justification: The Right to Information

The heart of Pyrcz's essay is its argument that the democratic right to information should take priority over the liberal right of consumer choice and that, as a result, journalists must be protected from the preferences of citizens. This argument is just wrong. In what way does consumer choice violate the right to information? This is never made clear in the essay, but there are two possibilities: (i) deliberate deception, or (ii) distortion through sensationalization.

Although the right to information is violated by deliberate deception, such deception has nothing to do with commercialization or with consumer choice. It can be forbidden in the same way as product misrepresentation is forbidden. Some might say that this violates the freedom of the press, but this view is mistaken. Freedom of the press is not an absolute principle; its value derives from its role in facilitating freedom of thought and expression for individuals. In some contexts, freedom of the press is the essential vehicle for individual thought and expression, but in other contexts what is claimed is the freedom to produce a commercial entertainment that has no direct relation to individual freedom of expression. In such cases, freedom of the press has no special value, and as a result it may be regulated in the same way as any other commercial activity.

This does not mean that the press *should* be regulated, but only that it is not as immune to regulation as it would be in cases involving genuine freedom of expression. Deliberate distortions of the news can be forbidden in the same way, and for the same reason, that product misrepresentation is prohibited in market transactions. In cases of deliberate deception, therefore, there is no need to make an issue out of the right of consumer choice. There is no conflict with this right and no basis for restricting it.

The situation is different with respect to the mass media. Here, the news is presented in a way that may be sensationalized, oversimplified, or vulgar. Although there is presumably no intention to deceive, the news is distorted for commercial reasons such as sales and ratings. This may be necessary, however, to make the news accessible for the intended audience, and the distortion may be insignificant.

How, then, is the right to information threatened by the right of consumer choice? Suppose a newspaper puts sports and scandal on its front page, and soft-core pornography just inside. So long as there are alternatives, people are free to buy the *Globe* if they want; hence a million others can buy the *Sun*, but this will not violate the *Globe* reader's right to information. In Pyrcz's view, however, the *Sun* reader's right is violated by reading the *Sun*. It doesn't matter whether there are alternatives or not. Reading the *Sun* violates the right because the reader has less information than if he or she had bought the *Globe*. From this perspective, what violates the right is the choice; hence, to protect the right, one must be protected from one's own choice. In the name of the right to information, therefore, a nonelected body will tell people what to read and forbid them the rest. Thus, the "right" to information is the right to read what others tell one to read.[4] Even if this were justified (and it is not), it is a travesty to call it a "right." It is regulation, control, and censorship, and it should be called by its proper name.

This is not to defend consumer sovereignty, which in this discussion is a red herring. It has nothing specifically to do with freedom of the press. The right of consumer preference is a general principle that can be used to oppose regulation in any situation. As a result, it is much weaker as a principle than are the freedoms of thought, expression, and publication. If there is a real objection to regulating the press, it will be raised in terms of freedom of thought. Those who object on the ground of consumer sovereignty do not have much ammunition and can be answered easily. For example, those who buy a television and then discover that there are bricks behind the screen cannot be answered with the comment, "Well, you bought it and you knew what you were getting, so there is no reason to complain."

The short answer to those who raise the principle of consumer sovereignty against the regulation of the press is that no one takes the principle seriously anywhere else, so why here? In any case, the principle is inapplicable as a defence of the press. If the news is not distorted, the press needs no defence, because there is no reason to regulate it. But if the news is distorted, consumer sovereignty would not defend it. People may buy distorted news, but not if they *know* it is distorted. The fact that they buy it doesn't mean that they want distorted news. What they want is *news*—honest information. As a defence of the media, then, the claim that it gives people "what they want" is either unnecessary or false.

The Importance of Individual Expression

There is no need to reject the market orientation of journalism completely or to insist that journalists be protected from the preferences of the public. People want the news to be accessible, that is, to be communicated in terms they can understand without first having to get a Ph.D. The preferences implied by this criterion—relating to scheduling, depth, style, and so on—differ among individuals and will probably best be met by some form of market competition.

In this, as in any other market, regulation is necessary to protect individuals from deception, especially to protect the quality of communication in relation to democratic norms. What Pyrcz calls the "right" to information would better be called a requirement. For him, the main problem in legislating this right or requirement is that it violates the right of consumer choice. This is too weak a concern to be much of a problem; the principle that must be respected is the right of individual expression.

Notes

1. Following the essay's usage, this critique refers generally to the presentation of information as news, public affairs, and analysis by all of the mass media. Unless the context indicates otherwise, "media," "press," and "journalism" are used in this wide sense, and examples drawn from one medium are intended to apply to all.
2. See, especially, Plato's dialogue *Gorgias*.
3. Mass-market newspapers usually have excellent sports sections; a quality sports section is a proven way to sell newspapers. This suggests again that the lower quality of the news presentations in these papers should not be blamed on commercialization itself or on the stupidities of the readers.
4. The same thing happens to "freedom" of the press in Pyrcz's account. He construes it as the *duty* to inform citizens; as a "duty," however, it is no longer freedom but constraint and obligation. If journalists do not exercise this freedom/duty adequately, in the opinion of licensing boards, they risk losing their livelihoods. Thus, "freedom of the press" as Pyrcz describes it is only the "freedom" to do what others require.

Discussion Questions

1. Does democracy require a citizenry that is as completely informed as possible? If so, is democracy really possible?

2. Is Pyrcz's defence of a college of journalists essentially elitist? If so, is this form of elitism at odds with democracy?

3. Are liberal rights fundamental to democracy, or is democracy the "bottom line" against which liberal political rights are properly rationalized?

4. Is Canadian journalism as hopelessly isolated from democratic citizenship as both Pyrcz and Carmichael are prepared to contend?

Further Readings

The literature on the press and on the mass media generally has proliferated in recent years. Those seeking a balanced and widely drawn introduction cannot do better than to read Ross Eaman's *The Media Society* (Toronto and Vancouver: Butterworths, 1987). Eaman surveys a wide range of issues in the politics of the mass media and provides a consideration of the theoretical bases necessary to develop a point of view on both the media's power in forming social consensus and the measures that may be required to constrain it. The author is sensitive to the challenge to democracy that the mass media may pose and discusses issues in this light.

Those with a taste for more provocative work would be more than satisfied by the splendid critical posture that Dan Nimmo and James Coombs bring to their *Mediated Political Realities*, 2nd ed. (New York: Longman, 1990). This book borrows from and builds upon the work of Marshall McLuhan. It is especially useful for those who would like to discover what this chapter's essayist is so concerned about in the trends he asserts are undermining journalism in Canada.

Those who want a closer analysis of the issues troubling journalism in Canada should consult the background papers to the Kent Commission, *Report of the Royal Commission on Newspapers* (Hull: Government of Canada, Ministry of Supply and Services, 1981). The background papers and the report are available in the government documents section of most university libraries and in most of Canada's larger public libraries.

CHAPTER 9

Democracy and the Obligation to Obey the Law

In this chapter's essay, Tom Pocklington argues a twofold thesis: there is no general obligation to obey the law, and the acceptance of this conclusion should have desirable political consequences. The only line of reasoning for an obligation to obey the law that is likely to be accepted nowadays, he maintains, is one that traces this obligation to the consent of citizens. Accordingly, he examines several versions of "consent theory," finds them all wanting, and concludes that there is no general obligation to obey the law. Moreover, he maintains that this conclusion should be accepted warmly rather than anxiously, because it is likely to improve both lawmakers and citizens.

In his critique, Greg Pyrcz argues that there is a viable consent theory of political obligation. He holds that participating in politics is analogous to participating in a game. Just as anyone who voluntarily participates in a game implicitly consents to abide by its rules, so a participant in the "game" of politics implicitly consents to abide by its rules. Since most Canadians participate in politics at least to some extent, and since obeying the law is part and parcel of the game of politics, they incur—by implied consent— an obligation to obey the law. Pyrcz finds it unnecessary to examine the political implications of Pocklington's argument about political obligation, because if the argument is unsound it should have no practical implications.

||E||S||S||A||Y||

Nowadays almost everyone believes that it is sometimes permissible, or even obligatory, to disobey the law for political purposes. Several democracies and near-democracies were born in revolution, and it would be profoundly inconsistent to celebrate their liberation while denying to subjects of other corrupt, oppressive, and unjust regimes the same right to rebel. But it is not clear that Canadian citizens are permitted to disobey the laws of their *own* communities, which, partly because they are liberal and democratic, Canadians regard as basically just. The right or duty to disobey the law apparently arises when the regime is profoundly unjust and oppressive. At first glance, then, this right or duty seems to have little or no direct bearing on the way Canadians live their lives.

However, on further consideration most of them would probably qualify this proposition somewhat. When citizens of a liberal democracy have been treated very unjustly for a long period of time, and when they have pursued many avenues of *legal* redress for their grievances with no success, most Canadians would say that these people were justified in engaging in at least some *moderate* illegal political actions. Typically, Canadians would say that these people are entitled to engage in *civil disobedience*, which has the following characteristics: it is public rather than clandestine; it is nonviolent; it is symbolic, in that it is designed to draw the attention of the government and the attentive public to unjust laws or policies; and those who engage in it willingly submit to arrest and trial. Thus, for example, many would defend most of the illegal activities of the American civil rights protesters of the 1960s and 1970s, even while regarding the American political system as basically just. The thread running through the standard definition of civil disobedience is that, though it involves lawbreaking, it does not disrespect, let alone challenge, governmental authority. It exhibits grievances against particular laws or policies while displaying fidelity to law.[1] It is generally believed that only this *limited* sort of political disobedience can be justified in a liberal democracy.

The general view, then, is that the requirements for defending political disobedience in a liberal democracy are fundamentally different from, and far more demanding than, the requirements for justifying resistance of, or revolt against, regimes that are neither liberal nor democratic. The difference is held to be as follows. In illiberal and undemocratic regimes, political disobedience is sufficiently justified by drawing attention to the inhumanity or injustice of the regime itself, or to the perversity of its policies, or even merely to the iniquity of some or most of its laws. In liberal democracies, in contrast, political disobedience is justified only if it can be shown that the evil or injustice motivating the lawbreaking is so serious, or that the authorities are so unwilling to mend their ways, that it is permissible to refuse to comply even though all residents of liberal democracies have a general moral obligation to obey the law. Unlike the subjects of other kinds of regimes, citizens of liberal democracies are justified in disobeying the law only if their reasons for disobeying it are strong enough to *override* their moral obligation to obey the law. Thus, for such citizens there is *always* a *presumption against* political disobedience. They have a moral political obligation that allows them to disobey only if their reasons are grave.

This essay will argue that there is no general moral obligation to obey the laws of liberal democracies as they now operate. This view may seem unsound and dangerous. It may seem unsound because it appears to place liberal democracies on exactly the same footing as the most despicable tyrannies. It seems to imply that citizens of liberal democracies have as much right to disobey the law as do the subjects of the most oppressive autocracies. Furthermore, it is likely to seem dangerous because it appears to license indiscriminate lawlessness. If there is no obligation to obey the law, *carte blanche* appears to be offered to those who would disobey the law indiscriminately and for the most selfish purposes no less than to Mahatma Gandhi or Martin Luther King Jr.

Since there seem to be grounds for concern not only about the soundness of the contention that there is no general moral obligation to obey the law but also about the political consequences of accepting and acting on that contention, two theses will be argued here: first, there is no general moral obligation to obey the law; second, this conclusion is not alarming in its political consequences. Since this essay will deal at some length with the second thesis, it deals with the first only in part. Although several lines of argument support the view that there is a general moral obligation to obey the law, at least in liberal democracies, the essay criticizes only variations of the most widely accepted of these, that is, arguments based on "consent," and simply assumes that other arguments for political obligation are also indefensible. This approach leaves room to argue that, though the conclusion that there is no political obligation is not dangerous, neither is it merely an armchair conclusion, a philosophical anarchism that has no political significance.[2]

The essay's argument is presented in five parts. The first part deals with the notions of obligation and political obligation. The second part explores the concept of consent and criticizes theories that attempt to ground political obligation in express consent. In the third part, theories based on tacit consent are considered and found to be no more convincing than those based on the express variety. Criticism of consent theories of political obligation is concluded in the fourth part, where the theory that consent can be inferred from receipt of benefits is examined and found wanting. The final part addresses the central question of this chapter: what if there is no moral obligation to obey the law?

Notions of Obligation

In the writings of moral, legal, and political philosophers, as well as in ordinary conversation, the term "obligation" is often used loosely. As often as not, "obligation" is used to refer to what a person should do, that is, anything it would be wrong not to do. In this very broad sense, it is one's obligation in any set of circumstances to do whatever one should do in that set of circumstances, "all things considered." For example, it is one's obligation not to wander around wrecking wheelchairs, because it would be wrong for one to do it, all things considered. This extraordinarily broad sense of obligation is mentioned here mainly to emphasize that it plays no part in the arguments discussed in the rest of this essay. There are two reasons for this. First, so broad a sense of obligation is utterly unhelpful; there is no point in speaking of an obligation not to wreck wheelchairs. The term "obligation" just gets in the way of saying what needs to be said: the conduct in question is wrong.

Second, those who maintain that there is a moral obligation to obey the law cannot be appealing to this sense of obligation. Proponents of a general political obligation usually acknowledge that there are circumstances in which it is permissible, if not obligatory, to disobey the law. They could not maintain this if they held that one should always obey the law, all things considered. They must hold that, at least under some circumstances, this obligation can be overridden or, as it is sometimes put, that it is "defeasible." Accordingly, it is a defining characteristic of obligations that they can be overridden. Proponents of the view that there is a general moral obligation to obey the law maintain that sometimes this obligation is defeated by weightier considerations, such as the existence of an extremely unjust regime or the persistent failure of a liberal democracy to redress the grievances of an oppressed minority.

Although one sense of "obligation" is so broad as to be practically useless, the distinction between a broad and a narrow sense of obligation is pertinent to this inquiry. It is most easily explicated by dealing first with the narrow sense. The main feature of an obligation in the narrow sense is that it is self-assumed, that is, the person who acquires the obligation does so by a voluntary obligating act. An example of an obligation in the narrow sense is a promise. If one person promises to lend another a certain book, that person acquires an obligation to the other to do what was promised. Moreover, at the same time the other person acquires a right against the first. The first person's obligation and the other person's right are *correlative*. They come into being at the same time and through the same act, and they are inseparable.

An obligation in the broad sense has the same characteristics as an obligation in the narrow sense, except that it is not self-assumed.[3] In particular, this sort of obligation, like the other, involves a correlativity between right and obligation: if A has an obligation to B, B has a right against A, and vice versa. But here obligation is not undertaken voluntarily, as in the example of the narrow sense of obligation, the promise. Examples of obligations in the broad sense are the obligations of parents to their children and of children to their parents, or one's obligation of gratitude to those who have benefited one, or one's obligation to assist people in distress when one is in a position to do so.

Obligations, in both the narrow and the broad senses, have the essential characteristic of defeasibility. Consider once again the example of the obligation in the narrow sense, the promise. If A promises to meet B at a certain time and place, A has an obligation to do so. But if, on A's way to meet B, A is called on to assist someone who has sustained a serious injury, A must do what is required, all things considered, and assist the victim rather than fulfil the obligation. This does not mean that A's obligation somehow disappears in the face of the more stringent requirement; A still has the obligation to meet B. It is just that the more powerful requirement *overrides* the obligation. The same condition holds for obligations in the broad sense. For example, one's obligation to pay special attention to the well-being of one's parents can be overridden by the need to tend one's ailing child. Thus, obligations in both the broad and the narrow sense can be overridden, and therefore they satisfy an indispensable condition for suitability as the basis for a theory of political obligation.

The claim that Canadian citizens have a moral obligation to obey the law is a claim *in either the broad or the narrow sense of obligation*. Several theories of political obligation rely on obligation in its broad sense. Examples are religiously based theories of obedience, such as the divine right of kings, and theories of natural law. These theories rely on the broad sense of obligation because they hold that citizens or subjects are morally bound to obey whether or not they have performed any voluntary obligation-incurring act. However, since the seventeenth century, most proponents of political obligation have appealed to the narrow sense of obligation. With the rise of individualism and the increasing emphasis on personal freedom, most theorists have found it implausible to suppose that any adult could be morally obligated to obey anyone else unless he or she voluntarily agreed to do so. By far the most widely accepted of the theories of political obligation that rely on the narrow sense of the term are the consent theories.

Theories of Consent

The theory that citizens have a moral obligation to obey the law based on their express consent is associated with some of the most famous modern classics of political philosophy, especially Thomas Hobbe's *Leviathan*, John Locke's *Second Treatise of Government*, and Jean-Jacques Rousseau's *Social Contract*. Moreover, this view suffers from no lack of recent adherents; it is elaborated by such theorists as Robert Nozick, John Plamenatz, Joseph Tussman, and Michael Walzer.[4]

The notion of "consent" has sometimes been assimilated into the notions of "promise" and "agreement." Although there are contexts in which these terms are interchangeable, in relation to political obligation the core meaning of consent is most closely related (as Hobbes clearly recognized) to authorization.[5] One acquires a moral obligation to obey the law by authorizing a person, or a group of people, or an institution to prescribe rules and regulations to govern one's conduct. It is *because* one has *voluntarily* authorized others to act on one's behalf that one has an obligation to obey.

The crucial premise underlying all consent theories is that all sane adults are naturally free and equal.[6] In consent theory, the claim that individuals are naturally free and equal is most importantly an assertion that people are all alike in that no one is "naturally" (by virtue of strength, pedigree, wisdom, special relationship to supernatural powers, or any other characteristic) the legitimate ruler of anyone else. This being the case, rightful government exists only when individuals consent to be ruled. All authority derives from the consent of the governed.

The version of consent theory that holds that citizens have a moral obligation to obey the law because they have personally and expressly consented to do so has been thoroughly and frequently discredited in the past couple of centuries. The most blatant flaw in the theory is that most people have never given their express consent. Admittedly, immigrants are often required to swear an oath of allegiance and some public officials formally vow to uphold the law, but they are rare exceptions. Most people have never been asked for their express consent, let alone given it.

Moreover, a single expression of consent is insufficient. People change their minds, often with good reason, and sometimes people *should* change their minds. Changing one's mind is not logically incompatible with the theory of express consent, but it is difficult for the theory to make room for it, since it leaves open the possibility that a one-time consentor might later become a dissenter and thereby not be subject to political obligation.

Finally, it has been argued, on the ground of express consent, that some people sometimes have a moral obligation to disobey the law.[7] Michael Walzer's central idea is that, though few people expressly consent to obey the state, many voluntarily join more limited groups, such as political organizations, churches, trade unions, and neighbourhood associations. It is much more plausible, Walzer argues, to maintain that people have consented to abide by the decisions of the more limited group than that they have consented to obey the laws of the state. Therefore, if the laws of the state conflict with the precepts of one's church, one may have a moral obligation based on consent to disobey the laws of the state. Although Walzer does not draw this conclusion, the reasoning seems to entail that *if the focus is on express consent*, most people are more likely to have moral obligations to disobey the law than to obey it.

There are several other serious defects in the theory of express consent as a defence of the claim that citizens have a moral obligation to obey the law. Those presented here, however, show that the theory is not worth pursuing further. Even the earliest consent theorists were aware of the frailties of theories of political obligation based on express consent. The standard way of trying to overcome the problems was, and for some theorists still is, to invoke the less demanding notion of tacit consent.

The Notion of Tacit Consent

John Locke, perhaps the most famous of all consent theorists, exemplifies the shift from express to tacit consent. In his *Second Treatise of Government*, he states forcefully the basic assumption of theorists of express consent: the sane adult residents of a "state of nature," that is, a society without government, are naturally free and are equal in their freedom. Accordingly, they can be governed legitimately only if they consent to be governed. Locke finds that the state of nature is attended by a number of "inconveniences" that make it advantageous to form governments. However, in view of everyone's natural freedom and equality, a legitimate government can be formed only with the unanimous consent of the citizens.

Even if it is conceded that small political societies were formed in this way or that the only kind of legitimate political society is one that acts as if it had been formed in this way, at least two serious problems arise. First, even for those hypothetical political societies that were formed initially by unanimous consent, how would public decisions be reached thereafter? It is inconceivable that all decisions should be ratified by unanimous express consent. Second, people form governments and thereby emerge from the state of nature only once. The question arises, how do members of succeeding generations give or withhold consent? Why is a citizen obligated to obey the laws of a regime that was authorized by a distant ancestor?

Locke was aware of these problems and tried to solve them. To solve the problem of showing that, once a political society is formed by express consent, subsequent governmental decisions are also based on consent, he argued that the initial unanimous consent was a consent to be ruled thereafter by whatever government enjoyed the consent of the majority. He presented a number of arguments in favour of majority rule, but whatever one thinks of those arguments,[8] they surely do not do the job Locke intended them to do. Whatever the merits of majority rule, it simply is not the case that one consents to laws, policies, practices, or institutions that one in fact opposes.[9]

Recently, J.P. Plamenatz produced a revised version of Locke's theory.[10] In brief, Plamenatz argued that voting, whether for a winning or a losing candidate, *implies* consent to the liberal democratic process and establishes an obligation (which can be overridden) to obey the law. According to Plamenatz, since the point of voting is to choose rulers and, indirectly, some policies within a liberal democratic regime, the act of voting implies consent, even from those who detest the winners and their policies.

This argument seems quite unsound. One of the most obvious objections, but no less powerful for that, has been advanced by Carole Patemen. She points out that in some parts of the world, notably Australia, voting is required by law. Can an Australian who deliberately spoils a ballot (to avoid a fine) be said to consent?[11] Even where there is no compulsory voting, Plamenatz's theory runs into trouble. Does one consent if one votes for a party that openly affirms its intention to abolish free elections? Does one consent to obey the laws of the Canadian, French, or British governments if one votes for a militant Québecois, Basque, or Scottish separatist party? No. Plamenatz does not rescue the thesis that majority consent can serve as a substitute for individual consent.

To encompass those who were not part of the initial founding consent, Locke appeals to the notion of tacit consent. The purpose of tacit consent in Locke's theory of political obligation is that it substitutes for express consent without requiring an express statement. When one consents tacitly, one consents by acting in a way that communicates one's consent without stating expressly that one does consent. Locke sees a difficulty here, namely, that of determining "what ought to be looked upon as a tacit consent, and how far it binds, i.e., how far any one shall be looked on to have consented, and thereby to have submitted to any government, where he has made no expressions of it at all.'"[12]

Locke's answer to this question is an implausibly sweeping conception of tacit consent. He maintains that citizens consent tacitly to the authority of a government merely by accepting the protection it provides. Thus, for example, people consent to governmental authority simply by accepting a night's lodging or by travelling freely on the highway.[13] These indications of tacit consent go "as far as the very being of any one within the territories of that government."[14] The trouble with Locke's notion of tacit consent is that through it he broadens the notion of consent to the point that it is unrecognizable. Giving consent is intelligible only in contrast to withholding it. But in Locke's theory, giving tacit consent is practically unavoidable and tacitly refraining from consent is practically impossible. Under these circumstances, the notion of tacit consent becomes meaningless.[15]

The notion is not, however, incurably empty. Consider the following example. A university has a rule that examinations can be given only at specified times, unless all the students consent to its being held at a different time. The professor asks the students whether they are opposed to their examinations being held on a date other than the one scheduled. None of them signifies opposition. On the face of it, this is an instance of genuine tacit consent. The students have actually consented, but through their silence rather than through express authorization.[16]

In *Moral Principles and Political Obligation*, A. John Simmons has provided a thoughtful discussion of the conditions necessary for tacit consent. He finds five conditions to be especially important:

(i)   The situation must be such that it is perfectly clear that consent is appropriate and that the individual is aware of this.

(ii) There must be a definite period of reasonable duration when objections or expressions of dissent are invited or clearly appropriate, and the acceptable means of expressing this dissent must be understood by or made known to the potential consentor.

(iii) The point at which expressions of dissent are no longer acceptable must be obvious or made clear in some way to the potential consentor.

(iv) The means acceptable for indicating dissent must be reasonable and reasonably easily performed.

(v)   The consequences of dissent cannot be extremely detrimental to the potential consentor.[17]

A crucial feature of Simmons's conditions is that they emphasize that tacit consent is intentional. Silence can be construed as consent only when it is meant to be so construed. In political contexts, this means that the simple silence of the absence of protest or resistance is not tacit consent. Just as a professor is not entitled to conclude that students tacitly approve of his or her teaching simply because they do not complain to the dean, so governments cannot conclude that citizens tacitly consent to laws simply because they do not defy them.

The conditions necessary for tacit consent are not available to most people in modern states, including the liberal democracies. Most people have no more opportunity to acquire a moral obligation to obey the law by consenting tacitly than by consenting expressly. At most, they can express their approval or refrain from engaging in acts of defiance. But this is not consent—express or tacit.

It may be that Locke's conception of tacit consent has been given unduly short shrift. His point is that the acceptance of benefits from a government, such as the police protection that makes it possible to travel freely on a highway, could be argued to establish a tacit obligation to obey the law. If people *willingly* accept such benefits, they *do* tacitly consent to sustain the government, and this consent *does* involve a moral obligation to obey the law. Arguments of this kind, which have been called "benefits arguments," have recently become increasingly popular among political theorists.

Benefits Arguments

Do citizens consent to a government and thereby acquire a moral obligation to obey its laws by accepting the benefits it provides? Like Locke, several recent political philosophers have argued that citizens do. Two of the most penetrating of these writers are Hanna Pitkin and John Rawls. Pitkin's argument is based on a reassessment of Locke.[18] She acknowledges that Locke stretches the notion of tacit consent to the point where it is no longer recognizable as consent at all. Nevertheless, she holds that *The Second Treatise of Government* contains the rudiments of a consistent and persuasive theory of political obligation that can be reasonably described as a consent theory. She argues that Locke's assumptions (about, for example, the nature of man, the strength and scope of natural rights, and the substance of natural law) are such that there is only one kind of political society to which rational adults *could* consent. In her interpretation, the heart of Locke's theory of political obligation is not a doctrine about the personal histories of individuals as regards their consent to government, but a doctrine about the *only possible* kind of government to which rational individuals could consent.

The crucial question is not what kind of political society people did or do consent to, but what they *should* consent to. Pitkin labels this the theory of "hypothetical consent." She regards the consent label as appropriate because the kind of government to which people should consent (that is, the only kind to which they hypothetically do consent) is a good, just government. Good, just governments are best conceived as those that confer a wide range of material and nonmaterial benefits on their citizens. Such governments have a variety of characteristics, such as responsiveness to popular demands, that are reasonably described as exhibiting consent in a broad sense. Pitkin argues that this theory, suitably elaborated, can form part of a satisfactory theory of political obligation.

But is the doctrine of hypothetical consent really a consent theory? It is not. When the question arises, central to any theory of political obligation, "Why does one have an obligation to obey the law?", Pitkin's answer must ultimately refer to what would, or should, be said by a hypothetical rational person. This person's reply must, in turn, refer to the goodness and justness of governments, that is, of governments that "deliver the goods" to their citizens, for it is to such governments that rational persons should consent. Therefore, actual consent, whether express or tacit, is not the foundation of any moral obligation to obey the law.

If citizens have an obligation to obey the law, it is not because they have consented to do so but because they are bound to obey good, just governments that provide the benefits that governments should provide. But most theorists now reject the view that any adult could be obligated to obey anyone else unless he or she voluntarily incurred that obligation. The current general view of government is that it may give citizens what it thinks is good for them, and it may be right. But if citizens don't want it, why should they be obliged to take it, or submit to the government's view of what is good for them? The doctrine of hypothetical consent clearly violates this outlook. It says that citizens should obey a good, just government, regardless of what they want or what they think is good for them.

John Rawls's monumental book, *A Theory of Justice*, has probably received more attention in the English-speaking world than any other work of political philosophy written in the twentieth century. As part of his theory of justice, Rawls elaborates a theory of political obligation that is applicable at least to liberal democracies and is based on "the traditional theory of the social contract as represented by Locke, Rousseau, and Kant."[19] However, consent, either express or tacit, plays no part in Rawl's theory, and Rawls makes no pretense that it does. The main idea he borrows from the traditional consent theorists is the fundamental premise that persons are "naturally" free and equal. His theories of justice and political obligation are based on the principles that would be agreed to by rational and self-interested hypothetical contractors.

In Rawls's theory, the *consent* of actual persons is replaced by the *assent* of hypothetical persons who are in several important ways unlike actual persons, and political obligation is based not on consent but on the fairness with which social institutions distribute benefits. More specifically, Rawls maintains that the "person" best placed to assess the justice or injustice of basic social and political arrangements is one who is ignorant of his or her own identity. In particular, this "person" does not know its position in society, for example, its income, wealth, rights, opportunities, responsibilities, or social status. It does not even know its own goals in life or its ability or disposition to achieve whatever goals it turns out to have. It is thereby unable to tailor principles of justice to provide itself with special advantages. It is genuinely "Everyperson," because it is no particular person; for this reason, above all, Rawls believes that it would choose sound principles of justice.

The leading principle of justice that would be chosen by Rawls's hypothetical person is that "each person is to have an equal right to the most extensive basic liberty compatible with a similar liberty for others."[20] As Rawls elaborates this principle, it becomes clear that he sees it as justifying the main features of the liberal democratic state.[21] He holds that the citizens of such a state have a moral obligation to obey its laws.[22]

This summary of Rawls's theory of political obligation is not intended to suggest that he somehow fraudulently passes himself off as a consent theorist. Although he adopts some of the fundamental ideas of the classical consent theorists, Rawls makes no attempt to base a theory of political obligation on consent. Instead, he travels much further along the path started by Pitkin. Like Rawls, Pitkin accepts some of the basic ideas of the consent theorists. However, although she sees that neither express nor tacit consent will do the job they were intended to do, she clings to the belief that something worthy of being called a consent theory of political obligation can be salvaged from the wreckage; hence the theory of "hypothetical consent." Rawls, in contrast, sees that consent can't do the job and uses some of the ideas of Locke, Rousseau, and Kant to construct a theory of political obligation quite different from theirs. A theory founded on the rational assent of a hypothetical person is a long way from a theory of tacit, let alone express, consent.

Neither express nor tacit consent provides the basis for a tenable theory of political obligation. Increasingly, political theorists are recognizing the futility of trying to resurrect consent as the basis for political obligation and, like Rawls, they are attempting to construct or revitalize theories that do not rest on consent. There is now a considerable number of theories of political obligation, ancient and modern. Limitations of space forbid even a cursory examination of them here, but suppose that *all* theories according to which citizens have a moral obligation to obey the law are defective.[23] What then?

Is There a Moral Obligation to Obey the Law?

Many people find the suggestion that there is no moral obligation to obey the law disturbing. They are likely to agree with the sentiments of the philosopher Kurt Baier:

> If there is no political obligation, then each person living in the territory of . . . a state in reason may and should consider each directive of . . . a government on its own merits: he can please himself whether to obey or disobey, following his inclinations or his own best interests—unless, of course, he has some special moral obligation to obey such directives, e.g., special favors received or a freely given oath of allegiance, and so on.[24]

This view is mistaken. It neglects the possibility that there may be a moral obligation to obey the laws of certain kinds of regimes but not others. Even if this possibility is ignored, it is still not the case that, if there is no moral obligation to obey the law, then (barring such special obligations as those incurred by the few who actually do consent) people may obey or disobey laws as inclination or calculation of advantage dictates. To say that there is no moral obligation to obey laws is not to say that moral considerations are irrelevant to the rightness or wrongness of obeying or disobeying; this is clear in the case of such acts as rape and murder. It is preposterous to suggest that people can please themselves as to whether or not to obey such laws. But this point does not hold only in regard to courses of action that are "wrong in themselves." How could it be maintained that the decision to drive on the left or right side of the road is a matter of moral indifference?

The relevance of moral considerations is not confined to uncontroversial laws. Should one obey or disobey a law that prohibits abortions except to save the life of the mother? Should one pay taxes to finance the testing of nuclear weapons? These questions are certainly controversial, and they cannot be answered without reference to moral considerations. The denial of a moral obligation to obey the law does not imply that the decision whether or not to obey particular laws is a matter of moral indifference.

Notwithstanding these considerations, there seems to be something right about Baier's view, namely, that if there is no moral obligation to obey the law, then it is permissible to consider each law on its own merits. This conjures up the vision of morally earnest political agents exhausting their waking hours to evaluate laws, and little imagination is required to make this vision even more distasteful. The question is not simply whether particular laws are good or bad, or just or unjust; it is whether they should be *obeyed*. Therefore, it is essential to consider not only what a law prescribes but also how it is administered, since a law that is good on paper can be perverted if it is badly interpreted and enforced. Moreover, even finding that a law is good and well administered does not mean that it should be obeyed. To mention only one possibility, disobeying that law may be justified as a means of protesting a law or policy that cannot be disobeyed, such as a policy of giving military aid to despotic foreign governments.

This vision, however, is unfounded. The vast bulk of the legislation of the modern state does not provoke agonizing moral decisions. Most of it is of a housekeeping nature and does not threaten to introduce new abuses. Moreover, the division of labour in the scrutinizing of governmental activity prevents gross abuses. Even the most politically attentive rely to some extent on others, such as callers to talk-radio shows or fellow party members, for intelligence of official skulduggery. The picture of citizens earnestly scrutinizing each and every law is a caricature.

Caricatures, however, exaggerate real characteristics, and it must be emphasized that it does make a difference whether there is a moral obligation to obey the law. If there is such an obligation, the burden of proof always rests on those who contemplate disobedience to show that the reasons for disobedience are sufficient to override the obligation to obey; the citizen is always on the moral defensive. But if there is no such obligation, the question whether or not anyone may (or should) disobey may (and should) be decided, as Baier put it, "on its merits." However, this does not mean that deciding on the merits of the case is simply a matter of acting on one's inclinations or calculations of advantage while being constrained only by the special obligations one may have acquired.

In deciding whether or not to obey particular laws, one must evaluate a range of considerations, including: (i) the goodness or badness of the laws (keeping in mind that good laws may be corrupted by bad administration and bad laws may be modified for the better by good administration); (ii) the relationship between the law(s) in question and other laws and policies (other things being equal, disobedience is more likely to be justified when directed against laws that are part of a syndrome of governmental wrongdoing); (iii) the likelihood that abuses can be remedied by legal rather than illegal means (other things being equal, the former will be more easily justified); (iv) the nature of the regime whose laws are in question (other things being equal, the better the regime, the easier it will be to defend compliance with its directives); and (v) the likelihood that obedience or disobedience will have good results. Thus, to say that there is no moral obligation to obey the law is not to say that in deciding whether to obey or disobey one has a moral *carte blanche*; but it does mean that the cards are not stacked in favour of obedience.

Consequently, the denial of political obligation does not carry with it the sinister implications attributed to it by writers like Baier. Considering laws on their merits would have two highly desirable consequences. First, if enough citizens were more hesitant about complying with bad laws, governments would be more careful in enacting laws in the first place. The second desirable consequence was stated eloquently by John Stuart Mill:

> The first element of good government being. . . the virtue and intelligence of the human beings composing the community, the most important point of excellence which any form of government can possess is to promote the virtue and intelligence of the people themselves.[25]

Few things would contribute more to the virtue and intelligence of citizens than their careful consideration of which laws they should obey and which ones they should ignore or resist.

Notes

1. In this essay, "political disobedience" refers to any illegal act or campaign intended to serve political purposes. Civil disobedience is thus one among several types of political disobedience. See John Rawls, *A Theory of Justice* (Cambridge, Mass.: Harvard University Press, 1971), pp. 364–68; Hugo A. Bedau, "On Civil Disobedience," *Journal of Philosophy* (1961), pp. 653–61. However, see also Bedau's remarks in Bedau, ed., *Civil Disobedience: Theory and Practice* (New York: Pegasus, 1969), pp. 218–19, which identify problems with a number of conceptions of civil disobedience, including his own.
2. Robert Paul Wolff, in *In Defense of Anarchism* (New York: Harper and Row, 1970), argues, as this essay does, that there is no political obligation. But his "anarchism" seems to be of the armchair variety and to have no political implications worth mentioning. In contrast, A. John Simmons, in his beautifully argued *Moral Principles and Political Obligations* (Princeton: Princeton University Press, 1979), though describing himself as a "philosophical anarchist," reaches conclusions that are politically weightier and more radical than he seems to recognize.
3. It is preferable to call obligations in the broad sense *duties* and to reserve "obligation" for voluntarily assumed requirements. This terminology has its own difficulties, because duties are often associated with positions in institutions (parent, comptroller, minister, shop steward, etc.), but its advantages outweigh its costs.
4. Robert Nozick, *Anarchy, State, and Utopia* (New York: Basic Books, 1974); J.P. Plamenatz, *Consent, Freedom, and Political Obligation*, 2nd ed. (Oxford: Oxford University Press, 1968); Joseph Tussman, *Obligation*

and the Body Politic (New York: Oxford University Press, 1960); Michael Walzer, *Obligations: Essays on Disobedience, War, and Citizenship* (New York: Simon and Schuster, 1971).

5. In *The Problem of Political Obligation: A Critique of Liberal Theory* (New York: Wiley, 1979) Carole Pateman laments that the voluntarism she sees as an essential ingredient of a democratic theory of political obligation has been reduced to a liberal "consent" that is, in liberal democratic regimes, at most an authorization for the rulers to govern the ruled. Simmons, in *Moral Principles and Political Obligations*, p. 76, suggests that acts of consent are "essentially authorizations of the actions of others."

6. In the classical consent theories and even in some recent statements, this means all sane *male* adults. See Pateman, especially the "Afterword" to the 1985 edition of her book.

7. Michael Walzer, "The Obligation to Disobey," *Ethics* (1967), pp. 163–75, which has been reprinted as chapter 1 of Walzer, *Obligations*.

8. Locke's arguments concerning majority role are given a penetrating discussion in Willmoore Kendall, *John Locke and the Doctrine of Majority Rule* (Urbana: University of Illinois Press, 1941).

9. This is not to say that there are never good reasons for abiding by the will of the majority. It simply means that majority consent is not necessarily one's own consent.

10. Plamenatz.

11. Pateman, p. 86.

12. Locke, *Second Treatise*, Section 119.

13. Locke.

14. Locke.

15. A couple of decades ago, Joseph Tussman attempted to revive the consent theory of political obligation while recognizing that a consent theory must acknowledge that many citizens never (and perhaps could never) actually consent. In what appears to be an appeal to tacit consent, Tussman described the nonconsentors as "child-bride citizens." It is difficult to see how child brides can be taken to have consented, explicitly or tacitly, and Tussman does not clarify the matter. See Tussman, especially pp. 36–37.

16. It is difficult to know without further information that this really is an instance of tacit consent. Suppose, that university students had good reason to believe that they would be penalized if they objected to the professor rescheduling the examination. That would clearly undermine the voluntariness of their conduct and thereby vitiate any claim that they had given consent *of any kind*. In other words, lack of voluntariness is not a problem peculiar to *tacit* consent; it relates to consent in general.

17. These five conditions are quoted directly from Simmons, pp. 80–81, but with some ellipses and changes in the style of presentation.

18. Hanna Pitkin's reassessment of John Locke is set out in "Obligation and Consent, I," *American Political Science Review* (1965), pp. 990–99. She defends the elaborated version of the theory of political obligation she finds in Locke in "Obligation and Consent, II," *American Political Science Review* (1966), pp. 39–52.

19. Rawls, p. viii.

20. Rawls, p. 60.

21. Rawls, pp. 61, 221–27, 356–62.

22. However, he does not allow that civil disobedience is sometimes justified in liberal democracies. Rawls, pp. 363–91.

23. Very few political theorists accept this view; the most impressive exception is Simmons. M.B.E. Smith also makes some telling points in "Is There a Prima Facie Obligation to Obey the Law?," *Yale Law Journal* (1973), pp. 950–76. Carole Pateman argues that there is no obligation to obey the laws of existing regimes but that there would be such an obligation in a genuinely participatory democracy. Robert Paul Wolff defends a "philosophical anarchism" with philosophically weak and politically insipid arguments.

24. Kurt Baier, "Obligation: Legal and Moral," in *Nomos XII: Political and Legal Obligation*, ed. J. Roland Pennock and John W. Chapman (New York: Atherton Press, 1970), p. 117.

25. John Stuart Mill, *Considerations on Representative Government* (New York: Liberal Arts Press, 1958), p. 42.

CRITIQUE

In this daring essay, Tom Pocklington argues that there are no compelling arguments to support a *prima facie* obligation to obey the law. This is true, he insists, even of the law generated in democratic institutions by democratic politics. Bolder still is the author's contention that this essentially anarchist conclusion is a desirable one. Pocklington is not opposed to public order *per se*. But, he maintains, any legitimate public order can only stem, at least morally, from what citizens voluntarily consider to be the merits of legislation. For Pocklington, only the weight of argument in the minds of citizens is sufficient for obedience to any and all laws. When citizens consider the merits of legislation to be insufficient, they may, at their pleasure, obey or not obey, at least when they are not morally obligated to disobey.

The release from the presumed general authority of the law that the essay favours might well be productive for citizens and enhance the quality and integrity of the law. Many democracies accept too easily the blind or fearful submission of some citizens and the habitual diffidence of others to the law. In doing so they leave little room for thoughtful, voluntary obedience and disobedience. In this respect, the moral and intellectual skills of citizens would indeed be quickened if they were given more to dissent. But whether it is compelling or not, the state of affairs favoured by Pocklington is simply not warranted. One of the arguments rejected by Pocklington is sufficient to establish most of the presumed authority of law from which he seeks to free citizens.

That argument deduces a general obligation to obey the law from citizens' voluntary participation in democratic politics and institutions. In this argument, the application of the principle of majority rule establishes a *prima facie* obligation, even for those who democratically express a minority opinion, to obey the law.

The Authority of Rules

Voluntary participation within a regime of politics and institutions is analogous to voluntary participation in a game. By voluntarily participating in a game, one agrees to play by the rules that define it. The game metaphor is all that is needed to establish a general obligation to obey the law, at least for those who freely participate.[1]

In this metaphor, one's first vote as the citizen of a democracy, one's first membership in a party or pressure group, or one's first assertion of the right to speak is no different from one's first hand of duplicate bridge. The similarity lies in the effect choosing to play has in indicating to others one's willingness to be governed by the rules of the game. Indeed, observing the rules of a game is largely what it means to play a game. If one is ever morally bound to authority, one is so bound by voluntary action; this Pocklington concedes. But just as with promises, one is morally bound to the rules of games that one has agreed to play, even when the terms of these games are not in one's favour or to one's liking.

It may be said that one need not play all or indeed any games. Nor must one play "democracy" or, for that matter, "tyranny" or "oligarchy," although one may be made to suffer their playing by others. Some games are simply better than others in the way they respect the essential dignities of human beings or in the good that stems from their playing. Nor must one make an extended commitment to any game. One's obligation to obey the rules of a democracy, including majority rule, lasts only as long as one can reasonably be said to be playing.[2] Moreover, playing one game does not imply an acceptance of the terms of authority of another, even an interrelated, game. A willingness to play "political economy"—to participate in and receive benefits from co-operative activity—does not mean that one must or indeed has decided to play "democracy," even when one plays "political economy" in a society governed by democratic principles and rules. Finally, one's use of public roads, public education, or universal medicare does not commit one to an obligation to obey the law, even those laws enacted by governments that can be credited with providing these goods.[3] All the goods that one person may give another or that one may leave for another to enjoy, though profoundly appreciated, do not create an obligation for the beneficiary to obey the giver. Only a voluntary decision so to do, if anything can, generates this authority.

The Rejection of This Model

Pocklington does not find this way of proceeding to a general obligation to law promising. What about a citizen's democratic activity in support of a nondemocratic outcome? How is one to understand a vote in favour of a revolutionary or separatist party or program? Is it consent to majority rule when the intent of such "democratic" activity is to undermine democracy?

This apparent contradiction appears to be sufficient to sink the model sketched above. However, it ought not to be abandoned quite so quickly. First, it is not clear that a vote for a revolutionary party is always genuine in its claimed intent to dismantle democratic politics and institutions. Few true revolutionaries seek their revolution through democratic practices, at least in well-entrenched democratic societies. It is more likely that a vote for a revolutionary party is either a vote in favour of radical reform of the laws currently legitimized by democratic procedure or an exercise in simple theatrical expression. However, the fact that these votes are not as contradictory as they appear to be does not prove that they could not be.

In a democracy, what does a vote for a separatist party indicate about whether a person is playing "democracy"? It typically is a vote against a majority; in most cases, it is against the application of majority rule. But these are special events in the life of a democracy. What is usually indicated by a vote for separation is not a desire both to play and not to play "democracy." Instead, it indicates a desire to redefine political boundaries. In the game metaphor, this is a vote for a break-off game. Continuing to play at the larger game is an indication, where one can do otherwise, that one is willing to play until a new game is established and toward its establishment.

At least one other strategy for starting a new game or for a smaller version of the same game exists: purposeful nonparticipation in the older or larger game, and a proclamation of one's commitment to the new or smaller one. This indication is given with ease and singular clarity in, for example, a basketball game that has had to deal with the problem of playground "self-determination."

Although it may not be wise to continue to play a game that one opposes until one succeeds in starting another, it is not logically contradictory to do so. It is logically possible to understand persons as playing "democracy" when they really favour some other game, even when they hope for and support the achievement of the latter. But is it logically possible both to play a game and not to have accepted its rules (the Pocklington dilemma)? Can one play a game ingenuinely?

It is tempting to assert that this is impossible. It might be asserted that those who do not really mean to play a game, but still act as if they are, are undeniably playing, even though they may not be aware of the significance of their actions. This is not unlike the case of people who make a promise and then deny any moral significance to having done so. The problem with this tempting conclusion is that for an action to be considered voluntary, it is best understood as requiring that the person doing it understands its social significance. However, the lack of such understanding in the minds of some people does not undermine the general obligation of others who have acted in the knowledge of this significance.[4] Thus, two classes of persons are not governed by a general obligation to obey the law: those who voluntarily choose not to play the game governed by the law and through which other law is generated, and those unable or unwilling to understand the significance of choosing to play a game. Most people fall into neither category.

The Obligation to Obey the Law

A general political obligation to obey the law does exist, despite Pocklington's charge that no such obligation can be supported by argument. The metaphor of games sheds light on the notion of implied voluntary acceptance of the authority of rules, including "majority rule." Pocklington's argument that this view is vulnerable to the contradiction of a rebel in democratic practice can be countered by arguing that the challenge posed by this apparent contradiction is merely a practical one. The unhappy result is that generally one can be obligated to obey what one opposes. This possibility should make one very cautious before deciding to play any game.

Notes

1. Democracy may be the regime most successful in generating this obligation, because it gives the citizen the most freedom to play or not to play. See Peter Singer's *Democracy and Disobedience* (Oxford: Clarendon, 1973).
2. This point is difficult but not impossible to discern. Telling evidence in the case of democracy is the failure to exercise any democratic rights or opportunities.
3. This account differs from the accounts given by Plato in the *Crito* and by John Locke.
4. It may be helpful to recall similar arguments that occur in some informal softball games. To the rebels who join in but refuse to acknowledge the authority of the rules and the significance of having decided to play, a player explains the notion of the game. The rebels are left to consider whether they wish to play this game. They fail to reach a decision but continue to "fool around," and the others simply play the game around them. The rebels are rightly treated as if they had chosen not to play. Tolerant players treat the rebels with respect and with concern for their well-being; but no claims the rebels make on the game's rules or protocol are treated seriously.

Discussion Questions

1. Does Pocklington's argument imply that no one has the authority to enact and enforce laws?

2. If there is no general obligation to obey the law, does it follow that it is permissible to disobey all bad laws?

3. Is Pocklington's argument just one more bit of evidence that liberal individualism, carried to its logical conclusions, is absurd?

4. Is Pyrcz's analogy between choosing to play a game and choosing to "play democracy" persuasive? Are there important differences between the rules of games and the rules of political systems?

5. If, as Pyrcz maintains, one must either play by the rules or not play at all, does this imply that civil disobedience is never justified in a democracy?

Further Readings

Paul Harris, ed., *Civil Disobedience* (Lanham, Md.: University Press of America, 1989), is the best collection of recent essays dealing with political obligation in relation to civil disobedience.

John Locke, in *The Second Treatise of Civil Government* first published in 1690, wrote the most influential treatise on political obligation by an English-speaking political theorist. Locke maintains that there is both a general obligation to obey the law and an occasional right of revolution.

Hanna Pitkin's "Obligation and Consent, II," *The American Political Science Review* (1966), pp. 39–52, is an interesting attempt to revive a kind of consent theory of political obligation. It is very thoughtful and imaginative in discussing the relationships between theoretical considerations and practical examples.

Plato's *Crito*, written in the fourth century B.C., is a short but deceptively complex dialogue on political obligation by the first, and arguably the greatest, political philosopher in the Western tradition. It should be read by all students of politics.

John A. Simmons, in his *Moral Principles and Political Obligations* (Princeton: Princeton University Press, 1979), presents a very carefully and clearly argued defence of the essay's thesis that there is no general obligation to obey the law. This is a difficult but rewarding book.

Peter Singer, in *Democracy and Disobedience* (Oxford: Clarendon Press, 1973), presents a clear and interesting argument defending the thesis that there is a powerful obligation to obey the laws of democratic political systems. This is a thoughtful and engaging book for the beginner.

To the owner of this book:

We are interested in your reaction to Carmichael, Pocklington, and Pyrcz, *Democracy and Rights in Canada*. With your comments and suggestions, we may improve this book in future editions.

1. What was your reason for using this book?

____ university course   ____ continuing education course
____ college course   ____ personal interest
                         ____ other (specify)

2. Which school? _____

3. Approximately how much of the book did you use?
     ____ ¼   ____ ½   ____ ¾   ____ all

4. What is the best aspect of the book?

5. Have you any suggestions for improvement?

6. Is there anything that should be added?

Fold here

· ·

43652

POSTAGE WILL BE PAID BY
Sheila Malloch
    Acquisitions Editor
College Editorial Department
HOLT, RINEHART AND WINSTON
    OF CANADA, LIMITED
55 HORNER AVENUE
TORONTO, ONTARIO
M8Z 9Z9

Tape shut